OPERATIONS RESEARCH SOCIETY
OF AMERICA

Publications in Operations Research

Number 7

PUBLICATIONS IN OPERATIONS RESEARCH

Operations Research Society of America

Editor for Publications in Operations Research
DAVID B. HERTZ

No. 1. QUEUES, INVENTORIES AND MAINTENANCE
Philip M. Morse

No. 2. FINITE QUEUING TABLES
L. G. Peck and R. N. Hazelwood

No. 3. EFFICIENCY IN GOVERNMENT THROUGH SYSTEMS ANALYSIS
Roland N. McKean

No. 4. A COMPREHENSIVE BIBLIOGRAPHY ON OPERATIONS RESEARCH
Operations Research Group, Case Institute

No. 5. PROGRESS IN OPERATIONS RESEARCH, VOLUME I
Edited by Russell L. Ackoff

No. 6. STATISTICAL MANAGEMENT OF INVENTORY SYSTEMS
Harvey M. Wagner

No. 7. PRICE, OUTPUT, AND INVENTORY POLICY
Edwin S. Mills

PRICE, OUTPUT, AND INVENTORY POLICY

A Study in the Economics of the Firm and Industry

by
EDWIN S. MILLS
THE JOHNS HOPKINS UNIVERSITY

JOHN WILEY & SONS, INC., NEW YORK · LONDON

PREFACE

This book is written by an economist for his fellow economists. Its subject is price theory and it is mainly concerned with the price and output decisions of firms in different kinds of markets. Specifically, its purpose is to formulate and test models which take explicit account of the effects of uncertainty and inventory holding on firms' decision making.

Even though the book is addressed mainly to economists, I hope it will be regarded as an interdisciplinary effort. It is, I think, very much in the spirit of the growing management science and operations research literature, and I have drawn freely from the work in those disciplines on production and inventory control. I hope that specialists in those areas will be interested in this study, and that it will improve the close relationship that they already have with economists.

Almost every economist of my acquaintance has been subjected to some part of this book at one stage or another. My interest in the role of inventories in economics dates from 1952, when Frank H. Hahn suggested it to me as a subject for my doctoral dissertation. My thesis, *The Theory of Inventory Decisions,* was supervised by him and W. M. Gorman. It was submitted in 1955 at the University of Birmingham, in whose library it resides, happily unpublished. To these two gentlemen I owe a professional debt too pervasive to permit specific acknowledgement. Parts of this book were read by William Brainard, Carl Christ, James Kindahl, Tjalling C. Koopmans, and Michael Lovell, to whom I am indebted for a number of specific improvements. In addition, Donald Hester and James Tobin patiently read the entire manuscript and made many helpful suggestions. My greatest debt, however, is to Robert Dorfman, who carefully read and criticized two versions of the manuscript.

Some preliminary computations were performed by John Carlson and Brian Brogan. Karen Hester helped in the preparation of the final manuscript and improved it both editorially and substantively.

v

Takeshi Amemiya prepared the index and helped in the final checking of the manuscript.

In two places the book draws heavily on previously published papers. Section 3 of Chapter 4 is based on my note, "The Use of Adaptive Expectations in Stability Analysis: Comment," *The Quarterly Journal of Economics*, LXXV, May 1961, pp. 330–335. The interested reader should also see "Reply," by Marc Nerlove, pp. 335–338, of the same journal issue. These two references were inadvertently omitted from the text. Chapter 5 is based on [56].

A number of organizations helped to support the research reported in this book. Most of the work was undertaken at the Johns Hopkins University, which supported and encouraged the research in many ways. Most of the computations were supported by funds from the Ford Faculty Research Grant of the Department of Political Economy at the Johns Hopkins University. The manuscript was completed while I was a Ford Faculty Research Fellow and a visitor at the Cowles Foundation for Research in Economics at Yale University. Some of the empirical research was supported by the Office of Naval Research on contract with the Cowles Foundation. I wish to thank all of these organizations for their generosity. I am particularly indebted to the Cowles Foundation for their hospitality and for providing an ideal environment in which to finish my book.

EDWIN S. MILLS

Baltimore
June, 1962

CONTENTS

Chapter 1

INTRODUCTION

1. Scope of the Book

This book is a study in the economic theory of prices and production. The question asked is the one traditionally asked by economists interested in this subject, namely: What considerations enable the economist best to explain the price and output decisions that firms make? Even though, as gladly acknowledged below, my debt to the operations literature is considerable, this book is not an operations research study. By this we mean that it is not intended to assist people who are responsible for making price and output decisions in firms and other organizations. Rather, it is an attempt to explain why firms make these decisions in the way they do. This can be stated in language now fashionable in economics by saying that it is a study in positive, as contrasted to normative, economics. There is of course an evident point of contact between the positive and the normative approaches in that both are concerned with the implications of rational behavior. This and virtually every other study in price theory attempts to explain price and output decisions by assuming that the firm is behaving rationally in one sense or another. On the other hand, operations research studies of price and, more usually, output policy attempt to suggest to firms what policies it would be rational for them to follow. Hence, from one point of view the tasks of the economist and the operations researcher are the same: to deduce the implications of rational behavior. Nevertheless, the point of view greatly influences the degree of abstraction, the amount of detail, and the emphasis placed on different factors in the analysis. The positive point

1

of view permeates the analysis in this book, and the models presented
will probably be of little normative value.

Nevertheless, the book is closely related to operations research,
and the reason is not hard to find. The purpose of the book is to incorporate inventory holding and uncertainty into the economists'
theory of price determination. What will be referred to as the "traditional" theory of price determination includes neither of these factors.
It assumes that firms make their price and output decisions on the
basis of a known, nonstochastic demand equation and without considering the possibility of holding inventories. For many purposes these
assumptions may be quite appropriate, but for many other purposes,
for example dynamic analysis or making quantitive short-run forecasts of firms' behavior, they clearly are not. Many economists have
of course recognized this and some have included these factors in more
or less fully developed models of firms' behavior. A few of these
studies are referred to at appropriate places in the following chapters.

Existing side by side with a growing recognition by economists of
the desirability of incorporating these factors in their models of firms'
behavior has been a mushrooming operations research [1] literature on
production and inventory control. Indeed, so vast has this literature
become that the subject is now a legitimate full-time specialty. So far,
the literature and the techniques it employs have had virtually no influence on the economists' theory of price and output determination.
The link between this book and operations research is the claim
that the techniques employed in the operations research literature
provide one way of incorporating the factors of uncertainty and inventory holding in the theory of price determination. Furthermore,
when these factors are included, the resulting models at least suggest,
if not imply, ways of predicting firms' short-run price and output
behavior.

There are probably several reasons why operations research studies
have had so little effect on price theory. One reason is certainly that
the operations research studies often do not appear to be concerned
with the economists' problem at all. For example, much of the operations research literature on production and inventory planning is con-

---

[1] The term "operations research" here really means "normatively oriented."
Important contributions to this literature have been made not only by operations
research specialists, but also by economists, statisticians, and mathematicians.
Indeed, many of the contributions on which this book relies most heavily have
been made by economists.

cerned with the problem of minimizing production and inventory costs when the quantity demanded is completely beyond the firm's control. Economists, on the other hand, are accustomed to assuming a goal of profit maximization rather than cost minimization. They assume, too, that the firm can affect demand by changing its price, and possibly by other means, of course. For another example, the production-planning studies in the operations research literature do not normally distinguish between different market types (competitive and monopolistic, and so on), whereas the economist is likely to regard the market type as having a major influence on the firm's policies. Finally, the planning literature deals almost exclusively with production, whereas the economist is likely to emphasize the interdependence of price and production decisions. The writer believes that these differences arise almost entirely from the difference, suggested above, between the points of view of the two groups rather than from important differences of opinion about the nature of the firm's objectives and the problems with which it is faced. Regardless of one's view on this matter, the fact is that these differences have hindered the flow of ideas, perhaps in both directions, between the two disciplines. It is thus clear that the planning literature does not provide the economist with ready-made answers to his problems. However, it is the hope and contention of this book that the techniques employed in the planning literature at least suggest ways of incorporating into the theory of the firm factors, such as inventories and uncertainty, in which economists are interested.

It may help to put this and other recent studies in their setting if this last point is made in a somewhat more general way. One cannot help but be struck by the condition of unbalanced growth which now exists in and around the literature of theoretical economics. Developments in the area of formal techniques of rational decision making have far outdistanced the application of these techniques to substantive economic problems. In the last decade or two almost revolutionary innovations have been made in formal theories of decision making under the headings of game theory, statistical decision theory, linear programming, personalistic probability, and dynamic programming. The result of all this has been that the economist now has at his disposal richer and more powerful tools for analyzing rational behavior than he had even a few years ago. Yet there has been relatively little use of these tools in the analysis of problems in which economists have traditionally been interested.[2] For example, we have virtually no analysis of the effect on firms' price and output policies of the use of different decision criteria such as expected utility maximization, various minmax criteria, safety-first, and so on. Furthermore, we have very little idea of which criteria are relevant or plausible in different kinds of markets, or which criteria lead to decisions that are systematically different from those indicated by the traditional theory of the firm. In other words, we have many different decision criteria but very little idea what sorts of decisions they lead to in various decision-making situations in economics.

This book presents an investigation of a very special and narrowly defined problem of this general type. One particular theory of decision making in uncertain situations is used to formulate models of price and output determination in perfectly and imperfectly competitive markets. Specifically, it is assumed that uncertainty enters the firm's calculations only through the demand for its products and in the form of a random variable whose distribution function the firm knows but cannot affect.[3] In the face of this situation the firm is assumed to choose price and output levels that maximize the mathematical expectation of its profits.[4] This problem falls under the heading of dynamic

[2] Two books have recently appeared which go a long way toward remedying this deficiency in at least two areas. The Dorfman, Samuelson, Solow study [19] demonstrates the applicability of linear programming to a wide range of economic problems, particularly those involving perfectly competitive markets in some way. The Shubik study [71] analyzes the application of game theory to the theory of the firm.

[3] Some economists would insist on calling this situation "risky" rather than "uncertain," following Knight's terminology which reserves the term uncertainty for situations in which probabilities are unknown to the decision maker. However, it is now well known that this distinction is very unclear. Recent work, particularly that of L. J. Savage [69], has shown that very weak restrictions on the consistency of choices, which Knight and his followers would certainly have to accept, imply that the decision maker acts "as if" he were maximizing the mathematical expectation of utility. Hence this distinction is not employed in this book. The severe restriction in this book is not the consideration of risk rather than uncertainty, but the assumption that utility is a linear function of profit.

[4] This term will frequently be abbreviated to expected profits. The word "expected" is used in at least three senses in economics. First is the value of a variable anticipated by some economic agent when his anticipations consist of a single number. Second is the mean value of his anticipations when these consist of a probability distribution that the agent attaches to some variable. Third is the mean value of the variable when the true probability distribution is attached

programming in the above list of formal decision theories.[5] Thus, the book can be viewed as an attempt to apply some special techniques of dynamic programming to problems in price theory. Similarly, the operations research literature on production and inventory control is largely an attempt to apply dynamic programming techniques to the normative problem of production planning.[6]

It is only too clear that, from a decision theory point of view, the models developed in this book are very special cases indeed. In no sense can this book be said to contain *the* theory of price determination under uncertainty. To begin with, the maximization of the mathematical expectation of profit is a very special decision criterion. It is a special case of the more general criterion of expected utility maximization, which is in turn only one of several plausible criteria for decision making under uncertainty. Furthermore, within the framework of the expected-profit criterion, some special assumptions are made in the chapters which follow. The most daring of these concern the way the firm views the distant future. Others concern the relation between the expectations of the firm and the observed values of the resulting variables, for example, the predictive errors that the firm makes. Thus, much of the appeal of the models to be presented depends on the persuasiveness of the assumptions on which they are based. There is no reason to think that the particular assumptions chosen here are "correct" in any sense or even that they are necessarily the best for the purpose at hand. Indeed, one of the basic arguments of this book is that once the restrictive assumptions of traditional price theory are dropped no natural or compelling set of assumptions is available. In conditions of uncertainty the decision criterion, the information available to the firm, and the approximations that the firm employs are all matters for empirical investigation. It seems natural to assume

to the variable. In this book, the term is rarely used in the first sense. Furthermore, the second two senses are equivalent in the following chapters since firms are always assumed to know the true probability distributions of relevant variables. When no confusion is likely, the abbreviation is used.

[5] The term "dynamic programming" was coined by Bellman to refer generally to models of multi-stage decision problems. However, usage is by no means consistent and the term is sometimes restricted to the description of special techniques which have been developed partly by Bellman [13] and partly by others [7] and [22] to solve these problems.

[6] The relation between dynamic programming and the operations research models of production and inventory planning is actually more complicated than this. See the next section.

that economists' understanding of price formation in these circumstances will grow gradually as theoretical and empirical investigations proceed. This book is intended to be a contribution in this direction.

Reasons for specific assumptions are given as they are made at various points in the book. There are, however, certain general criteria that have governed the approach adopted, particularly the unblushing use of the expected-profit assumption. These can be stated here.

(i) First and foremost is the availability of easily obtainable formal results. Implications of the expected-profit criterion are much easier to work out than are those of most other criteria for decision making under uncertainty. This is partly because probability theory is a highly developed subject compared with the techniques employed in other decision theories.[7] Even more, it is because an extensive literature is available concerned with the application of expected cost and profit criteria to problems of the type with which price theory deals. The argument here is that there is virtue in simplicity. The procedure should be to investigate thoroughly the implications of simple decision criteria and to abandon them only when considerable evidence accumulates that they lead to incorrect results. At present, such evidence is conspicuously absent, partly because the implications of the decision theories are largely unknown.

(ii) It is apparently easier to obtain specific empirical implications of the expected-profit criterion than of competing criteria. For example, in Chapters 5 and 6 a comparison is made between the prices and outputs that result when firms use the expected-profit criterion and those that result from the traditional theory. Such a comparison does not appear to be possible, without much more restrictive assumptions, when other criteria, such as minmax and safety-first, are used. In a similar vein, the expected-profit criterion appears to lead much more naturally to empirical econometric applications. The decision models to be presented in the following chapters suggest statistical studies which are intended to yield numerical predictions of firms' short-run price and output behavior and, in some cases, empirical tests of the theory itself. This provides a clear advantage over traditional price theory, which does not lead naturally to short-run predictions except of a qualitative nature. The desire to construct a theory that will lend itself to empirical estimation and testing, using only

---

[7] Many other decision theories using safety-first and minmax criteria also employ probability concepts. The point is that the manipulations required are much less familiar than those required for the expected-profit criterion.

the market observations usually available to economists, has had a strong influence on the choice of techniques and assumptions employed in this book. In several cases more restrictive assumptions have been made than were analytically desirable because they appeared necessary to obtain results which could easily be applied to available empirical data.

(iii) In an important sense, price and output policies which maximize expected profits dominate policies based on other criteria. It is assumed that the basic goal of the firm's price and output policies is to obtain as much profit over a fairly long period of time as is possible. Specifically, it is assumed that whenever two riskless policies guarantee different amounts of profit over the horizon, the more profitable policy is chosen. However, with one qualification, the average profit realized over a sample of decision periods will equal approximately the expected value of profits over the same number of decision periods, provided only that the sample is large enough. This means that, with the same qualification, the policy of maximizing the expected value of profits will guarantee larger profits than will any other decision criterion provided it is followed long enough. This is a well-known argument. The qualification is that this will only be true if realized profits in any interval of time are not so small that the firm is driven out of business altogether and is unable to take advantage of the law of large numbers. In this view other criteria are thought of as ways of achieving the basic goal of large, long-run profits, by making it as unlikely as possible that runs of bad luck will put the firm out of business.

The question to be asked here is, "Why should a run of bad luck put out of business a firm whose long-run profit prospects are good?" The answer seems to be related to some rather complicated assumptions about the capital market. If both borrowers and lenders attach the same probabilities to the firm's possible future profit levels, and both use the same rate of time discount, then a loan to a firm with good long-run prospects, that is sufficiently large [8] expected profits, is completely riskless. In other words, provided the discounted value of the firm's expected profits is sufficiently large, it is certain that any loan will be repaid if only the lender is sufficiently patient. The duration of the loan is not certain, of course. How large a loan the firm may need, and for how long, are matters that depend on the runs of low

---

[8] "Sufficiently large" here means large enough to cover the interest cost of any riskless loans the firm may need.

profits which happen to occur. That the loan will eventually be re-paid, with the accumulated riskless interest, there is no doubt. Thus, provided the capital market satisfies these stringent conditions, there is no reason [9] for the firm to take into account anything other than the expected value of its profits in making its decisions.

There are, of course, many reasons why the capital market does not behave in this way in reality. The fact that the borrower, being an "insider," has access to information about the firm's prospects that is not available to the lender (or that the borrower may conceal from the lender) may induce the lender to discount the firm's reported prospects. The fact that the lender is subject to other risks than that of default by the borrower, for example, he may suddenly need his principal if other loans of a genuinely risky character fail to pay off, may make the lender unwilling to commit his funds to the firm for an indefinite period. On the other hand, if the loan is a negotiable security and the rest of the market shares the lender's views about the firm's profit prospects, then the lender can recover his principal if he needs it by selling the loan on the market. Evidently there are many possibilities here, some of which do not appear to have been analyzed in the literature. Nor is it intended to incorporate in this book an elaborate analysis of capital markets. The only point to be made is that the existence of a well-organized capital market reduces the need for the firm to look at the higher moments of its probability distribution of profits.

(iv) Finally, the expected-profit criterion accords with what little the writer knows of the decision-making procedures actually employed by firms. Roughly, at least in making short-run price and output decisions, executives tend to average the results of different policies and choose the policy that promises the best average results. This fact is related to the point in the previous paragraph in that these decisions normally commit only a small fraction of the firm's total resources and therefore the probability of a disastrous outcome is negligible. The point is discussed more extensively in the next chapter, where available evidence is presented.

2. Relation to the Operations Research Literature

This section does not intend to survey extensively either the opera-tions research literature on production and inventory control or its

---

[9] Except the interest cost of riskless loans.

relation to economics. The former task is undertaken in several of the operations research textbooks, of which there are now a good number available.[10] The latter has been undertaken in an excellent semi-technical paper by K. J. Arrow.[11] In his paper Arrow shows that most of the considerations that are important in the dynamic programming approach to production planning are present in some form in the economics literature. At one time or another economists have considered the transactions, speculative and buffer motives for holding inventories of money and goods of various kinds. On this view the accomplishment of the dynamic programming studies has been to formalize, generalize, and integrate these considerations in models which include the costs of production, inventory holding, etc. These motives had certainly been noticed and taken into account informally by economists before the term "dynamic programming" had been thought of. However, only the development of the powerful mathematical tools associated with the name dynamic programming made it possible to show how these motives affect production policy in any but the most trivial situations. Since the knowledge that a factor is of practical importance to decision makers is of little predictive value unless the investigator has some idea how it affects decisions, the accomplishment of the dynamic programming literature must be regarded as considerable. That this literature has had very little effect on the thinking of economists does not detract from its importance.

The main point of this section is that only part of the operations research literature on production and inventory control can be said to be an application of dynamic programming techniques.[12] The reason is that dynamic programming techniques have their most obvious application to production problems in which the decision period is of fixed, discrete length, for example, when production decisions are taken the first of every month. Now it is by no means accidental that economists interested in production planning have been concerned primarily with the dynamic programming approach, that many of the dynamic

---

[10] See [16], [49], and [67].

[11] See Chapter 1 of [9].

[12] This statement depends of course on the precise interpretation given to the term dynamic programming. The sense in which the writer uses the term is described more fully in Chapter 6. Here it suffices to say that it refers to models in which the planning problem is a sequence of decisions in which earlier decisions affect later ones in a way that is only partly known when the earlier decisions are taken.

programming studies have been published in the economics literature by economists or others interested in economics, and that these techniques lend themselves most easily to price theory applications. The reason is that the assumption of a fixed decision period accords very nearly with tradition in economic theory and with the way most economic statistics become available. It is also the reason that the dynamic programming approach forms the basis for the models presented in this book.

There are, however, some production problems that do not fit easily into the dynamic programming mold. Indeed, most of the applied operations research studies of production and inventory control cannot be said to use dynamic programming techniques at all. The problems referred to here are mostly of the discrete run type, in which production takes place in discrete runs or lots rather than continuously. In this case the problem is to decide, not how much should be produced in a discrete period, knowing that another such decision will be made in the succeeding period, but rather how many units to produce in the next run, knowing that a similar decision will be made whenever the first run is exhausted. The run rather than the unit period is the basic decision element. The length of time between decisions is a random variable, assuming sales per unit time to be a random variable, whose probability distribution depends on the decision taken. In the dynamic programming approach the decision period is known and fixed independently of the decision taken. Now it may be that on a deeper view both the discrete and continuous problems can be formulated in dynamic programming terms.[13] The fact is that up to

---

[13] Production decisions are not, of course, of either the discrete or continuous type by the nature of the problem. Whether production should take place continuously or not is itself a decision problem that depends on the existence of short-run economies of large-scale production per unit time (resulting from increased specialization of the labor force, price breaks on purchased materials, etc.), on inventory costs, on set-up costs, and so forth. From a mathematical point of view, the desirability of discrete runs results from the presence of important concave segments of at least some of the cost functions involved. Although some progress has been made with problems of this type, most of the dynamic programming techniques apply to situations in which the functional relations are convex. Concavities are introduced by set-up costs, decreasing unit production costs, etc. Economists would do well to reflect on the fact that, even in the traditional riskless theory, a firm whose unit production costs are falling as output increases would profit by producing in alternate periods enough to satisfy two periods' demands, and remaining idle in alternate periods. At least this is true provided the economies realized in production costs offset the inventory costs

now this has not been the case. Discrete run problems are handled by a variety of miscellaneous techniques in the operations research literature,[14] none of which appears to be closely related to dynamic programming.

The relationship between this book and the operations research literature on production and inventory planning is as follows. The models used here are largely applications of rather simple dynamic programming techniques to price theory. These techniques are also frequently applied to operations research problems of production planning. Many production-planning problems, those involving discrete runs with no fixed decision period, are not, however, easily handled by dynamic programming techniques. In the operations research literature these problems are handled by a variety of methods. Thus, the models in this book are closely related to only a part of the operations research literature on production planning, namely, that part which applies dynamic programming techniques. The theory of price determination for discrete runs remains to be written.

3. Outline of the Book

The chapters of this book fall naturally into three groups. Chapters 1, 2, and 3 form the first group and contain preliminary and somewhat methodological material. Chapter 2 presents some of the intuitive and organizational factors which underlie the formal models developed in later chapters. Chapter 3 is a discussion of the place of expectations in econometric studies. Some recent techniques for estimating expectations and behavior relations in which expectational variables appear are discussed and criticized. Then a new technique, called the "implicit expectations" approach, is presented and analyzed.

Chapters 4, 5, and 6 form the second group; they present the basic theoretical models and constitute the core of the book. The purpose of these chapters is to introduce uncertainty and inventory holding into the decision making of firms in different kinds of market situations. Chapter 4 contains a detailed analysis of firm and market behavior in a perfectly competitive market. First the optimum policy of a firm in such a market is deduced and then the stability of the market

---

involved in this procedure. But alternation between production and idleness is the essence of a discrete run policy. This fact suggests that much of the existing theory of production with decreasing costs relies heavily on a literal interpretation of the assumption of a one-period horizon.

[14] For typical approaches to such problems see [47] and [57].

is investigated.   In Chapters 5 and 6 a model is constructed of the price and output policy of a firm in an imperfectly competitive market. Considerable attention is paid to the comparison of the policies deduced in these chapters with those indicated by the traditional, static theory of the firm.

Chapters 7 to 13 form the third group and are concerned with the application of the models to empirical data.   Chapters 7 and 8 form a transition from the theoretical to the applied parts of the book and have as their purpose the deduction of empirical implications of the models which can be estimated and tested.   Chapters 9 to 12 present four econometric industry studies designed to estimate and test the price and output decision rules implied by the model.   Chapter 13 summarizes and evaluates the findings.

Chapter 2

RATIONALITY
AND THE
"AS IF" PRINCIPLE

1. *Introduction*

This chapter and the next are concerned with topics that some readers may wish to classify under the heading of methodology. The subject considered is the place of expectations in economics. Specifically, there are two sets of problems with regard to expectations in economics, and most investigations are concerned primarily with one or the other of them. In the first place there is the problem of the nature and source of expectations: how they are to be described, on what they depend, and how the economist is to estimate them. In the second place there is the problem of the relation between expectations and behavior: by what rule decisions are made on the basis of expectations. The first problem has to do with the formation of expectations, the second with their use. In this chapter a special aspect of the second problem is discussed. The next chapter is largely concerned with the first question.

In neither place is any attempt made to present a complete or definitive discussion of the subject. In particular, there is no discussion in this book of the foundations of expectational and decision theories in the sense that no new fundamental decision criterion is introduced and no detailed comparison is made among existing criteria such as the maximization of expected utility, minmax procedures, potential surprise, and so on. As stated in Chapter 1, we are concerned only with working out the implications of the simplest probabilistic decision criterion, expected-profit maximization, in certain market situations of interest to economists.

The procedure in these two chapters is to discuss only special aspects of these questions that are important for the purposes of this book. This is particularly true in the present chapter. Here only one very special question is considered, the relation between the costs of estimation and computation on the one hand and the assumption that decision makers behave "as if" they were employing some model of rational decision making on the other hand. The point of view which is presented and criticized in the next two sections is undoubtedly to a large extent a straw man. Nevertheless, it will serve as a convenient peg on which to hang some of the intuitive-institutional-managerial considerations which have motivated the formal models in the rest of the book.[1]

2. Recent Developments in Decision Theory and the "As If" Principle

Economists have long argued whether or not it is justifiable to assume that households and firms will behave consistently with the various criteria of rational choice traditionally employed in economic analysis. Not only have there been discussions about which of several criteria of rational choice is appropriate to explain certain classes of economic decisions, but there has also been a skeptical minority in the profession that doubted whether sufficiently accurate explanations of economic behavior could be obtained by supposing that people would behave "as if" they were employing *any* criterion of rational choice.

Somewhat curiously, recent developments in formal decision-making techniques (especially in such areas as game theory, personalistic probability, statistical decision theory, linear programming, and dynamic programming) have apparently had the effect of adding to the ranks of the skeptical on this question. Beyond a doubt, these developments have been successful in helping people make decisions intelligently, as the mushrooming of operations research attests. The issue in doubt is the contribution of modern decision theories to positive economics, that is to the explanation of economic behavior.

In one sense these developments have facilitated discussion and evaluation of the various forms of the "as if" principle, since the formalization involved in recent work has made it easier to decide what restrictions on behavior are involved in any decision criterion. The clearest example of this, though others are available, is the controversy

---

[1] Since no comparison of alternative decision criteria is made in this book, reference should be made to the two excellent surveys of the subject by Kenneth Arrow in [3] and [5].

over measurable utility. Most of the earlier discussion was concerned with the admissability or acceptability of measurable utility without careful specification of the restrictions on choice entailed by the assumption of measurability. Much of this discussion was rendered obsolete by the work of von Neumann and Morgenstern [65], and more recently Savage [69], who showed that simple assumptions about the consistency of choices made in uncertain situations imply a utility function that is, in an important sense,[2] measurable. Furthermore, the assumptions involved appear to many people to be on the same level of intuitive acceptability as the usual assumptions of the riskless theory of consumers' choice.

In another sense, however, recent research on decision theory appears to have strengthened the doubts among economists that useful explanations of economic behavior can be obtained by using the "as if" principle. Recent developments have greatly increased the awareness in the profession of the complexity of the decisions we are trying to explain. We now realize, for example, more than we did twenty years ago, how difficult it is to formulate and solve a program of rational production and inventory policy. If it takes a highly trained mathematician and an electronic computer to solve even a simplified version of a real decision problem how, we ask, can an executive, untrained in mathematics, whose computer is an intuition trained by business experience, come up with the right answer? Similar examples of the complexity of relatively simple decisions could be given from other decision theories, such as game theory and personalistic probability.

It is difficult not to sympathize with this view. For example, researchers experienced in solving moderately complicated linear programming problems know how difficult it often is to conjecture the right solutions to such problems even if they have had considerable experience with the data in question. A more persuasive example concerns certain production-planning problems that commonly arise in business operations but for which mathematicians are unable to find even formal, as contrasted with numerical, solutions. (See Chapter 6 for a detailed outline.) Furthermore, industry's voracious appetite for linear programming studies, and for operations research in general, is indirect evidence of this point. The fact that it is profitable to employ experts to make such studies is evidence that the assumption that

---

[2] It is measurable in the sense that all the utility functions that can describe the choices made by an individual with a particular set of tastes, which satisfy the axioms of the model, are linear transformations of each other.

firms were previously behaving "as if" they were employing such techniques is a poor one.[3] Of course, to the extent that the results of such studies are actually used, the assumption that the firm is behaving "as if" it employed the technique in question is correct, since it is doing so.

Nevertheless, this chapter will argue primarily that recent developments in decision theory provide no real basis for the abandonment of the "as if" principle. On the general level on which the discussion usually takes place, a fairly convincing case can be made for its retention, at least if it is appropriately interpreted. Of course, such speculations as those in the next section can never be conclusive. The only way to discover whether the "as if" principle can be used to explain behavior is by trying to explain behavior with it. Nevertheless, in any investigation it is necessary to eliminate some possible techniques on general grounds prior to the accumulation of evidence from the investigation itself. The only argument here is that there is no reason to eliminate the "as if" principle on these grounds.

3. *Costs of Estimation and Computation and the "As If" Principle* [4]

Basically, this section argues that people become discouraged with the use of the "as if" principle by the complexity of modern decision theory because they forget that part of a rational decision is the rational consideration of what resources to invest in collection of information and computation of the decision. This means that the rule a decision maker can use rationally is the one that makes use of only the information it is worthwhile to collect and that requires only

---

[3] This evidence needs to be interpreted with care. It is worthwhile for a firm to make, for example, a programming study if it results in an increase in profit net of the cost of the study. Unless the firm is very small, a study which saves one per cent of costs may be an extremely profitable one, though the change in the firm's behavior as a result of the study may be small from the economist's point of view. A few operations research studies, e.g. [35], have compared the actual behavior of the firm with that which would have resulted had some formal decision rule been employed. Speaking generally, partly on the basis of personal experience, we would say that while the savings from such operations research studies are often large relative to the cost of the study, it is questionable whether the change in behavior resulting from the study should be considered large from the economist's point of view. Evidence, however, is much too scanty to warrant any general conclusion.

[4] The subject of this section has been studied intensively, from another point of view, by J. Marschak. See, for example [48].

those computations it is worthwhile to make. On this view it is an error to say that the rationality assumption is a bad one because rational behavior requires more information or computation than the decision maker can be expected to have available. If a decision rule requires too much information or computation, it is not rational to make decisions by that rule.

The terminological question which arises here about the meaning of rationality will not be argued. Certainly, rationality will not be defined narrowly, so that certain interesting decision-making techniques are considered irrational by definition, for example, because they do not employ all the information that might be relevant to the decision. Vaguely, the concept of rationality involves doing the best you can in the circumstances to get what you want. This seems to be the notion underlying the best work on the subject. The point is that the relevant circumstances include the costs of estimation and computation.

The implication of this view for the economist interested in explaining a decision maker's behavior is not that he should abandon the "as if" principle, but that he should search for the particular simplifications and approximations the decision maker has found it desirable to employ. In many cases this means that, for explanatory purposes, a rather simple decision rule is more relevant than a sophisticated one that may represent the solution to the "true" problem. The rest of the section is devoted to a more detailed development of this thesis.

In the first place, it is an indisputable fact that every piece of information that goes into an industrial price, production, or inventory decision has a price tag attached to it.[5] Two examples will illustrate this fact.

(i) Suppose a firm is considering whether to increase its output by 10 per cent and wants to know what extra cost this will entail. One of the reasons it may be difficult to estimate is that the distinction between inputs variable in the short run and those variable only in the long run is not given to the firm from the outside in the manner sometimes

---

[5] The cost of consideration may also be of relevance in the theory of consumers' behavior. For example, probably to some extent the demand for items which take only a small part of one's budget is price inelastic simply because of the psychological cost of deciding how to readjust the purchase pattern when prices change. Such time as one is willing to devote to consideration of the best allocation of expenditures must be used in the way that will yield the greatest "savings," i.e., give the most preferred bundle of goods. Largely, this means that one should pay most attention to items that take an important segment of the budget.

suggested by price theory textbooks. Generally speaking, any factor can be varied to almost any desired extent within any period of time, at a price. The firm always has to decide what factors it is worthwhile to vary for a given purpose, and this is not always easy to do. The firm in our example will certainly have to increase its inputs of direct labor and materials, and it will probably be able to estimate rather accurately and without too much difficulty the resulting costs. But what about its salaried administrative staff? To some extent the work of each major department—production, purchasing, sales, quality control—will be increased. As the operations of each major department expand, however, economies will be realized from increased specialization within the department, and proportionate expansion of staff should not be necessary. Furthermore, some of the functions of these departments are independent of the volume of output, at least within broad ranges.[6] If too little staff is provided, the work of these departments will suffer and profits will eventually be hurt. On the other hand, the provision of too much staff will obviously be wasteful.

In addition, there is a time factor to be considered, though this problem is usually at least mentioned in textbooks. The longer the projected higher output is expected to continue, the more of these overhead factors it will pay to vary. Thus, in a sense the solution to this problem requires a forecast of production in the indefinite future. But future production decisions depend to some extent on precisely the question at hand, i.e. the variation of costs with output.

Thus, the firm is faced with an extremely complicated estimation problem. It is likely that, instead of considering the problem in its true complexity, the firm will adopt simplifications and approximations in the form of one or more rules of thumb. Thus, it will have reduced a complicated problem to a simpler one that can be solved with data and techniques more nearly at hand.

(ii) Suppose that a firm normally makes a demand forecast one production planning period in advance, and that it is deciding its output for the coming period. It knows that its forecasts are normally subject to considerable error and that occasionally demand during a planning period exceeds the amount available for sale. This unfilled demand or "shortage" involves not only a loss of current revenue, but also a loss of goodwill and possible future sales. Logically, the decline

---

[6] **Many** activities concerned with planning and setting up production are independent of the volume to be produced.

in profit resulting from such a future loss of sales depends on the levels of marginal revenue and marginal cost in the future periods involved. These in turn depend on the pattern of future sales and output and it may be expensive or impossible for the firm to estimate or plan these variables far into the future. In addition, we again have the kind of simultaneity problem present in the first example. This simultaneity arises from the fact that the variable being planned (current production in the present example) depends on planned future values of the same variable,[7] and these in turn depend on the decision made concerning current production. Thus, again we have an extremely complicated problem which the firm will have to simplify in order to be able to solve. The simplification often suggested is to represent the cost of shortage by a conventional value intended to approximate the average profit lost from shortage.

The second example is discussed again in Chapter 6. Here it is to be noted that in both cases the cost of collecting information and of making computations has led the firm to approximate a complicated problem by a simpler one. Furthermore, this may be a perfectly rational thing to do. The result in both cases is that the economist's task of explaining the firm's market behavior is greatly simplified. Instead of having to estimate the complicated relationship which would govern the firm's behavior if the true decision problem had been solved, the economist needs to estimate only the simpler relation derived from the firm's need to approximate the problem.

In view of the above, it might reasonably be expected that a decision theory incorporating the costs of estimation and computation is to be presented in this book. This is not the case. The most important reason for not presenting such a theory is the lack of such a theory. Furthermore, such a theory is not necessary for the purpose at hand. Money and effort spent on estimation and computation are factor inputs just as are other kinds of labor which are usually identified as factor inputs along with different kinds of capital. It is possible, at least in principle, to estimate the firm's production-cost function without knowing why it was profitable for the firm to employ the particular input quantities that led to the observed costs. In the same way, it is possible to explain the firm's output policy without having a complete

---

[7] Planned future production affects current production because, other things being equal, the greater the production planned for the future, the less the need to carry inventories into future periods. Hence, the less the current production which is needed.

decision theory that explains why it is rational for the firm to make its decisions in a particular way. The economist is required to estimate, or guess, the particular approximations and simplifications of its problems that the firm has adopted.[8] This is not always easy to do, of course, and it places a great emphasis on empirical studies of how firms actually make decisions. Essentially, the argument here is that there is no natural or compelling model of rational decision making which all intelligent firms can safely be assumed to use. There are many decision techniques that a rational firm might employ, depending on a host of circumstances, and the discovery of the rules actually used, or good approximations of them, is an important subject for empirical study.

On the other hand, the discovery of good approximations to widely used decision rules should not be an impossible task. In particular, a small amount of information about the internal workings of firms should pay large dividends. Such information would concern the procedures for collecting various kinds of data, who makes what decisions, and what data is available for the purpose.

Consider again the two examples previously given. In both cases the internal information which the economist requires in conjunction with such external information as ex post observations of prices, outputs, etc., should not be too difficult to obtain. In the first example, the economist needs to discover the firm's policy about the expansion of salaried staff in response to changes in output. He should rather easily be able to discover whether, as far as this factor is concerned, the firm thinks of its average cost as approximately constant or as decreasing substantially as output increases. In the second example, the economist needs to know whether shortage cost is represented in the firm's thinking by a conventional cost parameter, presumably per unit of unsatisfied demand, or whether some more sophisticated procedure is used. Some evidence is provided simply by a knowledge of the information available about this cost. If the firm does not normally make sales forecasts beyond the current decision period then shortage cost is almost certainly handled in a mechanical fashion.

Finally, it should be stated that although the models presented in the following chapters, particularly those in Chapters 5 and 6, employ some special assumptions concerning the way firms simplify

---

[8] A very interesting example of an attempt to do this, based on the kind of casual empiricism which is so desirable at this stage, is a recent book by William Baumol [12].

their decision problems, these assumptions are not derived from extensive observation of decision processes within firms. To some extent the assumptions have been suggested by the author's very limited experience as an industrial consultant. To a greater extent they have been suggested by some of the planning literature in the operations research journals. Mostly, however, they have been suggested by the intuition and preconceptions imparted by a training in economics and statistics.

4. The Making of Price and Output Decisions

This section presents a summary of the writer's view of the process by which firms make short-run price and output decisions. This section is presented neither as evidence nor as formal assumptions. The evidence I have for and against the models presented in this book is contained in Chapters 9 through 12. The formal assumptions are presented in Chapters 4 to 6 containing the models themselves. This section is intended merely to provide the motivation for some of the subsequent assumptions. It provides the writer's view of the techniques employed in the making of short-run price and output decisions, techniques which the formal models in later chapters are intended to approximate in mathematical form. As a final warning it should be stated that the decision process described here does not take place in the sequence indicated. The decisions are made more or less simultaneously and continuously; the sequence refers only to the exposition.

In the first place, the firm has to decide how much information to collect. As argued above, the firm must consider the collection cost of each piece of information relevant to its decision. Nevertheless, the implications of the cost of collecting information are analyzed in this book only in the case of demand forecasting. Firms are assumed to behave "as if" they knew all cost parameters with certainty.[9] This

---

[9] Actually, a somewhat more general assumption will give the same result. Suppose some cost parameter c is a random variable whose frequency function is known by the firm. Provided c is distributed independently of output, so that its frequency function can be written $h(c)$, its mathematical expectation is

$$\bar{c} = \int_{-\infty}^{\infty} ch(c)\, dc$$

A firm concerned only with the mathematical expectation of profit can make its decisions only on the basis of the mathematical expectation $\bar{c}$ of c. All the cost parameters in the following chapters can be so interpreted. It is when the distribution of c also depends on output that trouble arises.

follows the tradition in economics of introducing uncertainty explicitly only on the demand side. The firm must decide how accurate a prediction of demand it is worthwhile to make. Very accurate forecasts of demand are of course more expensive than less accurate ones. Through intuition and experience the firm finds the point at which the extra profit resulting, on the average, from greater accuracy in the demand forecast equals the extra cost of a more accurate forecast. The distribution of interest to the firm is that of its forecast errors, actual demand minus predicted demand, and one measure of forecast accuracy is the variance of this error. As long as the cost of making forecasts with a given degree of accuracy does not change, it will not pay the firm to increase the accuracy of its forecasts. One of the conditions for equilibrium in the decision procedure is that the main characteristics of the distribution remain unchanged as long as the costs of forecasts do not change. In this view, the distribution of forecast errors should have about as much temporal stability as most of the firm's cost parameters. This is a very important point. In fact, the next chapter argues that this is all the economist needs to know about the firm's demand forecasts, at least for some purposes. In other words, even if nothing is known about the formation of the firm's expectations the economist may still explain and predict the firm's behavior.

On the basis of its demand forecasts, an estimate of the distribution of forecast errors gained from its recent forecasting experience, and estimates of the various costs involved in its operations, the firm tries to discover the price and output policy that will yield it the largest average profits. The averaging process here is over various possible forecast errors, each weighted by its probability. This policy is sought partly by observing the results of the firm's recent experience (Which policy gave the best results in similar circumstances in the past?) and partly by direct calculation (What would happen to production cost if output were increased by a certain amount?). Two questions can be raised about this view of the firm's decision making. First, is the firm interested only in the average, i.e., mathematical expectation, of profits? Second, can the combination of experience and intuitional calculation provide the firm with a policy that approximates the best one on this criterion?

The answer to the first question is partly contained in the discussion in Chapter 1, Section 1. Here, those arguments will be supplemented by a brief intuitional argument concerning the way price and output decisions are made. Price and especially output decisions of the short-run type discussed in this book are largely routine decisions,[10] at least in multiproduct manufacturing firms. They are made at short intervals of time, normally several times a year for each product produced, and therefore the sample of decisions available to the firm is quite large even if only a few years and a few products are involved. As a result, the actual average of profits within the sample is unlikely to deviate much from its mathematical expectation. Furthermore, successive decisions are made within a framework of similar external conditions. Thus it is more plausible to project recent experience with forecasting errors, and the decision maker can make decisions without having to reorganize his thinking each time. Finally, the proportion of the firm's resources risked in each decision is ordinarily quite small, at least in manufacturing, and there is undoubtedly some tendency to ignore the small probability of a large loss.

In discussing the second question we must first understand that the policy in question maximizes average profit within the model containing the simplifications and approximations that the firm finds it worthwhile to employ and not necessarily the true average profits. For example if, as in the second example above, the firm treats shortage in a mechanical way, the appropriate model for the economist to use is one that also treats shortage in this mechanical way. Then the question is whether the firm's policy approximately maximizes average profits within the model, not whether it maximizes true average profits obtained by a correct but more detailed consideration of shortage costs. Since these simplifications are made to facilitate the computation of an optimum policy, we presume that the simplifications are ones for which the firm has the necessary data and computational facilities. Nevertheless, it is not necessarily true, even on this interpretation, that the firm maximizes its average profits. In other words, the hypothesis still possesses content within the interpretation just given. On the basis of any given set of approximations and simplifications there are still many decision rules which the firm might employ, and it is still relevant to ask what techniques the firm must employ to estimate the policy suggested in this book.

In principle, the firm only needs to be able to estimate ex post the costs and revenues that result from different price and output policies in order to find its optimum policy. By experimenting with different price and output policies it can, with a sufficiently large sample of such

---

[10] See Katona's book [37] for the concept of routine behavior intended here.

decisions, find the policy that maximizes profits on the average for any given sales forecast. The averaging process involved consists of taking the profits that result from the various demands for each forecast, weighting these profits by their relative frequencies, and summing. Of course, if the firm had no information about the form of its cost and revenue functions except these observations, the procedure would require a very large number of such observations. The required number would depend on how many different demand forecasts were considered, the form of the distribution of forecast errors, and how well behaved the cost and revenue functions were.

Nevertheless, decision making on this purely trial and error basis is essentially the same as the "Monte Carlo" method,[11] which has been used with considerable success by operations research specialists in solving, among others, optimum production problems. Briefly, the Monte Carlo method is the technique of discovering important properties of a theoretical model by sampling from it. To take a trivial example: if we had a particular mathematically defined normal distribution whose mean we wished to estimate we might do so by taking a sample of observations from this particular distribution and calculating the sample mean. By taking a sufficiently large sample we might obtain as good an estimate of the true mean as we wished. This is the Monte Carlo method. Of course, in this case it would be much easier to deduce the mean of the distribution theoretically, a process that requires only an inspection of the mathematical formula since the mean of a normal distribution can be identified with one of the two parameters the distribution contains. In complicated mathematical systems, however, it is often difficult or impossible to find important characteristics in a formal way, and the Monte Carlo method is a valuable tool of analysis.

Applied to the present problem, the method consists of the experimental generation of different market situations and the evaluation of revenues and costs associated with various decisions. In this way it is

---

[11] The difference between Monte Carlo techniques and ordinary sampling is that the former samples from a theoretical model whereas the latter samples directly from the empirical population under investigation. Since World War II, Monte Carlo techniques have been widely used in pure and applied mathematics as well as in operations research. Reports of such investigations in operations research are frequently published in *Operations Research*. A good survey is presented in [31]. The sampling experiment in Chapter 8 is a small Monte Carlo study.

possible to discover the best decision in each situation. Specifically, the procedure considers a particular demand forecast and a particular price and output policy. A sample of actual demands is then generated from an assumed population distribution of actual demand around the forecast. For each member of the sample the resulting profit is computed and the average profit is found for this forecast and price and output policy. This procedure is repeated for the same forecast, but for different price and output policies. By comparing these results it is possible to estimate the price and output policies that give the best results for the demand forecast in question. The whole procedure is repeated for different forecasts.

This technique has been made feasible only by the advent of modern high-speed computers that can generate samples and do calculations rapidly. The number of observations necessary to obtain a good approximation to the best policy depends on the range of forecasts considered, the distribution of actual demands around the forecasts, and the complexity of cost functions involved. The point is that it is possible to obtain answers to such problems using only this crude trial and error procedure, and in some cases remarkably good approximations can be obtained using few observations.

The Monte Carlo technique is simply a capsule version of one way businesses can discover desirable policies from experience. By a comparison of ex post results of earlier decisions, the firm accumulates valuable information as to which policies are best in particular situations.

In fact, of course, the decision maker in business supplements the crude empiricism of the Monte Carlo method with much subtler techniques for finding desirable policies. A variety of techniques is employed to answer "iffy" questions about what would happen if different policies were followed without actually undertaking the policies in question. Education, training, and intuition, supplemented by engineering studies, are aids in finding desirable policies by predicting the effects of a great variety of different moves, most of which will never be made.

In summary, the view of decision making here is that it consists of a judicious mixture of sheer experimentation, intuition, and formal calculation. In the models presented the experimentation stage is ignored. We assume that at the time of observation the firm knows the policy that is optimum within the model containing the simplifications and approximations it decides to use. This leaves out the process of absorbing new information, or learning, though it would be desirable to have models in which learning was included.

5. *Conclusion*

None of the above proves the "as if" principle to be justified. It merely makes at least the writer feel that it is not obviously unjustified. Evidently, experience is concentrated within a restricted range of values of relevant variables and is a poorer guide to good decision making the farther outside this range one gets. Furthermore, it is difficult to accumulate much relevant experience if the number of decisions taken in similar situations is small. These facts make it more plausible to apply the above arguments to price and output decisions than to fixed capital investment decisions. Finally, it is more difficult to learn from experience if results are determined jointly by several decision variables rather than by just one. This raises the question of the extent to which decisions can be departmentalized, that is, made independently of each other in some sense. This is considered briefly in Chapter 6.

Chapter 3

THE ANALYSIS
OF EXPECTATIONS

1. Introduction

Questions pertaining to expectations have long been the subject of controversy in economics. Particularly since the late 1930's there has been a mushrooming of interest in expectations associated with the increased interest in dynamic analysis and in econometric studies. The purpose of this chapter is to discuss in a rather formal way the place of expectational analysis in economic investigations that attempt to combine theoretical and empirical material. The chapter is included because the approach to expectations in this book is somewhat different from the one usually adopted by economists. Whether this approach is desirable or not depends mainly on whether it is useful in empirical studies such as those which will be reported in Chapters 9 to 13. The general, formal considerations that appear to be relevant to the choice between alternative approaches to the handling of expectations are discussed here. In the course of the discussion important recent developments in the area are outlined and criticized. Then the particular approach to expectations that forms the basis of most of this book is outlined and discussed. It is only after the expectational concepts and assumptions introduced in this chapter have been incorporated in the specific decision theories developed in the four subsequent chapters that useful empirical estimates and tests can be attempted.

2. The Place of Expectations

Economics as a positive science is concerned with the explanation of certain observable quantities such as prices, employment, and investment. One of the things that makes the subject interesting is the fact that many economic phenomena are related to decisions whose outcomes depend on data that cannot be known until some time after the decision is taken.   Thus, for example, the profitability of a production decision depends on prices and sales that materialize only after resources have been committed to production.   For this reason, in order to make intelligent decisions economic agents must have expectations or predictions of the future events that affect the success of the decisions (prices, and sales in the above example).   Therefore, since the variable to be explained depends on a decision which in turn depends on expectations of future events, the economist's task requires as an intermediate step an investigation of the formation and use of expectations by decision makers.   Stated in this way, the argument is unexceptionable.   Clearly, before he can predict behavior the economist must have information about some characteristics of the decision maker's expectations.   What is not so clear, however, is precisely which characteristics the economist should attempt to discover.   The answer to this question depends on how the results of the investigation are to be used, what prior information is available concerning the decision process, and so forth.   This chapter shows that a somewhat different approach is available in estimating expectations from the usual one employed in econometric studies.   The circumstances in which this approach, which the author calls "implicit expectations," is preferable to the usual approach are discussed in some detail.   Before presenting this alternative approach it is useful to discuss some of the recent work in the more traditional vein.   Criticisms of this work lead naturally to the ideas advocated here, and they are presented in Section 4.

First, however, one point should be cleared up.   The assumption made in this book (see the discussion in Chapter 2, Section 4) is that decision makers are uncertain of the values, but not the distribution functions, of relevant future variables.   Hence an expectation consists in a specification of the entire distribution function of the future variable in question.[1]   Now virtually all applications of expectational analysis, whether theoretical or empirical, treat expectations as though they were numbers.   Within the framework of the present approach this can be interpreted in two ways.   First, it may be assumed that

---

[1] The point made in this paragraph really applies to all theories of expectations that do not assume certainty on the part of the decision maker.   Virtually no expectations, except those assuming certainty, can be completely characterized by a single number.

only the mean of the distribution, and not its other moments, varies from period to period. Hence the whole distribution is specified once the mean is established. Alternatively, it may be assumed that even though the other moments vary, decisions depend exclusively or mainly on the mean. This is often true, for example, in models of production planning, in which the production decision turns out to be independent of all higher moments of the distribution of random demand.[2] Even in cases in which higher moments enter the decision problem, the common procedure of ignoring all the higher order terms in a Taylor's expansion leads to the use of the mean of the distribution as a linear approximation. In this chapter the custom of treating an expectation as a number is followed. This facilitates comparison of the implicit expectations approach with other approaches. In later chapters, however, the entire distribution of the random variable will be introduced explicitly. Only when explicit assumptions to this effect are made, will higher moments be ignored.

3. Recent Investigations of Expectations

Roughly speaking, it can be said that during the 1930's much of the investigation of expectations, largely undertaken by Swedish economists,[3] was concerned with making and emphasizing the distinction between expected and realized values of variables, usually designated ex ante and ex post values. Although this is clearly an important preliminary step, it is useful only to the extent that the distinction makes possible an improved explanation of behavior. Therefore, there has been a gradual transition from the formal distinction between expectations and events themselves to the substantive questions of the dependence of behavior on expectations, and of expectations on past events. Since World War II the most interesting work concerning expectations has been concerned with some aspect of these two questions.

Specifically, two major lines of empirical investigation can be identified. On the one hand recorded expectational data have been utilized. On the other hand several techniques have been suggested for estimating expectations, and the behavior relations in which they appear, from the observed behavior of the decision maker. Most of this section will be concerned with the second of these developments, because it is more closely related to the approach adopted in this

---

[2] For an example, see [57]. For the general analysis of this problem, see [76], Chapter 8.

[3] Most of this work is summarized in the article by Ohlin [66].

book. However, since the present study has one point of contact, in Chapter 10, with the utilization of recorded expectations, the next paragraph outlines the relevant aspects of this development.

In recent years various governmental and private agencies have undertaken to record and publish the expectations of certain firms concerning variables, such as prices, sales, and capital investment, that are relevant to their decisions. The data are usually obtained by requesting firms to complete written questionnaires about their expectations and plans. Several interesting studies have been undertaken to determine the usefulness of such data in predicting both the variables in question and the decisions supposedly based on the expectations.[4] As the authors of the studies realize, such series are subject to all the limitations of information obtained by verbal report rather than by observation of economic behavior. Economists hold a strong presumption, probably justified, that observed behavior generally provides a better source of explanatory hypotheses than do verbal reports. Particularly in the case of sales forecasts there is a danger that goals or targets will be reported rather than forecasts. In many businesses sales forecasts serve, as do most accounting data, a partly normative function of attempting to stimulate personnel to better performance. In such cases a correction factor is sometimes applied, at least informally, when the forecasts are used, for example, to plan production. Of course, to the extent that this bias is present it will show in attempts to use the data to explain or predict the behavior of the firms. If alternative approaches involve less bias they presumably will be more successful in helping to understand behavior that depends on the expectations. Thus, ultimately, the question to be asked of published expectational data is whether they predict behavior better than available alternatives. Only the Modigliani-Sauerlender study cited above has considered this question thoroughly. The methods and conclusions of this interesting work are discussed in Chapter 10, where a similar comparison of the explanatory value of published expectational series is made with the implicit expectations approach.

The second recent major development concerning expectations has been the attempt to understand and estimate the generation of expectations by relating them to some plausible set of observable variables, in particular to past values of the variable that the expectation at-

---

[4] See [58], [23], [28] and [18]. Particular attention is directed toward the Modigliani-Sauerlender study [60].

tempts to predict. Hicks' "elasticity of expectations" [32] and Metzler's "coefficient of expectations" [50] are well-known examples of
this approach. More recently great interest has been shown in the
"adaptive expectations" formula employed by Cagan [15], Nerlove
[64], Friedman [27], and others. The idea behind the adaptive expectations formula is a very simple one: expectations are altered pro-
portionately to the error most recently observed. If x_n^e is the expectation of a variable x at time n, when x_{n-1} is known, then in the adaptive
expectations formula, x_n^e is given by

$$x_n^e = x_{n-1}^e + B(x_{n-1} - x_{n-1}^e) \qquad (1)$$

where B (>0) is a constant which determines the responsiveness of
expectations to expectational errors. Since the x^e's for previous periods
are also given by (1), it can be seen that x_n^e is a weighted sum of earlier
x's where the weights decline geometrically through time.

All three of these expectational formulas are simple autoregressive
systems involving particular weights for lagged values of the variable
being predicted. Even though autoregressive schemes have the advantage of keeping analysis simple, it is surprising that their use to
represent expectations has so much intuitive appeal to economists.
Empirical investigations by Kendall [38] and others suggest that for
many economic series only a relatively small part of the movement in
the variables can be explained by examining their autoregressive structure. In particular, the inclusion of terms lagged more than one period
seems to add very little to the explanation of the variable in question.
This means that autoregressive schemes contain very little predictive
information not already exploited by a naive forecast that employs
only the most recently observed value of the variable to forecast the
next period's value. Therefore, an expectation based exclusively on an
autoregressive scheme is likely to yield a poor forecast of the variable.
Furthermore, there is little support for the use of autoregressive schemes
on theoretical grounds. Most economic theory is based on the notion
that different economic phenomena are closely related, so that they
cannot be explained solely in terms of their own history. If it were
not so, economics would be a very trivial subject. Thus, on both
empirical and theoretical grounds, economists should have little faith
in the predictive value of autoregressive schemes. There is no evidence that forecasters and decision makers in business feel otherwise.

It might reasonably be argued that the criticism is superficial, because autoregressive schemes are really intended to govern only that

part of the expectation not derived from other variables (sometimes called the endogenous part). To investigate this possibility, consider the following generalization of (1). Let $V = (v_1, \cdots, v_R)$ be the vector of the R variables v_i thought by the decision maker to be relevant to the determination of x_n. Let V_n be the value assumed by the vector in period n. Some of the v_i may of course represent past decisions taken by the individual concerned, or lagged values of other variables. Then $X(V_n)$ is the function embodying the decision maker's knowledge of the effect of the v_i on x in period n. The generalization of (1) can now be written as

$$x_n^e = X(V_n) + B(x_{n-1} - x_{n-1}^e) \tag{2}$$

In considering the plausibility of (1) or (2) in the formation of expectations it is important to recognize that expectations are, from a statistical point of view, estimators. The function on the right hand side of (2) is an estimator of x_n and the value of x_n^e obtained from inserting particular values of the independent variables into the right hand side is an estimate of x_n. In keeping with economists' tradition of assuming rationality on the part of decision makers, it seems reasonable to require that an expectations formula assume that the individual in question will make efficient use of whatever information is at his disposal, V_n, x_{n-1} and x_{n-1}^e, in (2). However, the adaptive formula fails to satisfy this criterion in that in general it implies biased expectations. By observing his own past mistakes the decision maker could, with no additional outside information, improve his forecasts. Formally, this can be seen as follows. Define u_n as the expectational error in period n,

$$u_n = x_n - x_n^e \tag{3}$$

Subtracting x_n from both sides of (2) and using (3), we have

$$-u_n = X(V_n) - x_n + Bu_{n-1}$$

Now the expectational formula is an unbiased one only if the mathematical expectation of u_n equals zero for all n. It should be stressed that, for any n, the relevant expectation is conditional on all information available when x_n^e is to be determined including V_n and u_{n-1}. Hence for the purpose of this operation the first and third terms on the right hand side of the above equation are constants. Then the condition that $E(u_n) = 0$ reduces to

$$E(x_n) = X(V_n) + Bu_{n-1} \tag{4}$$

The expectation must be unbiased regardless of last period's expectational error and this requires that (4) should be an identity for all u_{n-1}. In order for this to be true B must equal zero and the function $X(V_n)$ must satisfy

$$E(x_n) = X(V_n)$$

Hence the adaptive expectation term drops out in (2) and we are left with the expectational equation

$$x_n^e = X(V_n)$$

In words, this result simply shows that if x_{n-1} or x_{n-1}^e contain information that will help in predicting x_n, then this information is used most effectively by building it into the function $X(V_n)$. If x_{n-1} and x_{n-1}^e are of no help in predicting x_n, or if their use is already exploited in $X(V_n)$, then no further help can be obtained from the error term u_{n-1}. In other words, if error terms contained some information of predictive value, better predictions could be obtained by utilizing this information and therefore having different error terms with no predictive value. The deficiency in the adaptive expectations formula is the same as the one that makes regression analysis yield poor predictions when autocorrelated error terms are not taken into account.

It should be noted that none of the above implies that adaptive expectations must necessarily be biased. Suppose, for example, that the variable x_n to be predicted is generated by an autoregressive scheme of the form

$$x_n = \gamma \sum_1^\infty (1 - \gamma)^{i-1} x_{n-i} + \epsilon_n$$

where ϵ_n is a stationary random variable with no autocorrelation and a zero mean. Then the expectation will be unbiased if it is generated by the similar scheme

$$x_n^e = \gamma \sum_1^\infty (1 - \gamma)^{i-1} x_{n-i}$$

However, as was pointed out above, the adaptive formula can be written in precisely this form. Hence, adaptive expectations are unbiased if, and only if, $B = \gamma$. The point is not that adaptive expectations must be biased. They, or any other autoregressive expectational formulas, may be right if the variable being predicted is generated by precisely the autoregressive scheme that the expectational formula posits. In contrast with the assumption always made in applications of autoregressive expectational schemes, the parameter of the scheme cannot be chosen independently of the way the variable being predicted is generated.[5]

Note also that the condition that expectations be unbiased does not require that the decision maker have any particular amount of information. His expectations do not have to be right and he does not even need to know the true mechanism generating x_n. The implication is that, whatever information is available, the adaptive expectations formula in general fails to make effective use of it. Using the same information it is possible to make a prediction of x_n whose error variance is smaller than that of the adaptive expectations formula simply by removing the bias in this formula. This argument does not depend on whether x_n is autocorrelated or not. Any autocorrelation observed in the x series can be used to form an unbiased estimate of x_n by including lagged values of x among the v_i in (2).

The above criticism applies specifically only to the adaptive expectations formula. However, it is a special case of a more general argument that applies to virtually all the autoregressive schemes used by economists to represent expectations. The theoretical use usually made of expectational equations is to deduce, with their aid, the behavior of a particular variable. Within a theory that assumes a considerable degree of rationality on the part of decision makers, this use provides an internal check on the expectational assumptions which, unfortunately, is rarely utilized. As has been emphasized by Fellner [25], a decision maker who is presumed to act rationally in other respects should not be presumed to continue forming expectations that lead to systematically wrong results. In other words, if the economist's theory implies that a variable is generated by a particular process then he should not assume that expectations of the variable are formed in a way inconsistent with this process. This is particularly important if, as in the usual model, the variable is generated by a relatively simple mechanism that an intelligent decision maker, who is familiar with the series, can estimate.

These remarks do not mean that economists should always assume that decision makers correctly predict the numerical values of relevant

[5] There are in fact important theoretical models in which the variable in question is autoregressive. One such, in which the model shows that expectations can be unbiased only if they are generated by the adaptive formula with an appropriate B, is presented in an important paper by J. Muth [61]. The above paragraph owes much to a reading of this paper.

variables. There may be a stochastic component of the variable that makes accurate numerical prediction impossible. Even if a more accurate prediction can be obtained, it may be so costly that it is not worthwhile. Here it is argued only that decision makers should not be assumed to retain systematic biases in their expectations such as the one present in the adaptive expectations formula. It is still possible and desirable to retain the assumption that individuals make considerable forecasting errors. The force of the argument in the previous paragraph is presumably greater when, as in making output, inventory, and price decisions, there is a large routine element in the decision process. The routine nature of these decisions permits the accumulation of a large sample of experience with which to eliminate biases in the expectational process.

It may still be argued that in spite of the above objections the adaptive expectations formula, or some other autoregressive scheme, yields better explanations of the data the economist is trying to investigate than do alternative approaches. This is an important argument, and in empirical studies such as those by Cagan [15] and Nerlove [64], the adaptive expectations approach has had considerable success. Nevertheless, this is an empirical question and the answer depends on the set of alternative approaches considered.

4. Implicit Expectations

The expectational analysis used in this book is free of the objections raised in the previous section. Although the writer feels that these objections are persuasive, the approach suggested here is obviously not the only way of meeting them. It is suggested as an approach that appears to offer as much chance of success as the available alternatives, at least in some circumstances and for some purposes. No stronger claim can be made without more persuasive evidence than is presented here. To avoid terminological confusion it is desirable to introduce formal notation at the outset. Time subscripts will be dropped except when they are significant.

Recall that the reason for the economist's interest in the decision maker's expectations is that the economist wishes to predict or explain decisions or behavior. However, the decision maker's behavior, y, is a function of his expectation

$$y = Y(x^e) \tag{5}$$

Of course more variables than a single expectation are normally relevant to decisions, but the presence of other variables in the behavior relation does not affect the following argument, except as noted below. The economist's problems arise from the fact that the expectation x^e is not directly observable. If the economist could observe x^e, then the estimation of $Y(x^e)$ from a sample of observations of y and x^e would be a straightforward, though not necessarily easy, statistical problem. If the behavior relation were known then, since y is observable, x^e could be estimated from the inverse function

$$x^e = Y^{-1}(y)$$

at least if Y were monotonic. The latter situation may indeed sometimes occur. For example, if y is the output and x^e the price expected by a firm in a purely competitive industry, the traditional theory of competitive price and output policy tells us that the output chosen will be the one that equates marginal cost and expected price. In this case the inverse function Y^{-1} would be the marginal cost function estimates of which may be available from accounting or engineering data. More commonly, the investigator must estimate both the expectation and the behavior relation from a single sample.

The usual approach in this situation starts from a recognition that the expectation is a function of some observable variables. To borrow some notation from Section 3, the decision maker's expectation is his estimate of the effect of a vector $V = (v_1, \cdots, v_R)$ on x,

$$x^e = X(V) \tag{6}$$

With this notation, the autoregressive schemes discussed in Section 3 are all special cases of the function X in which the v_i are lagged values of x. Using (5) and (6) we obtain

$$y = Y[X(V)] = G(V) \tag{7}$$

G is thus a composite function consisting of both the behavior and expectations functions. The usual procedure is for the investigator to form an estimate $\hat{G}$ of G by taking the regression of y on the set of variables he thinks likely to determine the decision maker's expectations. This involves guessing the set of variables $v_1, \cdots, v_R$, the form of the X function, and the form of the Y function. It is not generally possible to estimate separately the behavior relation Y and the expectational relation X from the estimate $\hat{G}$,[6] but for some purposes it does not matter. This procedure will be referred to as the explicit approach to expectations.

The approach adopted in this book starts with a recognition that an expectation, in addition to being a function of observable variables, is also the decision maker's estimate or prediction of a variable. As with any other estimate, an expectation has certain statistical properties which, in principle, are discoverable. This is perfectly obvious. What appears to be an innovation is the argument that, on certain assumptions about the statistical properties of the estimate, the economist can estimate both the behavior relation and the expectation itself in an indirect or implicit way. Recall the notation of equation (3), which defined the expectational error by

$$x = x^e + u$$

In words, u is the decision maker's error in predicting x. Substituting (3) in (5), we have

$$y = Y(x^e) = Y(x - u) \tag{8}$$

a relation of the error in the variable type, since the observed variable x differs from the true variable x^e by an error of observation u. Virtually all that is known about statistical properties of estimates of such relations is concerned with the case in which the Y function is linear. For most practical applications only linear estimates are feasible, and no nonlinear estimates are attempted in this book. (See, however, the discussion of approximations in Chapters 7 and 8.) Hence, further discussion will be restricted to the case in which the decision rule is linear in x^e, that is,

$$y = Y(x^e) = \alpha + \gamma x^e$$

Then, using (3), we obtain

$$y = \alpha + \gamma x - \gamma u = \alpha + \gamma x + \epsilon \tag{9}$$

where $\epsilon = -\gamma u$. Now (9) is a standard statistical specification of a linear structural equation connecting the observable variables y and x, and on certain assumptions concerning the statistical properties of ϵ

---

[6] Sometimes the expectations and behavior functions can be separated. Nerlove [64] presents examples in which this is possible, specifying X as the adaptive expectations formula.

standard least squares techniques will yield good estimates of α and γ. Assume for the moment that these properties, discussed below, are present and that we have least squares estimates a and c of α and γ from a sample of observations of x and y. We then obtain an estimate $\hat{y}$ of y from the regression equation,

$$\hat{y} = a + cx$$

This estimate is subject to a regression error e defined by

$$e = y - \hat{y}$$

the difference between the observed and predicted values of y. Now the regression error is an estimate of the true residual ϵ:

$$e = \text{est } \epsilon = \text{est } (-\gamma u)$$

Therefore,

$$e/c = \text{est } (-u) = -\hat{u}$$

From this we obtain an estimate $\hat{x}^e$ of x^e

$$\hat{x}^e = x - e/c = x - \hat{u} = \frac{y - a}{c}$$

We refer to $\hat{x}^e$ as the implicit expectation. The basic idea behind this calculation is very simple. The implicit expectations approach makes possible an estimate of the behavior equation without first obtaining an estimate of the independent variable x^e. Once the behavior equation has been estimated, however, the inverse function provides an estimate of the expectation as a function of the observed decision. We refer to $\hat{x}^e$ as the implicit expectation since it is an estimate of the value such that, if this were the true expectation, it would lead to the behavior actually observed.

Thus, provided the distribution of u is appropriate, the implicit expectations approach yields an estimate of the behavior relation and, indirectly, of the expectation itself. The desirable properties of the distribution of ϵ are a zero mathematical expectation, a constant variance, and independence of x and of its own lagged values.[7] Of course, if ϵ has these properties, so does u, and vice versa.

On what, then, does the choice between the explicit and implicit approaches depend? In the explicit approach, an incorrect specification of the expectations equation (6), the omission of some of the v_i or an incorrect guess as to the form of the X function, leads to a struc-

_____
[7] See [74], pp. 280–284.

tural relation in which there are errors of observation in the independent variable x^e. As stated above, in the implicit approach the use of x as a proxy for x^e also leads to an equation with errors of observation in the expectations variable. Hence, both approaches lead to essentially the same kinds of statistical problems, those that arise in estimating an equation containing observational errors in the variables. Both approaches entail the small sample bias in the estimate c of γ which is known to result in such cases. The choice between the two approaches depends on two considerations: first, the properties of the error distributions involved, that is, a comparison between the distribution of u and that of the error in estimating the X function in the explicit approach; second, the precise purpose of the investigation. Most of the remainder of this section is concerned with a discussion of these two considerations.

(*a*) *Distribution of Error Terms.* Roughly speaking, the more accurately the economist can specify the expectations function the greater the advantage in the explicit approach; the better the decision maker is able to predict x, the greater the advantage in the implicit approach. The consideration is the economist's ability to estimate the decision maker's expectations, compared with the decision maker's ability to forecast the variable in question. There are two limiting cases: (i) The decision maker knows the true nonstochastic mechanism generating x, so $x^e \equiv x$ and $u \equiv 0$; (ii) The economist knows the true nonstochastic expectations equation $x^e = X(V)$. Either (i) or (ii) can occur, or both, or neither. If both (i) and (ii) are true, the decision maker knows with complete certainty the true mechanism generating x, the economist knows it, and the economist knows that the decision maker knows it. In this case the problem evaporates altogether and the behavior relation can be estimated equally well by either the explicit or the implicit method. If (i) but not (ii) is true, the implicit expectations approach is preferable. In this case the decision maker is good at predicting x but the economist does not know how he does it. If (ii) but not (i) is true, the explicit approach is preferable. In this case the decision maker makes mistakes, but the economist knows how the decision maker forms his expectations. In general, neither (i) nor (ii) is true and the investigator must decide on the better approach. We contend that there are at least some reasons to think that the implicit approach may yield a better estimate of the behavior relation than the explicit approach.

It can be argued that the formation of expectations by firms, for example, is likely to be a more subtle process than most simple expectations formulas of economists assume. Almost certainly, the trained intuition of a person or group whose job it is to forecast a variable will be able to take account of more factors, in a more sophisticated way, than do most of the usual expectational formulas. Thus, although there may be some stable relationship between expectations and the observable variables on which they depend, it is not necessarily of a simple form easily estimated by available statistical techniques and data. Therefore the likelihood of a significantly incorrect specification of the expectational function X appears great. To the extent that incorrect specification occurs, the estimate $\hat{G}$ of G in (7) will be a poor one.

On the other hand, even if there is no simple or stable formula that generates expectations, there may still be considerable statistical stability in the expectational process. Stability requires that the probability of different forecast errors be approximately constant through time. It implies that the u terms are drawn from approximately the same distribution over considerable periods of time, and hence that at least two of the desirable properties, constancy of mean and variance, are present.

To a large extent the decision maker has an incentive to make forecasts whose errors have desirable statistical properties from the economist's point of view. As argued in Chapter 2, statistical stability of expectational errors can be regarded as an equilibrium condition for the profit-seeking decision maker. Thus, the profit motive leads to a distribution of u terms which is invariant through time. In addition, as argued in Section 3, the decision maker has an incentive to eliminate from his forecasts biases such as those due to autocorrelation of error terms. Thus the economist's and the decision maker's interests coincide here. The properties that make the forecast a good one from the decision maker's point of view also make it possible for the economist to estimate the decision maker's behavior relation using the implicit expectations approach.

(*b*) *Purpose of the Investigation.* The purpose of the investigation is relevant because the two approaches being compared use different data and yield estimates of different sets of relationships. The explicit approach requires observations of the behavior variable y and of the variables from which the investigator thinks the expectation is formed; $v_1, \cdots, v_R$ if the true set is known. It yields an estimate or prediction of the former on the basis of the latter, but generally not of the expectation itself. The implicit approach, on the other hand, requires observations only of y and x. It yields an estimate of the behavior relation and a prediction of y on the basis of x. Indirectly, it always yields an estimate of the expectation x^e, but not of the expectation function $X(V)$. Since different purposes require estimates of different relationships, one approach or the other may be better for a particular investigation.

One important advantage of the implicit expectations approach is that the investigator does not need to know the ways in which x, or the decision maker's expectation x^e of x, are generated to estimate the behavior relation $Y(x^e)$. All he needs is a sample of observations of y and x and the assumption of statistical stability of expectations. A price must be paid for simplicity, however. In this case, the implicit approach does not by itself yield a prediction of y in advance of the observation of x, which normally occurs simultaneously with, or after, the behavior itself. The implicit approach does predict y in the sense that it explains the effect of x on y, but not in the temporal sense. Therefore, if the purpose of the study is a temporal prediction of the behavior y, the implicit expectations approach is not sufficient for the purpose. Illustrations of this will be provided in Chapters 9 to 12, in which the implicit expectations concept will be used to "predict" price and output in several sets of empirical data. However, each prediction will be a function of the sales volume observed in the period to which the prediction applies, and the sales variable is not explained by the model. In order to provide temporal predictions of price and output the model would have to be closed with a third relation that explained sales, for example, a demand equation.

In practical terms, even the explicit approach may not make possible a temporal prediction of y if the v_i are not available to the investigator in time. It is conceivable that x might become available to the investigator before some of the v_i and hence the implicit approach would yield a prediction of y before the explicit approach, but not prior to the behavior itself. Indeed, some of the v_i may never become available to the economist. One important factor in determining a firm's expectations may be declarations of future purchases, made by potential customers to the firm's sales personnel. This, and other, information normally remains within the individual firm.

There is, however, a more important and basic aspect of this problem. Often, the purpose of the study involving the behavior relation

$Y(x^e)$ is the explanation of the variable x itself. In other words, the model being constructed often contains other relations that close the system by specifying x as a function of y, among other things. In this case the implicit approach makes possible a temporal prediction of y since the independent variable x in the behavior equation is a dependent variable in some other relation. The simultaneous solution of all the relations in the model gives x, and hence an estimate of y, as a function of the predetermined and exogenous variables in the model. An example is presented in Chapter 4. In that chapter, the expectation has to do with price in a purely competitive market. The behavior relation is a production decision giving the firm's output as a function of the expected price. When the model is closed with a demand equation, the price becomes an endogenous variable of which the model yields a temporal prediction.

There is one further factor which appears, at least superficially, to weigh against the use of the implicit approach. The appearance of a single expectational variable in the behavior relation (5) does not imply that other expectational variables are not sometimes relevant to behavior. For example, it is known [8] that a short-run production decision depends in principle on the distribution of demand expected for all future periods within the firm's planning horizon. In this case, continuing to assume that all expectations can be represented by numbers, the behavior equation (5) must be generalized to read

$$y_n = Y[x_n{}^e(n), x_{n+1}^e(n), \cdots, x_{n+N}^e(n)] \tag{10}$$

Here $x_i{}^e(j)$ is the expectation of x_i held at the beginning of period j, and N indicates the number of planning periods within the decision maker's horizon. In this more general case both the implicit and the usual forms of the explicit approaches require some modification. The natural extension of the implicit approach would be to write

$$x_i{}^e(j) = x_i + u_i(j - i)$$

and to assume that all expectations are statistically stable, but that the distribution of expectational errors depends on the number of periods in advance that the forecast is made. Of course, the larger is N and the larger the variances of the u's the larger the error to which the investigator's prediction of y is subject. More important, unless the model is closed, the prediction of y not only cannot be made in advance, it must be made N periods in arrears. This is because the

[8] Proved rigorously in [22].

behavior y_n is now predicted as a function of the observed values $x_n, \cdots, x_{n+N}$.

A similar revision of the explicit approach is required when (10) is the true behavior relation. In this case an expectational equation must be introduced for each of the $N + 1$ expectations, and the resulting composite function must be estimated.

Three factors explain why the indicated revisions are not usually undertaken in studies using the explicit approach, and why they are not undertaken in the studies in this book using the implicit approach.

(i) Statistically, there is not much hope of separating either the influence of the v_i on different future expectations or the influence of different future expectations on current behavior. In both cases the influences are presumably so interdependent (for example, a movement in $x_{n+2}^e(n)$ has a similar effect on y_n to that of $x_{n+1}^e(n)$) that available data and statistical techniques could not separate them. Another way of stating this is to say that one future expectation utilizes virtually all the available statistical information of value in predicting y.

(ii) There is considerable question about the amount of future information relevant to current decisions. It is an interesting and important question, only one systematic study of which is known to the writer.[9] The question is discussed in detail in reference to production decisions by firms in Chapter 6. There it is shown that, in more general conditions than might be expected, current production depends only on the expectation of sales during the one future period for which the production plan is being made.

(iii) There is some evidence that firms rarely consider more than the near future in making production decisions. Partly, the evidence is that explicit forecasts are normally recorded only very short periods ahead (see Chapter 6). If true, this fact is related to the discussion in Chapter 2. The cost of making forecasts with any predictive value far in advance may be greater than the increased profit or utility that an improved forecast would permit. It is also related to point (ii) above, for the effect on current production of forecasts of future demands is less when the demand is farther in the future.[10]

---

[9] That by Modigliani and Cohen [58].

[10] The rigorous form of this statement is the theorem, first proved in [22], that under very general circumstances the optimum policy and the resulting utility with an infinite horizon can be approximated to any desired degree by the optimum policy with a finite horizon provided only the horizon chosen is long enough.

In concluding this section, we must take account of the fact that in practice there are important sources of residuals in estimating behavior relations other than those which have been discussed above. The last few paragraphs have been concerned with observational errors in the expectations variable resulting from (i) the use of the observed value of the variable as a proxy for the expectation in the implicit approach and (ii) misspecifications of the expectations function in the explicit approach. Normally the economist also has to reckon with errors in the equation arising from misspecification of the behavior relation. The point here is that errors in the equation invalidate the use of the implicit approach to estimate the expectations themselves, but not to estimate the behavior relation in which they appear.

It has been shown that the essential step in calculating the implicit expectations is the association of residuals in the estimated behavior relation with estimates of the expectational errors. If residuals are partly from other sources they will not be good estimates of the expectational errors. The fact that regression residuals are partly the result of specification errors, however, does not prevent the economist from estimating the relation, provided the specification errors have the three desirable statistical properties specified. If specification errors do not have these properties, neither the implicit nor the explicit approach can result in good estimates of the behavior relation. Thus, the use of the implicit approach to estimate expectations is a much bolder step than its use to estimate a behavior relation, and the former should be undertaken only after careful consideration of the difficulties involved.

5. *Conclusion*

In this chapter we have argued that the assumption of statistical stability of expectations is as reasonable as the usual one, that the economist knows the true form of the expectations function. This alternative assumption makes it possible to estimate a behavior relation in which an expectation appears as an independent variable without prior information about the generation of the expectation. Indirectly, it yields an estimate of the expectation itself. The real "gimmick" in this procedure is the use of regression residuals to estimate expectational errors. To the extent that regression residuals result from other causes, such as a misspecification of the form of the behavior relation, the implicit approach will yield bad estimates of expectations. On the other hand, using the explicit approach, a misspecification of either the behavior relation or of the expectation function will yield bad results.

In fact, there is no fundamental reason to regard the two approaches as competitive rather than complementary. Initially, when little information is available concerning the form of the X function, one can use the implicit approach to estimate a behavior relation and the relevant expectation. Using this estimate of the expectation as a dependent variable one can try to find an expectational formula (6), and use this estimate to try to improve the prediction of the behavior variable. This possibility is an implication of the fact that both assumptions may be true; expectations may be statistically stable and also generated by some expectational formula that can be estimated.

The discussion in this chapter suggests a number of interesting empirical investigations, some of which are undertaken in later chapters. First and most obvious is a comparison of the behavior predicted by the implicit and explicit approaches. Second, the expectations themselves should be estimated using the implicit approach and compared, in cases where they can be calculated, with those yielded by alternative explicit approaches. Finally it would be interesting to compare the implicit expectations with published expectations if the latter are available. In addition it might be ascertained whether the implicit or published expectations provided better predictions of behavior.

Chapter 4

PERFECT COMPETITION

1. Introduction

This chapter is concerned with the behavior of the firm and the industry in a perfectly competitive market. The following chapters are concerned with similar topics for an imperfectly competitive industry. For the purpose of this book a firm is said to be in a perfectly competitive, "competitive" for short, market if it expects, for any reason, to be able to sell as much as it wishes in each period, at whatever price happens to rule in that period. The notion of a market is taken to include uniformity of price among all firms in the same market. It follows from this definition that, although the firm may be uncertain of prices in future periods, the sales level at each possible price is a nonstochastic decision variable, completely under the control of the firm. On the other hand, when imperfect competition is considered in succeeding chapters it will be natural to assume that the firm is uncertain of the sales that will result at each price set.

This distinction about the way uncertainty enters is a fundamental one, and it permeates the analysis at every point. The writer originally thought that, with or without uncertainty, the problem of programming the perfectly competitive firm's activity was much simpler than programming that of the imperfectly competitive firm. The writer's reason for believing this was the notion that a competitive market performs a considerable amount of computation that the firm would have to do otherwise. Specifically, it computes the prices at which, in one sense or another, supply equals demand. The writer is no longer convinced that this is an important simplification. In any case, it seems clear that there are important unsolved programming problems for firms in both kinds of markets. Some of them are described in detail below.

What is certain is that the kinds of programming problems involved, and in particular the considerations that govern inventory policy, are quite different in the two cases. In imperfect competition, inventory policy is closely related to the desirability of hedging against a demand which, at the price set, is abnormally high. In perfect competition this factor cannot enter since there is no uncertainty about the amount demanded at any given price. Instead, the competitive firm's inventory policy is related to the "speculative" consideration that, by producing ahead when price is expected to rise, it can take advantage of lower production costs and increase its profits.

The first purpose of this chapter is to introduce inventories into a model of the output and sales decisions of a firm in a perfectly competitive market. In the absence of uncertainty, this is not terribly difficult. Surprisingly enough, in spite of this and of the interest shown by economists in perfectly competitive markets, no one ever seems to have presented a complete analysis of the optimum output, sales, and inventory policy of a competitive firm on the rather general assumptions made in the next section. Most writers on the subject [1] have exploited the analogy between price discrimination and multiperiod planning and, although this analogy is certainly helpful, it suggests inessential restrictions. In the presence of uncertainty the programming problem is much more complicated and is largely unsolved. It is argued in Section 5, however, that important insights can still be gained from the results established for the certainty case.

The second purpose of this chapter is to use the decision-making model developed in succeeding pages to investigate the dynamic stability of the market as a whole. Recent years have seen a resurgent and continuing interest in the question of stability in economies characterized by perfectly competitive markets.[2] By the application of more rigorous and sophisticated techniques it has been possible to establish many important new results that were inaccessible with simpler techniques employed in earlier investigations of stability. Now from the point of view of decision theory the interesting thing about these studies is the contrast between the decision processes assumed in the static and dynamic parts of the analysis. The static decision theory employed, based on the assumptions of profit maximization by firms

[1] See [44], [70], and [72].
[2] See [8] and the references therein.

and ordinal utility maximization by consumers, involves a careful and rigorous working out of the implications of rational decision making on the two sides of the market. Great care is taken to introduce explicit motivational assumptions and to deduce exactly what behavior they imply. The dynamic analysis, on the other hand, is based on the assumption of simple, mechanical, nonrational behavior by buyers and sellers, for which no motivational assumptions have been introduced. Specifically, this is true in two respects.

The first has to do with the introduction of expectations. When future expected prices are introduced into the model they are normally assumed to be generated by one of the simple autoregressive schemes criticized in Chapter 3, Section 3. It is then assumed that these expected prices have an effect on current demand and supply that is symmetrical with the effect of current prices. In other words, the same restrictions, mainly concerning sign, are placed on the coefficients relating current demand and supply to expected prices as are placed on the coefficients relating current demand and supply to current prices.[3] Now the assumption that expected future prices have an effect on current behavior is presumably related to the possibility of inventory holding, at least on the part of firms. Otherwise, it is not easy to see why, in a competitive market, expected future prices should be relevant to firms' current output and sales policy. However, the possibility of holding inventories introduces an important asymmetry into the effect of expected future prices. Although a rise in future expected price may induce the firm to build up inventories, a fall in future expected price can induce it to unload inventory only if it already has some inventory. If expected prices are to be introduced it would seem desirable to do so within the framework of an explicit theory of inventory holding.

The second mechanical element in studies of dynamic stability relates to the assumptions made concerning price formation. The usual assumption is simply that the rate of change of price is an increasing function of the excess of demand over supply in the market in question. Here demand refers to nonspeculative demand, and supply refers to the usual sum of firms' marginal production cost curves. Now if the price in question is below the equilibrium and demand exceeds supply, some consumers are unable to buy the quantity they wish at this price unless firms hold inventories that they are willing to reduce. If the

[3] Two examples are [11] and [24].

price is above equilibrium and supply exceeds demand, then some firms are unable to sell the quantity they wish at this price and, presumably, inventories accumulate. Thus, again there appears to be an implicit inventory consideration hiding in the background. Yet the accumulation of inventories at prices above equilibrium affects neither production nor sales. In either case there is a breakdown of competition in the sense that someone is no longer free to buy or sell in unlimited quantities at the existing price. Thus, expectations are wrong. Yet firms and consumers are assumed to behave in a way that is reasonable only if buying and selling in unlimited quantities are possible; for example, making decisions on the static profit and utility maximization principles. This is an example of the practice, criticized in detail in Section 3 of Chapter 3, of assuming that economic agents will behave in ways that are rational only if expectations can be continuously proved wrong.

In the dynamic analysis of Sections 4 and 5 these deficiencies are removed. Inventory policy is introduced in the model developed in the next section as an integral part of the firm's planning. In addition, in the spirit of the discussion in Chapters 2 and 3, expectations are assumed to be correct in one sense or another. In particular, this requires that the firm's belief that it will be able to sell what it wants at whatever price materializes in the future be correct. For this to be true, however, the price must adjust each period in such a way that firms' output and inventory plans are consistent with consumers' purchase plans.

Now it may be that a satisfactory and thorough investigation would have to assume the breakdown of competition in disequilibrium, that is, the inconsistency of firms' and consumers' plans.[4] It may be that disequilibrium is intimately related to incorrect expectations. If so, the nature of the breakdown, and the resulting behavior, should be analyzed more carefully than has been done in the past. Nevertheless, it seems worthwhile to follow the procedure adopted here and to retain the essential assumption of competition, that the price adjusts to clear the market in each period even in disequilibrium, and firms are therefore able to carry out their planned behavior.

The first justification for this is to show that dynamic analysis with determinate results is possible in this case. We can develop a dynamic model whose stability properties can be established, and in which

---

[4] This has been argued by Arrow [6].

firms' expectations are always correct in either a numerical or a statistical sense. This model should help to answer the question of whether the stability or instability of such markets is necessarily associated with inaccurate expectations. The analysis in Sections 4 and 5 shows that, at least in the model analyzed here, a competitive market in which expectations are correct is necessarily an unstable one. If this conclusion is accepted it suggests that the reasons for stability in such markets, if any, must be sought in behavior that in disequilibrium is based on systematically incorrect expectations.

The second reason for retaining the assumption that the price clears the market each period is that things become rather complicated when it is dropped, that is, when we assume that firms can affect the price out of, but not in, equilibrium. Hence the retention of the competitive assumption, which greatly simplifies the analysis of Sections 4 and 5, is desirable in this case, as in others, on grounds of convenience.

The final justification is that the assumption maintains the traditional notion that one of the fundamental characteristics of a competitive market is that price moves quickly to the level that clears the market. On the other hand, this assumption has the disadvantage of assuming that a considerable amount of dynamic adjustment already has occurred before prices and sales are recorded, and it leaves this adjustment unanalyzed.

The plan of the rest of the chapter is as follows. Section 2 considers the production, sales, and inventory plan of a firm in a competitive market when its expectations are numbers rather than random variables. Although Section 2 is concerned with the individual firm, Sections 3 and 4 are concerned with the adjustment of the market as a whole. Section 3 investigates the implications, in a simple, cobweb-type model, of the assumption that expectations are correct. This section is intended simply to illustrate the remarks above and in the previous chapter about the consistency of actual and expected events when the latter are generated by a simple expectational formula, the adaptive expectations equation in this example. In Section 4 the stability of a market in which firms hold inventories and make plans according to the model developed in Section 2 is investigated. In Section 5 an attempt is made to generalize these results to the case in which expectations are stochastic. It is argued that the programming problem is formidable, but that an approximation, analogous to the one used in Section 4, can be obtained for the stochastic case. This approximation is then shown to yield results parallel to those found in Section 4.

2. Production and Inventory Policy in a Competitive Firm

In this section we consider the optimum production, sales, and inventory policy of a firm in a perfectly competitive market. It is assumed that expected prices are nonstochastic. The relevance of this model to the case in which the firm knows only the probability distribution of future prices is considered in Section 5. Although the model presented here has important nonlinearities not present in many similar models that have been studied in the literature, the techniques employed bear a strong family resemblance to those employed by others who have worked on such problems. The resemblance is particularly great to techniques that have frequently been employed in nonstochastic production-smoothing problems.[5]

For notational simplicity the firm is assumed to have a finite horizon of N periods within which it does not discount the future. The introduction of discounting with either a finite or an infinite horizon makes no essential difference, and the interested reader can easily rework the results with these changes. Although prices may be expected to change in the future, the firm does not expect its production and inventory cost functions to change over time. In addition, production costs in one period are assumed to be independent of the volume of production in other periods. Starting with period one, the firm's profits over the entire horizon can be written

$$\Pi_1^N = \sum_1^N p_n^e x_n - \sum_1^N c(z_n) - \sum_1^N r(I_n) \tag{1}$$

where p_n^e = price expected in period n, x_n = sales, z_n = production, both during the nth period, and I_n = inventory remaining at the end of the nth period. The total cost of producing z units in any period is $c(z)$, and $r(I)$ is the total cost of storing I units between any two consecutive periods. Both $c(z)$ and $r(I)$ are assumed to be strictly convex functions of their arguments, that is, marginal production and inventory costs are assumed to increase with the amounts produced and stored respectively.[6] Concavities in the two functions (decreasing marginal

---

[5] See especially the investigation by Modigliani and Hohn [59].

[6] It is also assumed that, for some admissable arguments, $c'(z)$ and $r'(I)$ can be made as large as may be necessary to satisfy (3a) and (3b) below.

costs) greatly complicate the analysis, and linearities (constant marginal costs) make the problem uninteresting. The reason for the latter statement is that if $r(I)$ were linear the firm would either store nothing or sell nothing each period. If $c(z)$ were linear the firm would either produce nothing or an infinite amount, or at least the amount that caused the breakdown of perfect competition, each period.

Before beginning the formal analysis, we should discuss one other assumption explicitly. In (2a) below, one of the constraints imposed on the firm's policy is $I_n \geq 0$. Although this non-negativity constraint is a natural and widely used one in the programming literature, it is often omitted in models of speculative behavior. There are three substantive interpretations which have been given to the notion of negative inventories.

(i) A firm may be thought to have the possibility of buying from other firms as well as of producing, thus making it possible to sell more than the sum of its own production and initial inventory. Although this may be possible for a single firm it is, by definition, not possible for the market as a whole and therefore should be excluded from a study aimed at the analysis of the entire market.

(ii) A firm, or the entire market, may be thought to have the possibility of postponing some deliveries for one or more periods.[7] The writer has two objections to this assumption. First, it is inconsistent with the notion, discussed above, that the observed price should clear the market in a competitive industry. Second, delivery postponement is profitable only if price is expected to fall in the future. That consumers in a competitive market should not only be willing to accept postponed delivery, but also to pay a higher price than that ruling when delivery is made, is an assumption not to be made without explicit justification. In fact such behavior can probably only be rationalized within a model containing a futures market. Then this interpretation becomes a special case of the next one.

(iii) A firm may be thought to make some of its sales on a futures market and some on a spot market. Although this fact modifies the form of the constraints in (2) below, it also introduces other constraints and complications. Others[8] have recently undertaken extensive analysis of futures markets, although without most of the complications introduced in this chapter by the multiperiod expectations horizon,

[7] The fact that Muth allows for this possibility is one of the main differences between his model [61] and the one in this chapter.

[8] See Telser [75] and Houthakker [36].

and such markets are excluded from this analysis. Excluding them preserves the analogy with the stability literature.

The firm's problem is to find the values z_n^*, x_n^*, and I_n^*, of z_n, x_n, and I_n respectively $(n = 1 \cdots N)$, which maximize (1) subject to the constraints

$$x_n, z_n, I_n \geq 0 \tag{2a}[9]$$

$$(n = 1, \cdots, N)$$

$$z_n - x_n = I_n - I_{n-1} \tag{2b}$$

This is a nonlinear programming problem and, as is often true, the non-negativity conditions (2a) cause trouble. In fact, the special structure of the problem, implied by the conditions of perfect competition, permits a rather simple solution. It is convenient here, as in many programming problems, to find the solution when some of the non-negativity conditions are ignored, and to modify the solution thus found in such a way as to satisfy them. Eliminate the x_n from (1) by (2b) and equate to zero the partial derivatives of (1) with respect to $z_n (n = 1, \cdots, N)$ and $I_n (n = 1, \cdots, N - 1)$. This gives us the following $2N - 1$ equations.

$$c'(z_n) = p_n^e \qquad (n = 1, \cdots, N) \tag{3a}$$

$$r'(I_n) = p_{n+1}^e - p_n^e \qquad (n = 1, \cdots, N - 1) \tag{3b}$$

The convexity assumptions ensure that each of these equations has at most one non-negative solution, and that the solutions are associated with a (local) maximum of (1) rather than with a minimum.

The usual price-equal-marginal-cost condition is (3a). It is stated in (3b) that the firm should hold for sale in future periods the amount that makes marginal storage cost equal to the expected price change between the two consecutive periods. Both of these are intuitively appealing but, as will be shown below, neither is a correct necessary condition for an optimum program in any period.

It is now convenient to introduce the concept of a fundamental solution of the firm's programming problem. The fundamental solution for period n consists of three values z_n°, x_n°, and I_n° of z_n, x_n, and I_n respectively. We define z_n° and I_n° below. Using (2b), x_n° is defined by

$$x_n^\circ = z_n^\circ - I_n^\circ + I_{n-1}$$

[9] Equation (2b) could be written more symmetrically with (2a) as $z_n - x_n \geq I_n - I_{n-1}$, allowing for costless disposal, but it would never be profitable.

Thus $x_n{}^\circ$ is the sales volume implied by the production decision $z_n{}^\circ$, the inventory decision $I_n{}^\circ$, and the arbitrary initial inventory I_{n-1}. The fundamental solution of the firm's programming problem consists of the set of fundamental solutions for all N periods.

We can now define $z_n{}^\circ$ and $I_n{}^\circ$. In any n for which non-negative solutions of (3a) and/or (3b) exist, those solutions constitute the values of $z_n{}^\circ$ and $I_n{}^\circ$. For example, if $z_n = \epsilon_n \geq 0$ is a solution of (3a), then $z_n{}^\circ = \epsilon_n$. Likewise for the inventory equations (3b).

It is clear, however, that under the conditions stated solutions may fail to exist for any or all of the $2N - 1$ equations (3a) and (3b). If no $z_n \geq 0$ satisfies (3a) for some n, this means that there is no output whose marginal production cost is as low as expected price. If no $I_n \geq 0$ satisfies (3b) for some n, there is no inventory whose marginal storage cost is as small as the expected change in price. This will certainly be the case if $p_{n+1}^e < p_n^e$. In any n for which the solution to (3a) fails to exist, we put $z_n{}^\circ = 0$. Likewise, in any n for which the solution to (3b) fails to exist, we put $I_n{}^\circ = 0$. Logically, these are simply definitions of the fundamental solution when solutions to (3a) and (3b) fail to exist. Intuitively the motivation is as follows. If price is too low to justify any production, then nothing should be produced. If there is some inventory from the previous period it may be sold currently, or stored for future use, or both, depending on what price is expected in the future. Likewise, if price is not expected to rise enough to cover the cost of storing even the smallest amount, both current production and existing inventory should be sold currently. While these intuitive arguments are appealing, we should remember that they are used merely to justify the definition of the fundamental solution. It does not necessarily constitute the firm's optimum program.

To summarize: the fundamental solution is built up from the solutions of (3a) and (3b) when these exist. Otherwise zeroes are used. Once $z_n{}^\circ$ and $I_n{}^\circ$ have been thus found, $x_n{}^\circ$ is the sales volume which they and I_{n-1} imply. It follows immediately that the fundamental solution always exists and that $z_n{}^\circ$ and $I_n{}^\circ$ are non-negative for all n. Under what conditions will the fundamental solution be the optimum program? It is obvious that the only way the fundamental solution can fail to be optimum is if $x_n{}^\circ < 0$ for at least some n. If $x_n{}^\circ \geq 0$ for all n, the fundamental solution is said to be feasible and, with the obvious terminal condition $I_N = 0$, it constitutes the firm's optimum program.

It should be clear that nothing in the definition of the fundamental solution implies its feasibility. Consider the simple example in which

$$c'(z) = z, \quad r'(I) = I, \quad I_0 = 0, \quad N > 2$$

$$p_1^e = p_2^e = 1 \quad \text{and} \quad p_3^e = 10$$

Then (3a) and (3b) give us

$$z_1{}^\circ = z_2{}^\circ = 1, \quad z_3{}^\circ = 10, \quad I_1{}^\circ = 0, \quad I_2{}^\circ = 9$$

Hence

$$x_1{}^\circ = z_1{}^\circ = 1, \quad \text{but} \quad x_2{}^\circ = 1 - 9 = -8$$

Thus the fundamental solution for period one is feasible, but that for period two is not. Hence the fundamental solution for the program as a whole is not feasible. The reason that nonfeasibility occurs is that (3b) tells the firm to store more than the production indicated by (3a), plus the amount available from last period's terminal inventory.

In order to see what the firm's optimum program is in case of nonfeasibility we must consider an optimization condition more fundamental than those expressed by (3a) and (3b). This condition is that it is never worthwhile to produce in the $(n + 1)$st period an amount whose marginal cost of production is greater than the marginal cost of producing a unit in the previous period and storing it. In other words, whatever else is true of the optimum production and storage quantities it certainly must be true that

$$c'(z_n{}^*) + r'(I_n{}^*) \geq c'(z_{n+1}^*) \tag{4}$$

The inequality runs in the direction indicated because the firm always has the option of producing now for future use, but not of producing later for current use. In particular, (4) holds as an equality in the special case in which production and inventory are the solutions of (3a) and (3b). Equation (4) is, however, more fundamental, and holds true even when (3a) and (3b) do not constitute the optimum program.

We can now demonstrate the relevance of (4) in the case of nonfeasibility. Suppose that the fundamental solution is nonfeasible. Choose a value j of n for which $x_j{}^\circ < 0$. Now from (3a) and (3b)

$$c'(z_j{}^\circ) + r'(I_j{}^\circ) = c'(z_{j+1}^\circ)$$

But, since $x_j{}^\circ < 0$, it follows that $z_j{}^\circ + I_{j-1} < I_j{}^\circ$ and hence [10]

$$c'(z_j{}^\circ) + r'(z_j{}^\circ + I_{j-1}) < c'(z_{j+1}^\circ) \leq c'(z_{j+1}^*)$$

[10] The second inequality follows from the fact that $z_n{}^*$ must be at least as great as $z_n{}^\circ$ for any n. If $z_n{}^\circ = 0$, this is obviously true. If $z_n{}^\circ$ is the solution of (3a), this is true because it would never pay to produce less than $z_n{}^\circ$. If less than $z_n{}^\circ$ were produced profit could be increased by producing and selling a larger amount in n since marginal cost would be less than price.

Thus the maximum amount that can in fact be stored if $z_j{}^\circ$ is produced violates the inequality (4). Thus it must be worthwhile to produce more than $z_j{}^\circ$ in period j. How much more? The answer to this is that enough should be produced in period j so that the marginal cost of production and storage in j equals the marginal cost of production in $j + 1$. This establishes the following theorem.

THEOREM I: If j is a value of n for which $x_j{}^\circ < 0$, then

$$z_j{}^* > z_j{}^\circ \text{ and } z_j{}^* \text{ must satisfy}$$

$$c'(z_j{}^*) + r'(z_j{}^* + I_{j-1}) = c'(z_{j+1}^*)$$

Before pointing out an important implication of this result it is worthwhile demonstrating a slightly more general theorem.

THEOREM II: Whenever $z_n{}^* > z_n{}^\circ$, $z_n{}^*$ must satisfy [11]

$$c'(z_n{}^*) + r'(z_n{}^* + I_{n-1}) = c'(z_{n+1}^*) \tag{5}$$

It is obvious that, if $z_n{}^* > z_n{}^\circ$, then (4) must hold as an equality, that is,

$$c'(z_n{}^*) + r'(I_n{}^*) = c'(z_{n+1}^*) \tag{4a}$$

Production of more than the amount that equates marginal production cost and current expected price can be profitable only because it is worthwhile to store some units for future sale. Since the firm always has the option of producing these units (those for future sale) during the next period, it will equate the cost at the margin of producing extra units in either of the two periods. This means that (4) holds as an equality (4a). However, Theorem II says more than this. It says that when $z_n{}^* > z_n{}^\circ$, not only does (4a) hold, but also $x_n{}^* = 0$ (that is, $I_n{}^* = z_n{}^* + I_{n-1}$). That this is correct can be seen as follows. Suppose that (4a) holds but that $x_n > 0$. We now propose to show that by reducing x_n, profit will be increased. If x_n is reduced, either (i) I_n increases, or (ii) z_n is reduced. Evidently (i) is not profitable since it would increase the left-hand side of (4a) and make it a strict inequality. This makes extra units available next period, but they could more cheaply be produced next period than this period. However, (ii) is profitable. If x_n and z_n are both reduced by one unit, revenue falls by

---

[11] Theorem II implies Theorem I, but not vice versa. This is because $x_n{}^\circ < 0$ implies $z_n{}^* > z_n{}^\circ$ but $z_n{}^*$ may exceed $z_n{}^\circ$ even if $x_n{}^\circ \geq 0$. The author is greatly indebted to F. H. Hahn and W. M. Gorman for setting him straight on this point.

$p_n{}^e$ and cost by $c'(z_n)$. But, by hypothesis, $c'(z_n) > p_n{}^e$. Hence costs fall by more than revenue and profits go up. Thus, it pays to reduce x_n either to zero or to the point at which $z_n{}^* = z_n{}^\circ$. This process establishes Theorem II.

We now have the key to the solution of the firm's programming problem. Since $z_n{}^*$ cannot be less than $z_n{}^\circ$, either $z_n{}^* = z_n{}^\circ$, where $z_n{}^\circ$ is determined as above, or $z_n{}^*$ satisfies (5). Before showing how a complete solution can be built up from these results, an important corollary of Theorem II should be pointed out.

Corollary: Whenever optimum production $z_n{}^*$ is other than the amount $z_n{}^\circ$ implied by the fundamental solution, then optimum current sales $x_n{}^*$ are zero.

The corollary follows immediately from Theorem II, since (5) says that when the premise is satisfied, $I_n{}^* = z_n{}^* + I_{n-1}$, or $x_n{}^* = z_n{}^* + I_{n-1} - I_n{}^* = 0$. This corollary means that whenever the firm violates the marginal-cost-equal-price rule, unless it does so in order to produce nothing, it will make no current sales. The converse is that if the firm is observed to make positive current sales then, unless current production is zero, it will obey the marginal-cost-equal-price rule. The case in which $x_n{}^* > 0$ will be called the "normal" case. In order to know whether the nth period is normal or not, the firm must, except as noted below, consider expected prices over its entire horizon. However, provided n and $n+1$ are normal periods, it follows that the firm's output and inventory policy can be "explained" by taking into consideration only $p_n{}^e$ and p_{n+1}^e. In other words, if n and $n+1$ are normal periods, the firm behaves "as if" it were considering expected prices only one period in the future. Although this argument never seems to have been stated explicitly in the literature, it has presumably been in the backs of the minds of many writers who have assumed that all future expected prices of a competitive firm can be represented by a single number.[12] The normal case appears to be closely related to the analysis of stability in competitive markets, and this concept will be used extensively in the discussion in Sections 4 and 5.

We are now in a position to derive the firm's optimum N-period plan. Starting in period one, it has an arbitrary initial inventory I_0. The two essential elements in the solution of the firm's programming problem are the fundamental solution and the roots of sets of equations like (5). However, over any interval of consecutive periods within the horizon

---

[12] See, for example, [11] and [24].

it is extremely important to know which calculation yields the optimum program. The reason is that finding the roots of sets of equations like (5) involves a high degree of simultaneity if many such equations are involved. The fundamental solution for period n, on the other hand, can be found by considering only I_{n-1}, $p_n{}^e$ and p_{n+1}^e. No problem of simultaneity is involved and the fundamental solution for the entire N periods can be found by considering consecutively periods 1, 2, $\cdots$, N. The natural question to ask in this situation is whether we can break up the N periods into subintervals that can be considered separately. The answer is "yes" in some circumstances, and these will be explored below. However, let us first indicate the solution in the general case in which simultaneity may be present over the entire horizon. The solution can always be obtained in the following way. Define the stage s computation as the determination of the $s + 1$ roots $z_n^{(s)}$ of the equations [13]

$$c'(z_n^{(s)}) + r'(I_0 + \sum_1^n z_i^{(s)}) = c'(z_{n+1}^{(s)}) \qquad (n = 1, \cdots, s)$$

$$c'(z_{s+1}^{(s)}) = p_{s+1}^e$$

(6)

There are N sets of equations like (6), obtained by putting $s = 0$, 1, $\cdots$, $N - 1$. The sth set yields a program for the first $s + 1$ periods, in which the firm sells nothing until the $(s + 1)$st period. In particular, if $s = 0$ then (6) reduces to (3a) when $n = 1$. In this case, provided the solution $z_1^{(0)}$ exists, it is the same as $z_1°$, the fundamental solution. The firm's optimum first period output is

$$z_1{}^* = \max_s z_1^{(s)} \qquad \text{where } s = 0, 1, \cdots, N - 1 \qquad (7)$$

Essentially, what this calculation does is to tell the firm the farthest period in the future for which it is worthwhile to start accumulating inventory in period one. The amount $z_1^{(s)}$ is what it would pay the firm to produce in period one if it contemplated sales only during and after the $(s + 1)$st period, and if its production obeyed the intertemporal efficiency condition specified by (4a). That $z_1{}^*$ is, as indicated by (7), the largest of the $z_1^{(s)}$ can be seen as follows. Suppose $z_1{}^* = z_1^{(q)}$. In (6)

---

[13] If there are any values of s for which no value $z_{s+1}^{(s)}$ of z_{s+1} satisfies this equation, then this set of $s + 1$ equations can be ignored. They play no further part in the determination of the optimum program.

put $s = q$. By successive substitution among the $s + 1$ equations in (6) we get

$$c'(z_1^{(q)}) = c'(z_2^{(q)}) - r'(I_0 + z_1^{(q)})$$

$$=$$

$$\vdots$$

$$= p_{q+1}^e - \sum_{i=1}^{i=q} r'\left(I_0 + \sum_{j=1}^{j=i} z_j^{(q)}\right)$$

The right-hand side of this equation can be called the "corrected" value of p_{q+1}^e, that is, corrected for the cost of storing the marginal unit from period one until period $q + 1$. Thus, in this form the equation determines the value of z_1 that equates marginal production cost in period one to corrected marginal revenue in period q when an optimum production program is planned in the intervening periods. Thus, the notion behind (7) is that the firm should sell period one's output in that temporal market whose corrected marginal revenue is greatest. Furthermore, the amount that should be produced for that market during period one is the amount that equates marginal production cost and corrected marginal revenue.

Equation (7) having established z_1^*, x_1^*, and I_1^* follow easily. Optimum first-period sales are

$$x_1^* = \begin{cases} x_1{}^\circ & \text{if } z_1^* = z_1{}^\circ \\ 0 & \text{if } z_1^* = z_1^{(q)} \quad \text{where } q > 0 \end{cases} \Bigg\}$$

The optimum first-period inventory is

$$I_1^* = \begin{cases} I_1{}^\circ & \text{if } z_1^* = z_1{}^\circ \\ z_1^* + I_0 & \text{if } z_1^* = z_1^{(q)} \quad \text{where } q > 0 \end{cases} \Bigg\}$$

Equation (7) having established that $z_1^* = z_1^{(q)}$, the other roots of (6) when $s = q$ give us the optimum production quantities $z_n^* = z_n^{(q)}$ for the intervening periods $n = 2, \cdots, q + 1$ as well. The intuitive consideration here is that if it pays to hold period one's production until period q, it certainly pays to hold the production of intervening periods until at least that time. Optimum sales and inventory levels for the intervening periods are

$$x_n{}^* = 0,$$
$$I_n{}^* = I_0 + \sum_1^n z_j{}^*$$

for any n in the interval $1 < n \leq q$, if such n exist.

This process completes the determination of the optimum plan for periods one through $q + 1$. The procedure for finding the optimum program for periods $q + 2$ through N is as follows. It is exactly the same as the one above, except that we now start with period $q + 2$ instead of with period one. Sets of equations ($N - q - 1$ sets, the sth of which contains s equations, where $s = 1, \cdots, N - q - 1$) exactly like (6) must be solved simultaneously, except that they now start with period $q + 2$ instead of with period one, as do the equations in (6). The application of the criterion (7) to these new sets of equations will then lead to an optimum production z^*_{q+2} for period $q + 2$. By proceeding in exactly the same way as before, the entire optimum program over some new interval, for instance from $q + 2$ to $q' + 1$, can be determined. Then a third interval starting with $q' + 2$ must be ascertained until, in this way, the entire N periods are covered. This procedure breaks the N periods into a series of not more than N subintervals. Each subinterval contains exactly one period in which positive sales are made. The normal case, as defined above, is that in which there are N such subintervals.

This procedure clearly involves extremely heavy computations if N is at all large. Computation of the optimum program is feasible only provided some shortcuts can be found that will limit the degree of simultaneity involved. Several sets of considerations can be established which reduce drastically the computational burden implied by the procedure outlined above.

(i) The first relevant consideration is that the firm is normally interested in determining each period only the first-period solution of the N-period program. Only period one's plan must actually be executed in period one, and next period the firm will normally have a new N-period horizon, commencing with that period, and it will again take only the first period decision of the new program. This calculation is of course much simpler than the determination of the entire N-period program.

Most of the attention in the next paragraphs and, indeed, in the rest of the chapter will be concentrated on the problem of finding the first period's optimum program. According to the procedure outlined this still involves an extremely burdensome computation. Each of N sets of nonlinear equations, the sth set involving $s + 1$ equations, must be solved simultaneously. Now the essential purpose of all this computation is to find the value of q, as defined above. Once this has been ascertained, the most that is required is the solution of one set of $q + 1$ simultaneous equations. Therefore the problem is to find ways of discovering q without solving all N sets of simultaneous equations. The following paragraphs are directed toward this goal.

(ii) The most important case is, of course, that in which the fundamental solution of the entire program is feasible, that is, $x_n{}^\circ \geq 0$ for $n = 1, \cdots, N$. In this case $z_n{}^* = z_n{}^\circ$ for all n, and no simultaneity is involved. In this case every period is normal. A sufficient but by no means necessary condition for feasibility is $p_n^e \geq p_{n+1}^e$ for $n = 1, \cdots, N - 1$. Roughly, if expected prices rise slowly relative to marginal storage cost, the fundamental solution is likely to be feasible.

(iii) Suppose that $k_1 \leq N$ is the largest n for which $x_n{}^\circ < 0$, that is, suppose $x_n{}^\circ \geq 0$ for $n \geq k_1$. Then $q \leq k_1$. In this case only k_1 rather than N sets of simultaneous equations must be solved. The maximum degree of simultaneity is the number of periods until the last nonfeasibility is observed in the fundamental solution.

(iv) Suppose k_2 is the smallest value of n for which $x_n{}^\circ < 0$, that is, suppose that $x_n{}^\circ \geq 0$ for $n < k_2$. Then either $q = 0$ or $q \geq k_2$. This means that it is never worthwhile to save all of current production for sale in a period earlier than that in which the earliest nonfeasibility occurs. In particular, if nonfeasibility never occurs then the fundamental solution is optimum.

(v) Suppose $p_m^e = \max_n p_n^e$ and that $m < N$. This means that the highest price expected over the horizon occurs in period m, which is before the final period. In this case $q \leq m$, since it evidently does not pay to start accumulating inventory for sale in any period after m until m has passed. Any inventory accumulated by period m will realize more revenue at that time than later.

(vi) Finally, the computational burden is reduced if special forms of the cost functions are introduced. Consider the following marginal cost functions, used extensively in the analysis of Sections 4 and 5:

$$c'(z) = cz, \; r'(I) = rI \qquad \text{where } c, r > 0$$

In this example the total production and carrying cost curves are quadratics and marginal costs are straight lines through the origin. The fundamental solution is given by

$$z_n{}^\circ = p_n^e/c \quad \text{and} \quad I_n{}^\circ = \max \left((p_{n+1}^e - p_n^e)/r, \, 0 \right) \qquad (8)$$

The simultaneous calculations are now within bounds for even quite large N. For example (6) reduces to the matrix equation.[14]

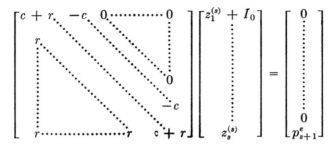

Furthermore, the determination of q is greatly simplified in this case. $z_1^{(n)}$ can be found from $z_1^{(n-1)}$ and $z_1^{(n-2)}$ by a simple linear difference equation.

3. Dynamic Stability without Inventories

In this and the following sections the decision model developed in the previous section is used to investigate the dynamic stability of a single competitive market. No consideration is given to the question of stability in multiple markets. The main focus of the discussion will be the relation between stability and the accuracy of expectations. The usual approach in studies of stability is to assume that expectations (the p^e terms in the model in Section 2) are generated in a par-

---

[14] It may be useful to indicate briefly how the solution presented here differs from those of other writers who have included inventories in models of a perfectly competitive firm. The two things that appear to be new in this analysis are: (1) The precise conditions for the normal case in which the effective horizon is two periods, and (2) the theorem that, if expected prices beyond the second period affect the first period's production, then no first period sales are worthwhile.

The two classical papers on the subject of speculative inventory holding are by Shaw [70], and Smithies [72]. Shaw presents the correct solution when the horizon is two periods and, in the terminology used here, $x_1° \geq 0$. His diagrams are restricted to the case of linear marginal production and storage costs, but this is not crucial to the argument. He considers the possibility $x_1° < 0$ uninteresting "in view of the timorousness and lack of resources of the competitive producer." Smithies was the first to give a rigorous analysis of the case, with a continuous time parameter, of a firm with a downward sloping demand curve and proportional storage costs. Essentially the same model, in discrete time, is considered by Lutz and Lutz [44]. Both of these studies derive the usual price discriminator's condition that marginal revenue and marginal cost should be equal within and between all periods. They restrict consideration to rightward shifts in demand and this ensures the non-negativity of I_n. Neither considers in detail the special case of perfect competition.

ticular way and to ask what time-path of actual prices will result. In this study the approach is to ask what expectations must be if the behavior they induce makes those expectations turn out to be correct.[15] Does this behavior lead to a stable or an unstable market adjustment? In particular, is it possible for a competitive market to be unstable even though expectations are correct?

In this section we consider the rather simple case of a market with no inventories. Although the case is essentially trivial, it may be useful to apply the analysis first to a transparent example. In Section 4 inventories are introduced, and it is shown that the assumption of numerically accurate expectations leads to a richer and more interesting analysis. In Section 5, the results of Section 4 are generalized to the case in which expectations are correct in a statistical rather than in a numerical sense.

In this as in other studies of stability it is easier to obtain results if linear approximations of certain relationships are employed. This fact means that the results obtained are valid only in the vicinity of the equilibrium position, and it is true of all the results in the remainder of the chapter. In particular, the firm's marginal production cost will be approximated by the linear form used in the example in the previous section, $c'(z) = cz$. In the next section, when inventories are introduced, the marginal carrying cost is also approximated by a linear form, again as in the example. Both here and in the following sections the addition of a constant to these marginal costs leaves all the stability analysis unaffected. Since in this section the firm is assumed not to hold inventories, its program in the nth period is completely specified by the first relation in equation (8)

$$z_n = p_n^e/c \tag{8a}$$

One of the important assumptions employed in the rest of the chapter is that all firms in the industry have the same price expectations, an assumption already contained in the notion that expectations are correct. Thus the aggregation of the firms' supply curves into an industry curve presents no problem. Assuming that all firms' marginal production costs are proportional to output, even though the coefficient c be different for different firms, the industry output will be determined by an equation of the form (8a). Industry output will be

---

[15] For an interesting application of this technique to a different problem see [30].

$\Sigma z_n = p_n^e \Sigma (1/c)$ where the sums are over all firms, not over time. In this situation there is no point in changing notation, and in the further analysis (8a) will refer to industry totals. Precisely the same remarks apply to the aggregation of inventories, and the second relation in (8) will be used to represent total industry inventory in the following sections. In the absence of inventory holding, industry sales x_n^S are the same as industry production z_n. The industry demand curve is also assumed to be linear in the current actual price

$$x_n^D = a - bp_n \qquad (9)$$

The actual and expected prices that clear the market in period n are those that satisfy

$$x_n^D = x_n^S \qquad (10)$$

Equations (8a), (9), and (10) do not yet close the model since (8a) contains expected price while (9) contains actual price. A determinate time-path of price would result if an additional relation between expected price and actual past prices were introduced. For example, the simple textbook version of the cobweb model is the case in which $p_n^e = p_{n-1}$.

Express (8a), (9), and (10) in the form

$$a - bp_n = (1/c)p_n^e \qquad (11)$$

It is obvious that in this model expectations can be accurate only if the system is in equilibrium. Putting $p_n = p_n^e$ in (11) gives us $p_n = \bar{p}$ where

$$\bar{p} = \frac{ac}{1 + bc} \qquad (12)$$

is the equilibrium price. In fact, for the accuracy of expectations in any period it is both necessary and sufficient that price be equal to its equilibrium level.

Now let us close the model by assuming that expected prices are generated by the adaptive expectations formula [16] (1) in Chapter 3

$$p_n^e = (1 - B)p_{n-1}^e + Bp_{n-1} \qquad (13)$$

It is clear from the above discussion that when the expectations generated by (13) are inserted in (11) the resulting time-path of actual price

[16] (11) and (13), except for notational changes, constitute the model considered by Nerlove [63].

must be such that expectations are in fact wrong except when the market is in equilibrium, that is when $p_n = \bar{p}$. This was proved to be true regardless of the way in which expectations are formed. In fact, in this case, the time-path of expectational errors has exactly the same form as the time-paths of both the actual and expected prices. This fact can be seen as follows. Between (11) and (13) either p_n or p_n^e can be eliminated, resulting in a difference equation in the remaining variable. In this case, whichever variable is eliminated, the ensuing equation is of the same form

$$v_n = (1 - B - B/bc)v_{n-1} + aB/b \qquad (14)$$

where v_n equals p_n or p_n^e. The solution of (14) is

$$v_n = (1 - B - B/bc)^n(v_0 - \bar{v}) + \bar{v}$$

where $\bar{v} = \bar{p}$ and v_0 is the initial condition (either actual or expected price in period zero). From this equation we get a similar equation for the expectational error in period n

$$p_n^e - p_n = (1 - B - B/bc)^n(p_0^e - p_0)$$

Here p_0^e is the expected price, and p_0 the actual price, in period zero. Thus, starting with an arbitrary initial expectational error $p_0^e - p_0$, the time-path of the error term is of exactly the same form as that of both the actual and expected prices. In particular, if actual price converges (the market is stable) then so does the error; if the initial error is positive ($p_0^e - p_0 > 0$), then so are all succeeding errors. This is an example of the use of a simple autoregressive expectational equation to deduce the time-path of the variable of which the expectation is an estimate (see Chapter 3, Section 3). Yet the mechanism generating the variable leads to a time-path such that the expectations cannot possibly be correct. Not only that, but the expectational errors follow a time-path as simple as that of the variable itself. Presumably an intelligent decision maker would be able to observe at least that his expectational errors were all biased in the same direction and would then refrain from using the simple routine that led to the situation.

In closing this section it should be emphasized that these remarks are directed at the use of virtually all mechanical expectations formulas in stability analysis. Exactly the same criticisms would apply if the textbook cobweb model were used, in which $p_n^e = p_{n-1}$. The adaptive expectations formula has served merely as a peg on which to hang a much more general criticism.

4. Dynamic Stability with Inventories: Nonstochastic Case

In this section the possibility of inventory holding is introduced in the dynamic model considered in the previous section. This possibility complicates the analysis considerably, but we can still obtain definite results on the assumptions introduced above. Formal results in this section will be restricted to the normal case, defined in Section 2 as one in which the firm behaves as if it looked only one period ahead in formulating its plans. This is the only case relevant to an investigation of stability in the vicinity of equilibrium since, as was shown in Section 2, when the normal case breaks down the firm sells nothing. When this happens price rises to the level which cuts off all demand, and this is evidently not a point in the vicinity of equilibrium. In any case the meaning of the analysis becomes doubtful when we reach prices at which no sales are made.

In this normal case the production and inventory plan followed by the industry in period n is completely specified by equations (8).

This plan can be expressed by

$$z_n = p_n^e/c \tag{15a}$$

$$I_n = \max\{(p_{n+1}^e - p_n^e)/r, 0\} \tag{15b}$$

Here the price terms are all expectations held when the production and inventory decisions in the period in question must be made. Employing the convention introduced in the previous section, we shall reinterpret the symbols in (15) as industry totals. Industry sales are

$$x_n^S = z_n + I_{n-1} - I_n \tag{16}$$

Substituting (15) in (16) we get

$$x_n^S = p_n^e/c + \max\{(p_n^e - p_{n-1}^e)/r, 0\} - \max\{(p_{n+1}^e - p_n^e)/r, 0\}$$

The linear demand curve (9) and the condition (10) that the price clear the market each period are again assumed. In this section we seek the implications of the assumption that all price expectations are numerically correct, that is, $p_n = p_n^e$ for all n. In the next section the model is generalized to include the case in which the distribution function, but not the numerical values, of future prices are correctly anticipated. Dropping the superscripts, using the definition (16), and substituting (15a), (15b), and (9) in (10) we get

$$a - bp_n = p_n/c + \max \{(p_n - p_{n-1})/r, 0\}$$

$$- \max \{(p_{n+1} - p_n)/r, 0\} \quad (17)$$

Equation (17) is the relation that price must satisfy if expectations are to be fulfilled each period. It is the fundamental dynamic relation on which all subsequent analysis in this section is based. It is a second order nonlinear difference equation, but fortunately one whose stability properties are easily deduced. Its solution, the time-path of price, and of course of expected price, depends on two arbitrary initial prices p_0 and p_1, whose values are given to the market exogenously.

The equilibrium price in the market is the stationary solution of (17) obtained by putting $p_n = \bar{p}$ for all n. The equilibrium price this yields is the same as the one found in the model of the previous section, equation (12), in which there were no inventories. The reason is that in equilibrium the firms hold no inventories and the price that clears the market is unaffected by the cost of carrying inventory. If the initial prices p_0 and p_1 are both equal to $\bar{p}$, this price will continue until some exogenous force disturbs the market.

What happens if the equilibrium is disturbed? Superficially, the possibility of inventory holding against an expected price rise appears to be a destabilizing factor in the market. An expected increase in price induces the firm to withhold some current production for future sale, and it is this behavior that makes price rise and fulfills expectations. In fact, the connection is more than superficial, and in any case in which correct expectations are possible (17) is explosive in an upward direction. More specifically, the following theorem can be proven.

THEOREM III. For any initial conditions p_0 and p_1, neither of which is equal to $\bar{p}$, but for which a solution to (17) exists, price is unstable in an upward direction.

The mathematical proof of this theorem is tedious, though it involves only elementary algebra, and it is relegated to Appendix A. The following literary proof appears to be rigorous, and the proof in the appendix follows it step by step.

It is convenient to consider two cases separately according to the relation between the initial prices p_0 and p_1.

(i) Suppose $p_0 < p_1$. In the first place, $p_2 < p_1$ is inconsistent with (17), that is, once price starts to rise expectations of a fall cannot be correct. If price in period one exceeds that in period zero, firms will have some inventory on hand at the end of period zero. On the other hand, if price is expected to fall in period two below its period one level, firms will unload this inventory in period one. Not only that, but production will be less in period two than it was in period one since the price is lower and therefore a smaller output equates price and marginal cost. Thus, even if no inventory is held at the end of period two, the amount put on the market in period two must be less than that put on the market in period one. Since the demand curve is downward sloping the price must be higher than that which ruled in period one and therefore expectations of a lower price cannot be correct. The argument can be summarized by saying that if $p_0 < p_1$, expectation of a decline in price in period two would lead firms to put less on the market than in period one, and the price would be higher rather than lower.

In the second place, a continuous rise in price is always possible and can be consistent with correct expectations. If $p_0 < p_1$, and firms expect p_2 to be greater still, there is always some value of p_2 which, if expected, will induce firms to hold in inventory at the end of period one just the amount that makes p_1 clear the market. The same reasoning applied to the next period ensures that the price expected in period two actually materializes. Together, these results imply that there is a unique price p_2 which, if expected, will materialize, and that this price exceeds p_1. The same reasoning applied to period three shows that $p_3 > p_2$, and inductively that every price exceeds the preceding one.

(ii) Suppose $p_0 > p_1$. Here there are two subcases.

(a) Suppose $p_0 > p_1 > p_2$. This case is impossible. If it were true there would be no inventory at the end of period zero and none at the end of period one. Hence, in period one production equals sales and this is possible only if $p_1 = \bar{p}$. But we cannot also have $p_2 < \bar{p}$ since the amount available for sale in period two would be less than the amount available in period one, and would therefore bring a higher price. If $p_0 \geq p_1$ and $p_1 = \bar{p}$, then $p_2 = \bar{p}$ is also a possibility, and the market remains in equilibrium.

(b) Suppose $p_0 > p_1 < p_2$. This case is also impossible. Here we would have no inventory at the end of period zero but a positive amount at the end of period one. But production in period one would be less than it was in period zero. Hence the amount put on the market in period one cannot be as great as the amount put on the market in period zero, and it would therefore bring a higher price, contradicting the assumption that $p_0 > p_1$.

Together, (a) and (b) prove that (ii) is impossible, and this fact completes the proof of the theorem.

The force of Theorem III appears to be that if we wish to retain the essential characteristic of competition, that the price clears the market each period, we must search for stabilizing factors in such markets among expectational hypotheses which, in one sense or another, permit incorrect expectations. If this argument is accepted, it becomes important to ask what kind of expectational errors should be introduced. In the spirit of the discussion in the previous chapter, an obvious case to investigate is one in which expectational errors are statistically stable. This task is undertaken in the next section.

5. Dynamic Stability with Inventories: Stochastic Case

Until now no account has been taken of the effect of uncertainty on the behavior of the firm or market. It is the purpose of this section to do so. As we pointed out in Section 1, only uncertainty concerning price, and not quantity demanded, is relevant in a perfectly competitive market. We assume that this uncertainty can be represented by

$$p_n = p_n^e + u_n \tag{18}$$

where u_n is a random variable which is identically and independently distributed from period to period and has a zero expected value. Thus p_n^e is the expected value of p_n, though it is convenient for the moment to leave unspecified the exact information on which this expectation is conditional. Since we assume that all firms have correct expectations, it is not necessary to distinguish between the actual and anticipated distributions of p_n: (18) represents both. It should, however, be noted that (18) involves a reinterpretation of the symbol p_n^e. In previous sections it has represented the numerical value that price was expected (with certainty) to assume in period n. In this section it represents the "expected value" of price, in the usual sense of the average of all values that p_n might assume, each weighted by its probability.

Equation (18), and the cost functions introduced in Section 2, still do not completely specify the firm's decision problem. We must also specify the information available at the time each decision is made. The following classification will indicate some of the possibilities:

(a) The firm might be able to observe p_n and then decide on z_n and x_n.

(b) The firm might have to decide on z_n before observing p_n (but after observing p_{n-1}), but be able to make its sales decision x_n after observing p_n.

(c) The firm might have to decide on both z_n and x_n before observing p_n (but after observing p_{n-1}).

(d) The firm might have to decide on all z_n and x_n for $n = 1, \cdots, N$ before observing p_1.

These possibilities are listed in order of increasing degree of "precommittal" required. The kinds of problems involved in programming the firm's operations are quite different in the four cases. Case (d) is essentially the same as the nonstochastic case considered in Sections 2 to 4, and the analysis of those sections applies completely.[17] Cases (a) to (c) represent basically different decision problems from the nonstochastic case.[18] In some ways case (b), in which the firm makes its production decision before knowing p_n but decides how much to sell and store after observing p_n, is the most plausible, and this case is analyzed in the remainder of the section. This case takes into account the fact that in competitive markets production decisions normally entail more precommittal than do sales decisions. Unfortunately, the firm's programming problem is still a very complicated one which is largely unsolved.[19] Hence the following approach will be used.

In Sections 3 and 4 we found that to analyze the stability of the market a two-period approximation had to be used, which assumed that each period's decisions were made only on the basis of prices anticipated in that period and in the next one. A precisely analogous

[17] This is because the firm must commit itself at time zero to all future sales and production levels within its horizon. For this purpose the expected price $p_n{}^e$ is a "certainty equivalent" and the techniques of Section 2 apply.

[18] Case (c) has, however, an important characteristic in common with the nonstochastic case. This arises when, as was true in the stability analysis of Section 3 and is true in the stability analysis below in this section, the two-period approximation is used, in which the firm makes its sales, output, and inventory decisions each period only on the basis of prices anticipated in that and the next period. In this case, $p_n{}^e$ and p_{n+1}^e are certainty equivalents for p_n and p_{n+1} respectively in the making of the nth period's decisions and the results of Section 4 apply completely.

[19] Any finite-horizon programming problem such as this one is solvable in a sense. One can, in principle, always start at period N and work backward to period one. What is meant in the text is that it has not been possible to characterize the solution in a way that is useful for the purpose of stability analysis.

assumption will be made here, namely that each decision is made on the basis of exactly one anticipated price. This means that z_n is chosen, taking into account the possible values that p_n may take; x_n and I_n are chosen after p_n has been observed, taking into account the possible values that p_{n+1} may take.[20] We may thus interpret p_n^e as the expected value of p_n, conditional on the realized prices of all previous periods. The form of the dependence of p_n^e on earlier observed prices is deduced below. In this case p_n^e and p_{n+1}^e are certainty equivalents for the nth period's decisions. The programming problem for case (b), and for the other cases as well, becomes trivial. In addition to this assumption, the linear marginal production and inventory cost functions from Sections 3 and 4 will also be used here. With all these assumptions, the firm's behavior can be summarized as follows.

$$z_n = p_n^e/c \tag{19a}$$

$$I_n = \max\{(p_{n+1}^e - p_n)/r, 0\} \tag{19b}$$

$$p_n = p_n^e + u_n \tag{19c}$$

$$x_n^s = z_n + I_{n-1} - I_n \tag{19d}$$

The form of (19a) follows from the fact that z_n must be set before observing p_n. Hence, marginal production cost is equated to the expected value of p_n, that is, p_n^e. The form of (19b) follows from the fact that the period n sales and inventory decisions are made after observing p_n. Hence the firm equates the expected value of the price change to marginal storage cost if p_{n+1}^e exceeds p_n and carries no inventory otherwise.

In defense of the two-period approximation the following argument should be made. It is clear that, were the firm to look ahead more than one period, it could not be induced to carry less inventory than is indicated by (19b). Equation (19b) indicates the inventory that is profitable if the firm knows it must sell next period. If, instead, it were to take account of the fact that next period it will have the option

---

[20] Unfortunately, here we no longer have the comfort provided by the theorem proved in Section 2 for the nonstochastic case to the effect that in any period in which the model with the truncated horizon does not provide the optimum policy, no sales would be made. In the present case the "correct" value of z_n would exceed that indicated by the two-period approximation whenever p_{n+1}^e was large. Whether sales would be made in any period would depend on whether the price that materialized was abnormally high or not, i.e., on the realized value of u_n for that period.

of keeping the inventory longer, inventory carrying could not be made less profitable. Hence, the inventory level indicated by the "correct" programming problem must be at least as large as that indicated by (19b). Now it is clear that in the models considered in this chapter the possibility of instability arises from the fact that, if firms expect price to rise, they take goods off the market to hold in inventory for future sale, thus raising the price. Hence, if the market where firms' actions are governed by (19) is unstable, the presumption is created that if the "true" model were used, in which firms store as much or more, the market would be even more unstable. This is a presumption rather than a proof, but it provides some confidence in the following results.

In order to complete the model, it remains only to introduce a demand equation. For this purpose the linear form (9) used in previous sections is used again, except that a random term is added to provide the "source" of the uncertainty represented by (19c). The equation can be written

$$x_n{}^D = a - bp_n + \epsilon_n \tag{20}$$

where ϵ_n has the same properties as u_n, namely an identical and independent distribution from period to period, and a zero mean.[21] Obviously, ϵ_n and u_n are related, and their relationship is explored below. It should be pointed out that ϵ_n and p_n cannot be independent, for ϵ_n affects the quantity demanded at each price and, given the supply equation, it affects the price which clears the market.[22]

The model is completed by introducing the identity

$$x_n{}^S = z_n + I_{n-1} - I_n \tag{21}$$

and the market-clearing condition

$$x_n{}^S = x_n{}^D \tag{22}$$

---

[21] There is no substantive difference between (20) and the alternative representation

$$x_n{}^D = a - bp_n{}^e + \epsilon_n'$$

In view of (19c), (20) can be written

$$x_n{}^D = a - bp_n{}^e - bu_n + \epsilon_n$$

Putting $\epsilon_n' = \epsilon_n - bu_n$, the two forms are seen to be equivalent.

[22] This is precisely the reason that in statistical models of simultaneous estimation of economic relationships all the endogenous variables are dependent on all the random terms.

Finally, recall the convention introduced in Section 3 that the same variables are reinterpreted as market totals for stability analysis. We are now ready to investigate the stability of the market represented by equations (19) to (22).

The substitutions that led to (17) now give us the fundamental difference equation

$$a - bp_n + \epsilon_n = p_n^e/c + \max \{(p_n^e - p_{n-1})/r,\, 0\}$$
$$- \max \{(p_{n+1}^e - p_n)/r,\, 0\} \quad (23)$$

Together with (19c) showing the relation between the p's and the p^e's, it constitutes the system whose stability properties are to be investigated. It is a nonlinear stochastic difference equation, a type whose behavior is generally very difficult to analyze. Quite definite statements, however, can easily be established about this particular system. The analysis is similar to that undertaken in the previous section, and the algebra is relegated to Appendix B.

The stationary solution of (23), defined by the equalities

$$p_n = p_{n-1} = p_n^e = p_{n+1}^e, \qquad \epsilon_n = u_n = 0$$

is the same as (12),

$$\bar{p} = \frac{ac}{1 + bc} \quad (24)$$

Partly as an exercise, first consider the possibility that p_n is a purely random process so that lagged values of price are of no use in predicting current price. Here, $p_n^e \equiv \bar{p}$ for all n and $p_n = \bar{p} + u_n$. In this situation firms treat each price as a random deviation from the equilibrium price, and observed prices have no effect on anticipations. If this were true, it follows from (19a) that z_n would assume the same value, $\bar{p}/c$, in each period. However, when p_n was less than $\bar{p}$, p_{n+1}^e ($= \bar{p}$) would exceed p_n, and firms would store some of their current production for future sale. If the next period's price, p_{n+1}, exceeded $\bar{p}$, firms would put not only that period's production but also their accumulated inventory on the market. This means that at any $p_{n+1} > \bar{p}$ more will be put on the market in period $n + 1$ if p_n was less than $\bar{p}$ than if p_n exceeded $\bar{p}$. Hence the amount put on the market in period $n + 1$ depends on p_n and, since the realized value of p_{n+1} obviously depends on the amount supplied in $n + 1$, p_{n+1} also depends on p_n. Hence the distribution of price is not independent from period to period, a fact that contradicts the anticipations on which this behavior was based. The argument shows that if current price is assumed to have no effect on future price, firms will behave in such a way that current price does affect future price, thus contradicting anticipations.

We must now consider what time paths of p_n might be solutions of the system. A complete analysis requires separate consideration of several possibilities classified according to the arrangement of the two initial prices on which the solution of (23) depends. This process is tedious and is presented only in Appendix B. Furthermore, the analysis follows that of the previous section step by step, and requires mainly changes in interpretation. In any case, the basic argument is very simple, and it is common to all the possibilities.

The behavior of the dynamic system (23) and (19c) can be summarized as follows. Only when expected price rises consistently and explosively do anticipations lead to behavior that implies an actual time-path of prices that is consistent with anticipations. Thus, with some reinterpretations to allow for the fact that the system is now stochastic, the conclusion is the same as that reached in the previous section, namely that in the vicinity of equilibrium the market must be unstable in an upward direction. This conclusion is established as follows.

First, consider the possibility of consistently declining anticipated prices. When price is expected to decline on the average (that is, $p_{n+1}^e < p_n$), it is not worthwhile for firms to hold inventories. Furthermore, the lower the anticipated price, the smaller the amount that firms find it worthwhile to produce, since marginal production cost rises with output. Therefore, the lower the price, the less, on the average, is supplied. But average demand is greater at lower prices. Therefore, a smaller supply cannot, again on the average, clear the market at a lower price.

Essentially the same argument applies to all possible sets of initial conditions, and the more detailed analysis of the following case will serve as a typical example. The other possibilities are considered in Appendix B. Suppose $p_0 < \bar{p} > p_1$, and that $p_{n+1}^e < p_n$. Clearly, $I_n = 0$ since in each period firms expect next period's price to be lower than the current price. In this case, z_2 is the amount that will be placed on the market in period two. However, z_2 will clearly be less than the amount that would clear the market on the average if p_2^e were as high as $\bar{p}$. Hence this smaller amount cannot, on the average, clear the market at a price lower than $\bar{p}$, and p_2 cannot therefore, on the average, be as low as p_2^e. Thus, expectations are contradicted.

This argument applies step by step to other cases, for example, those in which the initial prices are both above the equilibrium level $\bar{p}$. In this case the argument shows that the amount that firms put on the market is more than can be sold, on the average, at $\bar{p}$ ($<p_2^e$) and therefore the realized value of p_2 cannot, on the average, be as great as p_2^e.

Now consider the reverse situation in which price rises are anticipated, that is, in which $p_{n+1}^e > p_n$. Here the situation is quite different. As price rises through time, so does production. However, the price rises also induce firms to put some of their production in inventory in anticipation of further rises. Provided prices rise on the average at the appropriate rate, the amount that firms find it worthwhile to take off the market for speculative purposes is equal to the amount that results in the price rises whose anticipation induced the inventory accumulation in the first place. Hence, the anticipations of rising prices are confirmed, and firms have no reason to alter them.

Again, an exhaustive classification of possibilities is tedious, and the following is presented as a typical case for more detailed analysis. Suppose $p_0 > \bar{p} < p_1$ and that $p_{n+1}^e > p_n$. Clearly $I_n > 0$ since, in each period, the expected value of price in the next period is greater than the current price. Now it is easy to show that there exists some relation between p_n and p_{n+1}^e, which induces firms to put on the market just the amount that, on the average, will be demanded at the anticipated price. To see this, fix p_2^e ($>\bar{p}$) and therefore z_2. Now if p_3^e were only slightly above p_2, then firms would put on the market in period two nearly the total amount available to them, $z_2 + I_1$. But since $p_2^e > \bar{p}$, z_2 is greater than the amount that would be demanded on the average at the lower price of $\bar{p}$. Hence, on the average, p_2 could not be as great as $\bar{p}$, and this contradicts the expectation $p_2^e > p_1 > \bar{p}$. On the other hand, suppose p_3^e were very large relative to p_2. This would induce firms to make I_2 nearly as large as $z_2 + I_1$. Thus, the amount that firms put on the market in period two would be less than would be demanded on the average at p_2^e, and therefore p_2^e could not on the average be the market-clearing price. The foregoing shows that, for fixed p_2^e, a p_3^e too small in relation to p_2 will lead to a distribution of realized prices in period two with an average less than p_2^e, while a p_3^e too large in relation to p_2 will lead to a distribution of realized prices in period two with an average greater than p_2^e. It follows that, for some intermediate p_3^e ($>p_2$), the distribution of realized prices in period two will have a mean equal to p_2^e. Furthermore, in this example, the larger is p_2^e the larger must be the difference $p_3^e - p_2$ in order that expectations be realized. This is because, the larger is p_2^e, the larger will z_2 be. However, a larger p_2^e means on the average a smaller demand. Hence, the larger is p_2^e the more the firms must put in inventory if p_2 is to clear the market on the average at a level p_2^e. However, in order to induce firms to add larger amounts to inventory, the difference $p_3^e - p_2$ must be larger. Roughly, this last point can be summarized by saying that the higher the price is the faster it must rise.

When the initial prices are below $\bar{p}$, the analysis is exactly the same except that in this case firms must be decumulating inventory, at a slower and slower pace, until p_n^e rises above $\bar{p}$.

We can summarize as follows. Starting from any pair of arbitrary initial prices, only expectations of price rises lead to market behavior which, statistically, fulfills the expectations. Thus on the average price must rise. Furthermore, the higher the price the larger the amount by which price must, on the average, rise. Thus in this statistical sense the market must be unstable in an upward direction.

In conclusion it might be worthwhile to make several brief comments of a more general nature on speculative markets.

First, in common with all models of stability in the vicinity of equilibrium, this model contains assumptions that are clearly invalid when departures from equilibrium are extreme. Obviously the assumptions of linear demand and marginal cost curves are less accurate the larger the departure from the initial point. Perhaps more important are the assumptions that are emphasized by recalling that profitability of inventory speculation in this model refers only to "paper profits." It is obvious that the speculative inventories cannot be profitably decumulated by the market. When deviations from equilibrium are no longer "small" market behavior may be changed. For example the capital market may no longer supply funds at a constant interest rate for the purpose of carrying speculative inventories. Alternatively, firms may no longer be satisfied to plan their operations with a one-period horizon, or large inventories in the hands of firms may lead to pessimistic expectations. Even though no expectations may exist that can be realized the market may become "chaotic." These and other factors provide nonlinearities in the real world, which become important when divergences from equilibrium are large and presumably prevent price from moving farther away from equilibrium.

Second, it has often been realized in the literature that expectations of economic phenomena may be self-confirming. What does not seem to have been sufficiently appreciated is that not all expectations can be self-confirming. Depending on the characteristics of the market in question, for example on whether inventories can be carried, some kinds of expectations will be self-confirming and some kinds will not. In the model considered here, only very special kinds of expectations induce firms to behave in a way leading to the confirmation of expectations. In this model, though not necessarily in others, the only expectations that can lead to their confirmation result in a statistically unstable market.

Third, it is often said that correct expectations must stabilize the market because they induce speculators to reduce supply when price is low and to increase supply when price is high. This argument rests on a confusion between the systematic and stochastic parts of price movements. It is true in the model considered in this section that the more firms alter their inventory in response to deviations of p_n from p_n^e the smaller, on the average, will be such deviations. However, this notion considers only the effect of speculation in ironing out random fluctuations in price. The more fundamental aspect of speculation is that speculation is profitable whenever current price is low relative to anticipated future prices. This notion has to do not with the random but with the systematic component of price. In this sense, at least in the vicinity of equilibrium, speculation can clearly be destabilizing, even though it is based on correct expectations of the future trend of prices.

APPENDIX A

The purpose of this appendix is to prove the theorem in Section 4, that price is unstable in an upward direction when it is determined according to (17), i.e., when

$$a - bp_n = p_n/c + \max \{(p_n - p_{n-1})/r, 0\}$$

$$- \max \{(p_{n+1} - p_n)/r, 0\} \quad (17)$$

An elementary proof of this theorem is made possible by the fact that (17) is piecewise linear, that is, for any given set of initial conditions p_0 and p_1, p_2 is a linear function of p_0 and p_1. The nonlinearity lies in the fact that different initial conditions will imply different linear equations. The following proof parallels that in the text at each step.

(i) Suppose $p_0 < p_1$. In the first place, $p_0 < p_1 > p_2$ contradicts (17). From (17), this double inequality would imply

$$a - bp_1 = \frac{p_1}{c} + \frac{p_1 - p_0}{r}$$

or

$$p_1 = \frac{cp_0}{bcr + r + c} + \frac{acr}{bcr + r + c} \qquad (25)$$

A consideration of the properties of the difference equation

$$p_n = \frac{cp_{n-1}}{bcr + r + c} + \frac{acr}{bcr + r + c} \qquad (25a)$$

of which (25) is the special case in which $n = 1$, establishes the assertion (i). Equation (25a) is stable and converges monotonically to the stationary solution $p = \bar{p}$. Hence there are three possibilities:

(a) If $p_0 > \bar{p}$, then (25a) indicates that $p_1 < p_0$, which contradicts the assumption $p_0 < p_1$.

(b) If $p_0 < \bar{p} < p_1$, then again (25a) indicates that $p_0 < p_1 < \bar{p}$ and we have a contradiction.

(c) If $p_0 < p_1 < \bar{p}$, then in this case (25) is satisfied. However, it leads to the relation $p_2 < p_1 < \bar{p}$ and it is shown under (ii) that this set of prices, taken as initial conditions for the determination of p_3, is inconsistent with (17).

In the second place, a continuous price rise is possible. From (17), if p_2 is to exceed p_1 it must satisfy

$$a - bp_1 = \frac{p_1}{c} - \frac{p_2 - p_1}{r} + \frac{p_1 - p_0}{r}$$

or

$$ep_2 - e_1 p_1 + ep_0 + a = 0 \qquad (26)$$

where

$$e = \frac{1}{r} \quad \text{and} \quad e_1 = b + \frac{1}{c} + \frac{2}{r}$$

This is a special case of the second-order equation whose solution is

$$p_n = \mu_1{}^n K_1 + \mu_2{}^n K_2 + \bar{p} \qquad (27)$$

where

$$\mu_1 = [e_1 + (e_1{}^2 - 4e^2)^{1/2}]/2e, \quad \mu_2 = [e_1 - (e_1{}^2 - 4e^2)^{1/2}]/2e$$

Note that $e_1 > 2e > 0$. Hence $e_1{}^2 > 4e^2$. It follows that both μ_1 and μ_2 are real and positive and that $\mu_1 > 1$. K_1 and K_2 depend on

p_0, p_1, μ_1 and μ_2. Therefore (27) is an explosive system, and furthermore some sets of initial prices will give K's resulting in a continuously rising price.[1]

(ii) Suppose $p_0 > p_1$. There are two possibilities.

(a) $p_0 > p_1 > p_2$; this is impossible. From (17) this would imply $p_1 = \bar{p}$. But, applying the same reasoning to the next period, we get $p_2 = \bar{p}$, which contradicts the assumption $p_1 > p_2$.

(b) $p_0 > p_1 < p_2$; from (17) this requires

$$a - bp_1 = \frac{p_1}{c} - \frac{p_2 - p_1}{r}$$

or

$$p_2 = (1 + br + r/c)p_1 - ar \qquad (28)$$

This is a special case of the difference equation that has the solution

$$p_n = (1 + br + r/c)^n(p_0 - \bar{p}) + \bar{p} \qquad (29)$$

This is explosive since $1 + br + r/c > 1$. If $p_0 < \bar{p}$, it indicates $p_2 < p_1$, contradicting the premise. If $p_0 > \bar{p}$, (29) indicates $p_2 > p_1$. Then, when the p_2 indicated by (29) materializes, the initial conditions for determining p_3 are p_1 and p_2. Since $p_2 > p_1$, this is again the case discussed under (i), in which upwards instability must ensue.

APPENDIX B

The purpose of this appendix is to establish algebraically the conclusions reached in Section 5 concerning the stability of the system

$$p_n = p_n^e + u_n \qquad (19c)$$

and

$$a - bp_n + \epsilon_n = p_n^e/c + \max\{(p_n^e - p_{n-1})/r, 0\}$$

$$- \max\{(p_{n+1}^e - p_n)/r, 0\} \qquad (23)$$

The easiest way to analyze this system is as follows. Take p_0 and p_1 as initial conditions and consider the following four possibilities.

(i) $p_1^e > p_0$, $p_2^e > p_1$. Eliminating p_n^e and p_{n+1}^e by (19c), (23) tells us that in this case p_2 must satisfy

---

[1] It is easy to see that if (27) governs the behavior of the system for a sufficiently long time, it will cause the breakdown of the normal case on which it is based.

$$a - bp_1 + \epsilon_1 = \frac{(p_1 - u_1)}{c} - \frac{(p_2 - u_2 - p_1)}{r} + \frac{(p_1 - u_1 - p_0)}{r}$$

or

$$ep_2 - e_1 p_1 + ep_0 + a + \epsilon_1 + \frac{u_1}{c} + \frac{u_1}{r} - \frac{u_2}{r} = 0 \qquad (30)$$

Except for the random terms, this is the same as (26) in Appendix A, and e and e_1 ave the meanings assigned to them there. Equation (30) also tells us what the relationship between ϵ and u must be. In order that (19c) be satisfied by (30) it is necessary and sufficient that

$$\epsilon_1 = -(1/c + 1/r)u_1$$

We know from Appendix A that the characteristic equation of (30) has two real, positive roots, at least one of which is greater than one. Therefore, taking the expected value of p_2 from (30), we know that if anticipations satisfy condition (i), p_2^e will exceed p_1 and, statistically, an explosive upward movement of price results. Thus, if anticipations satisfy (i), an unstable upward movement of price results, and if an unstable upward movement of price results, anticipations continue to satisfy (i). If p_2 is generated by (30), it and p_1 become initial conditions and (30) can be used to generate p_3. Therefore, anticipations specified by (i) are self-sustaining and lead to the market behavior specified in the text.

(ii) $p_1^e < p_0$, $p_2^e > p_1$. In this case, using (19c), (23) reduces to

$$a - bp_1 + \epsilon_1 = \frac{(p_1 - u_1)}{c} - \frac{(p_2 - u_2 - p_1)}{r}$$

or

$$p_2 = \left(1 + br + \frac{r}{c}\right)p_1 - ar - \left(\epsilon_1 + \frac{u_1}{c}\right)r + u_2 \qquad (31)$$

Except for the random terms, (31) is the same as (28) in Appendix A. In this case, in order that (19c) be satisfied, the random terms must be related by

$$\epsilon_1 = -u_1/c$$

There are now two possibilities. If $p_1 < \bar{p}$, (31) indicates that $p_2^e < p_1$ (since the coefficient of p_1 is greater than one) and this contradicts (ii), that is, these expectations cannot be self-fulfilling. If $p_1 > \bar{p}$, (31) indicates $p_2^e > p_1$ and p_2 can be generated by (31). If this occurs, p_1 and p_2 are initial conditions for the determination of p_3 and, provided

$p_3^e > p_2$, (i) is again relevant and p_3 is determined by (30). If $p_3^e < p_2$, given that $p_2^e > p_1$ and $p_1 > \bar{p}$, it is shown under (iii) that expectations cannot be realized.

(iii) $p_1^e > p_0$, $p_2^e < p_1$. In this case, again using (19c), (23) reduces to

$$a - bp_1 + \epsilon_1 = \frac{(p_1 - u_1)}{c} + \frac{(p_1 - u_1 - p_0)}{r}$$

or

$$p_1 = \frac{cp_0}{bc + r + c} + \frac{acr}{bcr + r + c} + \frac{\epsilon_1 + (1/c + 1/r)u_1}{bcr + r + c} \qquad (32)$$

which, except for the random terms, is the same as (25) in Appendix A. Thus, if expectations were as specified in (iii), the system would need only one initial condition, for instance p_0, and (32) would generate p_1. However, it is easy to show that (32) cannot lead to the realization of expectations. First, recall that the coefficient of p_0 in (32) is between zero and one. Then there are two possibilities.

(a) $p_0 > \bar{p}$. In this case, (32) indicates $p_1^e < p_0$, contradicting (iii).
(b) $p_0 < \bar{p}$. In this case, (32) indicates $p_0 < p_1^e < \bar{p}$.

However, if we then use the same form as (32) to generate p_2 from p_1, we get $p_2^e > p_1$, contradicting (iii). This case shows that once price rises have been anticipated, firms cannot then anticipate that price will begin to fall. Roughly, this is because, in the last period before the first anticipated price decline, firms would unload all their inventories. Since production would also decline next period, supply would clearly be greater in the period preceding the anticipated price decline than it would be in the period in which the decline takes place. But, this larger supply could not, on the average, clear the market at a higher price and therefore the anticipated price decline cannot take place.

(iv) $p_1^e < p_0$, $p_2^e < p_1$. It is obvious that this is impossible. In this case we would have $I_0 = I_1 = 0$ and, on the average, the market would be cleared in period one only if p_1^e were equal to $\bar{p}$. But if this were true, $p_2^e < p_1$ could not be realized.

We can now summarize these results as follows. There always exist anticipations of rising prices which lead to behavior that fulfills the expectations in question. In some cases, an initial anticipation of a price decline, followed by anticipations of price rises in subsequent periods, can be sustained. No other anticipations can be sustained.

Chapter **5**

IMPERFECT COMPETITION:
ONE-PERIOD HORIZON [1]

1. General Remarks

In the last chapter the output, sales, and inventory policy of a perfectly competitive firm was investigated on the assumption of expected profit maximization. In the model considered there, the basic motive for inventory holding was the desire to sell each period's output at the most profitable point in time. This means that when price is expected to rise in the future, some of current output is retained in inventory for future sale. When price is expected to fall, not only current output but also existing inventory is sold. This represents an essentially speculative theory of inventory holding. In an imperfectly competitive firm, in which larger quantities can be sold, on the average, only at lower prices, there is a qualitatively different motive for inventory holding. It arises from the fact that, not knowing how much will be demanded per period at any price it might set, the firm has an incentive to produce a quantity that makes possible some remaining inventory at the end of the period. The firm can guarantee that no inventory will be left only by producing so little that on the average profitable sales are missed. It can guarantee that no potential sales will be missed only by producing so much that an unprofitably large inventory is left on the average. This set of considerations is usually referred to as the "buffer" motive for holding inventories. The inventory problem is to decide how much risk of carrying different amounts in inventory is worth taking.

---

[1] This chapter is based on the author's article [56].

The answer depends on the cost of carrying inventory, the relation between selling price and cost of production, the shape of the probability distribution of demand, and the length of the firm's planning horizon. The crucial point is that the firm's output and inventory policy must be integrated with its pricing policy. It cannot decide on an inventory policy until it knows by what amount price exceeds marginal cost. If price is sufficiently high relative to marginal cost it is worthwhile to produce enough to make the probability of shortage arbitrarily small. On the other hand, the optimum price cannot be ascertained without knowledge of the cost of carrying a large inventory made likely by the setting of a high price. The purpose of this and the next chapter is to analyze the relations among the price, output, and inventory policies of a firm in an uncertain and imperfectly competitive world. Particular interest focuses on a comparison between the policies followed by such a firm and those followed by a firm in an analogous imperfect, but riskless, world. In particular, do prices and quantity sold differ systematically because of the introduction of uncertainty? In order to facilitate such a comparison the model to be considered will be specialized early in the analysis in a way that permits a simple contrast.

The introduction of a planning horizon consisting of two or more decision periods severely complicates the analysis, and almost all the difficult problems in production and inventory control arise from the "multistage" nature of such models (see Chapter 1 of [9]). Indeed, exact solutions of such problems are known in only a relatively small number of special cases, for example, those in which the probability distribution of demand is stationary through time.

There are two distinct sets of intertemporal relations that ought to be included in the analysis. The first, which operates through the firm's price policy, arises from the fact that current prices may affect future demand. A firm that charges high prices may build up a reputation as a high price firm, and this could shift its demand curve to the left (or, conceivably, to the right) in the future. This effect might be called the "complementarity" relation between the present and future demand for a firm's product. It is not peculiarly relevant to the presence of uncertainty, and the tradition of ignoring it, well established in price theory, will be followed in this and the next chapter.

The second set of intertemporal relations operates through the firm's production and inventory policy, and it is more closely related to the presence of uncertainty. If the firm follows a policy of producing an amount that is small relative to expected current demand, there is a large probability that it will incur runout or shortage cost. This probability arises from the fact that a customer who is unable to make a purchase at the announced price, at least without a delay, is likely to shop elsewhere in the future if there are other firms that run short less frequently. Hence a low inventory policy has an effect on future demand and profit. On the other hand, if the firm produces an amount that is large relative to expected current demand then there is a large probability that it will end the period with a considerable inventory. This affects future profitability in that it permits the firm to lower future production and costs without increasing the probability of shortage. Fitting these intertemporal relations into models of production and inventory control is often extremely difficult, and there are important unsolved problems in this area. However, it is often possible to take account of them, in some cases approximately and in some exactly, by supposing that the firm is concerned only with current profits, but that the firm imputes a value to any inventory remaining at the end of the period and imputes a cost to any demand that goes unsatisfied during the period. This is discussed in detail in the next chapter, but, since the procedure adopted does not affect the analysis in a fundamental way, the main results in this chapter are obtained on the assumption that the firm has a one-period horizon. This assumption facilitates the exposition and comparison with the riskless theory; the alterations required can be indicated simply in the next chapter.

2. Alternative Specifications of the Model

It is assumed throughout that the firm knows the probability distribution of demand at each price it might set. Quite generally, the demand curve facing the firm in any period can then be written

$$x = X(p, u) \tag{1}$$

where x is the quantity demanded, p, as before, is the price set, and u is a random term. Thus, for each pair of values of p and u the firm knows the resulting x, but it is unable to predict x in advance because it does not know which of its possible values u will take. However, it knows the distribution function $f(u; p)$, which gives it the probability that, when price is set equal to p, x will take any value. Knowing $f(u; p)$ the firm can also calculate the frequency function

$$F(a; p) = \int_{-\infty}^{a} f(u; p) \, du$$

giving the probability that u will not exceed a, and hence x will not exceed $X(p, a)$.

In addition, it is assumed that the firm commits itself to a price and output each period before observing the value of u relevant to that period. This assumption is crucial to the analysis that follows, and we should realize that other possibilities exist. In some markets firms may be able to wait until demand has materialized for the period before committing themselves to either or both of these decisions. If the firm observes u before committing itself to p and z there is, of course, no uncertainty involved in the decision process, and the traditional theory applies. Similarly, if the firm commits itself in advance to only one of the two decisions, waiting until after u is observed before making the remaining decision, the analysis is not essentially affected by the presence of uncertainty. For example, suppose the firm chose its level of production knowing only the probability distribution of demand, then set its price after observing u for that period. In this case the firm maximizes expected profit by calculating, from (1) and $f(u; p)$, the probability that p will be the highest price obtainable from a sale of x units. It then produces the amount z which maximizes the expected value of profits when each such price is weighted by its probability. When u materializes for the period, the firm sells its z units at the price that clears the market, that is, at the price p where $z = X(p, u)$. What makes this model uninteresting is the fact that z and the expected value of p are exactly the price and output of the riskless theory if the demand curve of that model is interpreted as the expected value of demand, with u integrated out, at each price. Thus, in this case uncertainty plays no essential role in the decision process. It plays no such role because expected profit depends only on the expected value of price, and the expectations can be interpreted either as means of stochastic variables or as subjectively certain predictions. The firm's policy is the same in either case. Similar remarks apply if the firm precommits itself to p and decides on z only after observing u.

Thus, to make the model interesting, precommittal to both p and z must be assumed. In fact, casual empiricism suggests that firms in imperfect markets typically precommit themselves to price at least to the extent that they precommit themselves to production. Indeed, in many firms production rates are varied from month to month, and prices are reviewed only annually unless some major change, for example, in costs or product design, occurs. The frequency with which any decision is made depends on the cost of taking the decision and on the rapidity with which the data on which the decision depends become outdated. Certainly there is no general reason why the optimum decision interval should be the same for price and output decisions. However, the whole idea of a decision period of fixed discrete length is an approximation, and the case of coterminous price and output decision intervals is a natural starting point both on grounds of theoretical interest and of empirical plausibility.

The representation of the stochastic demand curve by (1) allows for the possibility that the probability distribution of u may be different at different prices. In principle, this almost has to be the case. If the expected value of demand tends toward zero at sufficiently high prices, the probability distribution of demand around the expected value can hardly be the same at very high as at moderate prices, since demand cannot be negative. Nor is there any particular difficulty in working out the conditions for a maximum expected profit in this general case. Nevertheless, a special form of (1) is employed throughout the following analysis, because it facilitates comparison with the riskless theory. The natural comparison to make is between the price and output decisions taken when uncertainty is present and those that would be taken if the expected value of demand at each price were certain to occur. The comparison is much easier to carry out if u is assumed to be additive and independent of p. Then (1) can be written

$$x = X(p) + u \qquad (1a)$$

The additivity restriction is in the spirit of Chapter 2. The firm makes a forecast $X(p)$ of the demand that will be forthcoming at price p, and the properties of the distribution of u characterize the forecast errors the firm makes. Assuming u to be independent of p means that the firm is as good at forecasting sales at one price as at another. Although this has a certain plausibility it can only be a good approximation near the range of prices contained in the firm's relatively recent experience. On this assumption, the distribution function $f(u; p)$ can be shortened to $f(u)$. Likewise, the frequency function $F(a; p)$ can be shortened to $F(a)$. Furthermore, it was argued in Chapter 2 that it is also reasonable to assume $E(u) = 0$, and this assumption is incorporated in the analysis below. Analytically there is no loss of generality since, if u had a nonzero mean, it could be included in the function $X(p)$ and redefined as a deviation from its mean.

Using the specialization (1a) the natural comparison between this model and the riskless model is between the decisions taken and those that would have been taken if u were identically zero, that is, if $X(p)$ were expected with certainty to be the quantity demanded at price p. In making the comparison, $X(p)$ will be referred to as the riskless demand curve, $\overline{R}(p) = pX(p)$ as the riskless total revenue, and the derivative

$$\frac{d\overline{R}(p)}{dp} \frac{1}{X'(p)} = \frac{X(p)}{X'(p)} + p$$

as the riskless marginal revenue.

3. Equilibrium Conditions

As was stated in Section 1, the analysis in this chapter is carried out on the assumption that the firm has a one-period horizon. The modifications required by the presence of a longer horizon are discussed in the next chapter. The one-period assumption not only facilitates exposition, it also sharpens the analogy with the riskless case. One further restriction, also removed in the next chapter, is placed on the model. Whatever price and output the firm sets, there is in general some chance that the quantity demanded will exceed or fall short of the amount produced. In the latter case there will be a positive inventory of unsold goods at the end of the period. Since the firm has a one-period horizon it attaches no utility to such inventory. In addition, however, we assume that inventory involves no cost either, that is, it is disposed of in a way that neither yields revenue nor incurs cost. Likewise, being interested only in current profits, the firm does not have to worry about the loss of goodwill or future sales owing to an inability to meet current demand. The firm produces whatever amount makes current expected profit as large as possible and then sells as much of this production as is demanded at the price it has set. If more is demanded than is produced, some demand goes unsatisfied. If less is demanded than is produced, the inventory is disposed of without cost.

Even in this situation uncertainty has a genuine influence on the firm's decisions. In the first place, it is not generally true that the firm sets a price that equates riskless marginal revenue and marginal cost. Depending on the shapes of the cost and revenue curves and on the probability distribution of u, the price may be either higher or lower than its riskless level. In the second place, it is not generally true that the firm produces the amount that clears the market, on the average, at the equilibrium price. In other words, if the firm's best price and output are p^* and z^* respectively, it is not generally true that $z^* = X(p^*)$. Output z^* may exceed or fall short of $X(p^*)$, again depending on the shapes of the cost, revenue, and probability functions involved.

Fundamentally, differences arise from the fact that the expected value of total revenue depends not only on the expected demand at the equilibrium price but on all the moments of the probability distribution $f(u)$. Revenue arises from sales, not demand, and if demand is greater than the amount produced, total revenue is pz rather than px. Hence, expected revenue is not p times expected demand, but p times expected sales, which depends on the mean of demand truncated at the point $u = z - X(p)$, since $u - (z - X(p))$ represents shortage when the difference is positive. Formally, the revenue realized is

$$R^*(z, p) = \begin{cases} px & x \le z \\ pz & x \ge z \end{cases}$$

and the expected value of total revenue is

$$E(R^*(z, p)) = pX(p)F(z - X(p)) + p\int_{-\infty}^{z-X(p)} uf(u)\, du \\ + pz[1 - F(z - X(p))]$$

It is convenient to write this equation in the equivalent form

$$E(R^*(z, p)) = pX(p) - pD(z, p) \tag{2}$$

where $D(z, p)$ is the "shortage function" representing the mean amount of unsatisfied demand. Written out in full it is

$$D(z, p) = \int_{z-X(p)}^{\infty} (u - z + X(p)) f(u)\, du \tag{3}$$

Clearly, $D(z, p) \ge 0$ for all z and p. Mathematically this fact is evident from the definition (3). In words, it is because, as (2) says, the expected total revenue is price times mean demand minus price times the mean amount of unsatisfied demand. If z or p were large enough to make a demand in excess of the amount produced impossible, no sales would be missed whatever demand materialized, and mean total revenue would be price times mean demand. In general it is neither profitable nor possible to produce enough to meet all possible demands. Hence a positive quantity representing the amount of demand unsatisfied on the average must be subtracted from the total amount demanded on the average to get the total number of units sold on the average.

The expected profit associated with a price p and an output z is (2) minus $c(z)$, the total cost of producing z units

$$E(\pi) = pX(p) - pD(z, p) - c(z) \tag{4}$$

The firm wishes to find the values of p and z that jointly maximize expected profit (4). Formally, the maximum occurs at values that simultaneously equate to zero the partial derivatives of (4) with respect to p and z. Since price affects only revenue and not costs, for any z, expected profit is maximized by finding the price that maximizes expected revenue. This requires

$$\frac{\partial E[R^*(z, p)]}{\partial p} = \frac{d\bar{R}}{dp} - pD_p(z, p) - D(z, p) = 0 \tag{5}$$

Here $D_p(z, p) = X'(p)[1 - F(z - X(p))]$ is the partial derivative of $D(z, p)$ with respect to p. Equation (5) says that, at any output, price is in equilibrium when a small decrease in price increases the revenue that would be realized from sales equal to the expected demand, by the same amount that it decreases the expected revenue received because of increased likelihood of shortage. In other words, a fall in price increases the average amount demanded, and expected total revenue would increase if all demand resulted in sales. However, for any fixed output a fall in price also increases the average amount of shortage, which reduces expected total revenue. The equilibrium price balances these two effects. As in the riskless theory, the equilibrium price occurs where $d\bar{R}/dp < 0$, that is, where the riskless demand curve is elastic. If this were not so, if $d\bar{R}/dp > 0$, revenue could be increased with certainty by raising price, regardless of the level of output. If price is raised by dp there are only two possibilities. If $x \leq z$, revenue increases by $d\bar{R}/dp > 0$. If $x > z$, revenue increases by zdp. Hence revenue increases with probability equal to one, and it pays to increase price at least to the point at which the riskless demand becomes elastic.[2]

---

[2] This also follows directly from (5). Using the usual definition of elasticity, $e = -X'(p)p/X(p)$, a little manipulation of (5) gives $e = 1/F(z - X(p)) + D(z, p)/X(p)F(z - X(p)) \geq 1$, since the first term exceeds one and the second is non-negative.

For any p, maximization of (4) with respect to z involves both cost and revenue terms. Equilibrium output must satisfy

$$-\frac{\partial E\,(\pi)}{\partial z} = pD_z(z,\,p) + c'(z) = 0 \qquad (6)$$

$D_z(z,\,p) = -[1 - F(z - X(p))]$ is the partial derivative of $D(z,\,p)$ with respect to z. Equation (6) says that, for any p, z is in equilibrium when a small increase in z increases expected revenue by the same amount that it increases production cost. If z is increased by one unit revenue increases by p if $x \geq z$, and it increases by zero otherwise. The former occurs with probability $[1 - F(z - X(p))]$, making the expected value of the increase in revenue $p[1 - F(z - X(p))]$. This must be equated to marginal cost. Equation (6) is analogous to the marginal-revenue-equals-marginal-cost criterion of the riskless theory. It says that, when uncertainty is present, marginal cost, evaluated at the output in question, should be equal to some fraction of price, and that the fraction is the probability that demand will exceed production. It is shown in the next section that the fractional relationship between marginal cost and price bears an interesting relationship to the analogous equality in the riskless theory. Equation (6) can also be written

$$F(z - X(p)) = \frac{p - c'(z)}{p} \qquad (6a)$$

Expressed in words, (6a) means that the firm's price and output policy should make the probability of shortage [3] equal to the ratio of marginal cost to price. In the riskless case, when the firm is in equilibrium, the right side of (6a) is the reciprocal of the elasticity of demand and has been employed by Lerner [41] as a measure of the degree of monopoly power possessed by the firm. When uncertainty is present the right side of (6a) does not bear this relation to the elasticity of riskless demand, since z is not in general equal to $X(p)$. Furthermore, (6a) shows that the Lerner measure depends on the shape of the probability distribution of u as well as on the structure of the industry.

From (6a), it can be seen that, for any z and p, $0 \leq F(z - X(p)) \leq 1$, implies $0 \leq c'(z) \leq p$, inequalities that also hold in the riskless theory. In particular, a firm should never produce an output that makes marginal cost greater than price, whether there is uncertainty or not. A second

---

[3] Shortage occurs when $x > z$, which has a probability of $1 - F(z - X(p))$.

set of inequalities for z, which follows immediately, is min $(u) \leq z$ $- X(p) \leq$ max (u). It never pays to produce less than the minimum or more than the maximum than can possibly be sold at the price set. If the first inequality were violated profit could be increased with probability one by increasing z, since sales would increase with certainty and $c'(z) \leq p$. If the second inequality were violated costs could be reduced, without jeopardizing revenue, by reducing z, since z is more than can possibly be sold and $c'(z) \geq 0$.

It is also clear from (6a) that there is no presumption that equilibrium output clears the market on the average at the equilibrium price. The market is cleared on the average if $z = X(p)$ and this equality does not hold generally when z and p assume their optimum values. For example, if $f(u)$ is symmetrical so that $F(a) \gtrless \frac{1}{2}$ according as a $\gtrless 0$, then from (6a), $z \geq X(p)$ if and only if $p \geq 2c'(z)$. In words, an extra unit of output adds $c'(z)$ to cost. If output is already at the level $X(p)$ this unit can be sold only fifty per cent of the time on the average. Thus, in order to make the extra output worthwhile, each sale of this marginal unit must add twice as much to revenue as to cost. Clearly, therefore, whether $f(u)$ is symmetrical or not there are many cases in which it is worthwhile for the firm to set price and output levels that result in shortage on the average. This fact does not, however, provide an incentive for the firm to raise its price or for new firms to enter the industry unless they have lower costs or information allowing them to make better forecasts of demand. In general, it requires a strangely shaped probability distribution to induce a firm with a marginal cost nearly as high as its price to produce enough to clear the market on the average. As will be shown in the next chapter, the incentive to clear the market is provided by long-run considerations involved in the durability of inventory and the fear that unsatisfied customers will shop elsewhere in the future.

The paradigm for the present case is the vendor of newspapers on a busy corner who cannot return unsold papers and operates on a small markup. Today's papers will be worthless tomorrow, and it almost certainly pays him to buy fewer papers than can be sold on the average.

4. Comparison with the Riskless Model

The simultaneous solution of (5) and (6) yields values z^* and p^* of z and p that maximize expected profit. What can be said about p^* and z^* compared with the values they would take if there were no uncertainty, that is, if u were identically zero? For example, can price ever be lower with uncertainty than without, and if so how does output compare with its riskless level? The special restrictions that have been placed on the random component of demand permit a simple analysis of this problem.

If there were no uncertainty, equilibrium price and output would be $\bar{p}$ and $\bar{z} = X(\bar{p})$ where $\bar{p}$ equates riskless marginal revenue and marginal cost

$$\frac{d\bar{R}}{d\bar{p}}\frac{1}{X'(\bar{p})} = c'(\bar{z}) \tag{7}$$

An equation similar to (7) can be obtained for the uncertainty model by combining (5) and (6). Recall that $D_p(z, p)$ in (5) can be evaluated as $X'(p)[1 - F(z - X(p))]$ and note that, from (6a), $[1 - F(z - X(p))] = c'(z)/p$. Making these two substitutions in (5) and dividing both sides by $X'(p)$, we get

$$\frac{d\bar{R}}{dp^*}\frac{1}{X'(p^*)} = c'(z^*) + \frac{D(z^*, p^*)}{X'(p^*)} \tag{8}$$

This equation shows that in the risky situation the firm equates riskless marginal revenue not to marginal cost but to marginal cost plus a second term, which in general is not zero. We must also remember that in (8), unlike the riskless case, it is not generally true that $X(p^*) = z^*$. Now let us examine the second term on the right hand side of (8): $D(z, p) > 0$ and, in the normal case, $X'(p) < 0$.[4] Hence this term is nonpositive. It follows from (8) that z^* and p^* will equate riskless marginal revenue to something less than the marginal cost of producing z^*. This fact can be stated as a theorem:

Define $p°$ such that [5]

$$\frac{d\bar{R}}{dp°}\frac{1}{X'(p°)} = c'(z^*)$$

Then $p^* \le p°$. In words, $p°$ is the price that makes riskless marginal revenue, evaluated at that price, equal to marginal cost evaluated at the equilibrium output.

---

[4] The reader can easily work out the analogs to the following results for the case in which $X'(p) > 0$, but the second order conditions for a maximum of (4) continue to hold.

[5] Here and in what follows the equality $p^* = p°$ holds only if z^* is large enough to make shortage impossible.

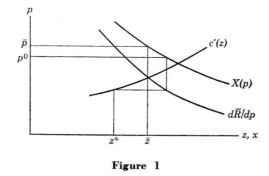

Figure 1

All the corollaries below are immediate consequences of this theorem, obtained by further specializing the model. It is convenient to treat separately the three cases that arise, according to whether marginal cost is constant, rising, or falling.

(a) *Marginal cost constant.* This is the simplest case. If marginal cost is constant, it is the same at z^* and $\bar{z}$. Hence $p^\circ = \bar{p}$ and the theorem says $p^* \leq \bar{p}$; that is, we have the rather remarkable result:

Corollary A: If marginal cost is constant then the equilibrium price cannot be higher than it would be in the riskless case.

This does not indicate where z^* lies in relation to $\bar{z}$. Numerical examples in Section 5 show that z^* may lie on either side of $\bar{z}$ depending on the shape of the riskless demand curve and of $f(u)$. In general the steeper the demand curve the higher the price relative to marginal cost and the greater the loss in missing potential sales. Therefore, it pays to make z^* large relative to $X(p^*)$ and hence large relative to $\bar{z}$ since Corollary A implies $X(p^*) \geq \bar{z}$.

(b) *Marginal cost rising.* This case is a little more complicated. If $z^* \leq \bar{z}$, it follows from the theorem that $p^\circ \leq \bar{p}$ and hence $p^* \leq \bar{p}$. That is, if equilibrium output is less than or equal to its riskless level, equilibrium price is also less than or equal to its riskless level. Likewise, even if $z^* \geq \bar{z}$, if $X(p^*) \geq \bar{z}$ then $p^* \leq \bar{p}$. Even if equilibrium output is greater than its riskless level it is still possible that average demand will be greater than its riskless level and therefore price will be less than its riskless level. These results can be summarized as

Corollary B: If marginal cost is rising, either $z^* \leq \bar{z}$ or $\bar{z} \leq X(p^*)$ implies $p^* \leq \bar{p}$.

It follows from Corollary B that shortage on the average implies that the price is lower than its riskless level.

Thus, when marginal cost is rising the only circumstance in which we cannot prove that price is lower than its riskless level is when output is greater than its riskless volume but expected demand is less than the equilibrium demand in the riskless case. We might conjecture that we could also show either that this curcumstance is inconsistent with the maximal conditions (5) and (6) or that price would still be lower than its riskless level even when this circumstance holds. We know that when marginal cost is constant price is less than its riskless level whatever relation z^*, $\bar{z}$, and $X(p^*)$ bear to each other. It seems plausible that this result should also hold when marginal cost is rising. That the conjecture is false is shown below by a numerical example.

It is, however, possible to impose further conditions on $c(z)$, $X(p)$, and $f(u)$ which imply that price is necessarily below its riskless level. For example, suppose that $c'(z) = cz$, $X(p) = a - bp (c, a, b > 0)$, and $f(u)$ is symmetrical. We know that $p^* \geq \bar{p}$ requires

(i) $z^* \geq X(p^*)$, and this in turn requires

(ii) $p^* \geq 2c'(z^*)$, since $f(u)$ is symmetrical.

Finally, from the theorem proved above we know that

(iii) $p^* \leq p^{\circ}$

Since p° is a function of z^*, inequalities (i) to (iii) are three relations that must hold between p^* and z^* if p^* is to exceed $\bar{p}$. Written out, they are

(i) $p^* \geq a/b - (1/b)z^*$

(ii) $p^* \geq 2cz^*$

(iii) $p^* \leq (a/2b) + (c/2)z^*$

From the fact that all the constants are positive it follows that no two of the inequalities are inconsistent with each other for all p and z. However, for some values of c, a, and b the three will be mutually inconsistent for all p and z. In this case p^* cannot exceed $\bar{p}$, because the maximal value p° of p is less than the minimal value $2c'(z)$ of p that would permit $p^* \geq \bar{p}$. Figure 2 shows the three sets defined by these inequalities, and their intersection is the shaded area. The three inequalities are inconsistent when their intersection is empty. An easy

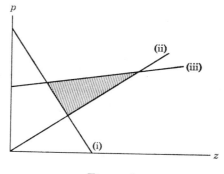

Figure 2

calculation shows that this situation occurs if and only if $bc > 1$. This condition says that if the product of the slope of the marginal cost curve and the absolute value of the slope of the demand curve is greater than one then p^* must be less than or equal to $\bar{p}$. Roughly, if either the marginal cost or the demand curve is very steep, then $p^* \leq \bar{p}$. This is independent of the form of $f(u)$ provided only that it is symmetrical. It is interesting to note that in the very situation that tends to create a high price (steep marginal cost and demand curves), the presence of uncertainty ensures a price lower than it would otherwise be.

We can now construct an example showing that price can be higher than its riskless level when marginal cost is rising, thus disproving the conjecture made above. The procedure is, first, to choose b and c so that bc is less than one. Next, suppose that $f(u)$ is the rectangular distribution with parameter λ. This distribution is described in detail in Section 5. It implies that u can fall anywhere in the interval $-\lambda < u \leq \lambda$ with the constant probability $1/2\lambda$, but that u never falls outside this interval. Next, solve (5) and (6) for p^* as a function of λ and then find a λ which makes p^* large. Using $X(p) = 20 - 0.5p$ and $c'(z) = 0.5z$, a tedious calculation shows that when $\lambda = 7$, $p^* = 25$, $X(p^*) = 7.5$ and $z^* = 11.0$. But $\bar{p} = 22$ and $\bar{z} = 9$. Hence $p^* > \bar{p}$.

(c) *Marginal cost falling.* This case is symmetrical with that of rising marginal cost considered in (b), provided the second-order conditions for the maximum continue to hold, and it need not be discussed in detail. The analog to Corollary B is

Corollary C: If marginal cost is falling, either $z^* \geq \bar{z}$ or $X(p^*) \geq \bar{z}$ implies $p^* \leq \bar{p}$.

Here the observation of average excess demand does not imply $p^* \le \bar{p}$. The circumstance in which we cannot show that $p^* \le \bar{p}$ is $z^* \le X(p^*) \le \bar{z}$.

5. *An Example and Some Policy Implications*

It is of interest to consider a special case, which is sufficiently simple to allow explicit representation of the functions involved in the results of the previous sections. Suppose the total cost and riskless demand curves are linear so that $c'(z) = c$ and $X(p) = a - bp (c, a, b > 0)$. Further suppose that $f(u)$ is the rectangular distribution

$$f(u) = \begin{bmatrix} 0 & \mu < -\lambda \\ \dfrac{1}{2\lambda} & -\lambda \le \mu \le \lambda \\ 0 & \lambda < \mu \end{bmatrix}$$

Then,
$$F(a) = (a + \lambda)/2\lambda$$
and
$$\int_{-\lambda}^{a} uf(u)\,du = (a^2 - \lambda^2)/4\lambda, \text{ for } -\lambda \le a \le \lambda$$

In this case (6) can be solved for z as an explicit function of p.

$$z(p) = X(p) + 2\lambda(\tfrac{1}{2} - c/p) \tag{9}$$

This illustrates the remark made above that $z^* \ge X(p^*)$ when $f(u)$ is symmetrical only if $p^* \ge 2c'(z^*)$. If $z(p)$ from (9) is substituted for z in $D(z, p)$ in (3), the latter takes the particularly simple form

$$\phi(p) = D(z(p), p) = \lambda c^2/p^2 \tag{10}$$

If $\lambda = 0$, there is no uncertainty, $\phi(p) = 0$ and (8) reduces to (7) giving $p^* = \bar{p}$. Likewise if c is very small $\phi(p)$ tends toward zero and p^* tends to $\bar{p}$. If marginal cost is zero it pays to produce enough to make shortage impossible and to charge the same price as in the riskless case. Again, if $X(p)$ is very steep p^* will be large relative to c and $\phi(p)$ will be small so that $\bar{p}$ and p^* will be approximately equal. The larger the price relative to marginal cost, the more worthwhile it is to reduce the risk of shortage by producing more.

Substituting $\phi(p)$ from (10) and the linear cost and demand equations in (8), we get

$$a + bc - 2bp - \frac{\lambda c^2}{p^2} = 0$$

so that p^* is a root of the cubic

$$\theta(p) = 2bp^3 - (a + bc)p^2 + \lambda c^2 = 0 \qquad (11)$$

The graph of this function is shown in Figure 3. If any non-negative price is to satisfy (11), two of its roots must be positive and one negative. This is true because $\theta(0) = \lambda c^2 > 0$ and θ goes to plus and minus infinity as p goes to plus and minus infinity respectively. Furthermore, p^* must be the larger of the two positive roots, because one of the roots occurs at a price less than marginal cost and thus cannot be p^*. This can be seen as follows. At $p = c$

$$\theta(c) = (\lambda - (a - bc))c^2 = [\lambda - X(c)]c^2 \qquad (12)$$

Now $X(p) - \lambda$ is the smallest amount that can be demanded when the price is p. Since the price is always at least as high as marginal cost, $\lambda < X(c)$ is necessary in order that there exist at least one price at which the minimum demand is positive. Hence, the term in square brackets in (12) is negative and $\theta(c) < 0$. This means that there must be one positive root greater than marginal cost and one less. Hence the larger positive root is p^*.

The following numerical examples illustrate the quantitative importance of uncertainty in reducing price. Suppose $X(p) = 20 - 2p$ and $c = 5$. Then

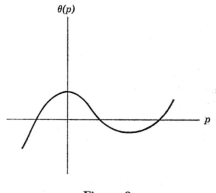

Figure 3

	if λ = 2	if λ = 5		if λ = 0
p^*	7.25	7.0	$\bar{p}$	7.5
$X(p^*)$	5.5	6.0	$X(\bar{p})$	5.0
z^*	4.7	4.0	$\bar{z}$	5.0

Thus, uncertainty lowers the price from the riskless level of 7.5 by about 3 per cent when $\lambda = 2$ and about 7 per cent when $\lambda = 5$. Output is 15 per cent smaller than average demand when $\lambda = 2$ and 35 per cent smaller when $\lambda = 5$. These output levels represent a reduction compared with the riskless output of 6 per cent and 20 per cent respectively. If demand were less elastic, output would be greater than the average amount demanded. Suppose $X(p) = 20 - p$, $c = 5$, and $\lambda = 5$. Then we have

	if λ = 5		if λ = 0
p^*	12	$\bar{p}$	12.5
$X(p^*)$	8	$X(\bar{p})$	7.5
z^*	9	$\bar{z}$	7.5

Equation (11) also indicates how p^* varies with λ, the measure of uncertainty. For $\lambda = 0$, $p^* = \bar{p}$. For $\lambda > 0$, $p^* < \bar{p}$ and p^* falls continuously as λ increases. When $\lambda = X(c)$, the maximal value λ can take, $\theta(p)$ has a local minimum equal to zero at the point $p = c$. This is then a repeated root, and the equilibrium price equals marginal cost. However, at a price equal to marginal cost (6a) tells the firm to produce $X(c) - \lambda = 0$. Since price only covers marginal cost and there is a chance that some of any production will be unsold, any output greater than zero adds more to cost than to expected revenue. Expected profit can only be reduced by production, and it is better not to produce at all. Thus, even though there exists an amount of uncertainty, as measured by λ, which will induce the firm to lower its price to marginal cost, there are no welfare implications since the firm will not produce anything at this price even in the short run. Any welfare analysis of the amount of uncertainty requires an evaluation of amounts of excess demand as well as of prices exceeding marginal cost.

There is also a moral for the theory of price control policy to be learned from this analysis, though it is not restricted to the example considered in this section. Suppose the authorities follow the Lange-Lerner rule and allow a monopolist to produce and sell whatever amount he wishes but forbid sales at any price in excess of marginal cost. The riskless model then tells us that the monopolist will behave like a perfectly competitive firm by producing and selling the amount that makes marginal cost equal to price. In the risky situation, however, (6a) tells us that the monopolist will produce only the amount he is certain to be able to sell. This is sure to imply shortage on the average, though it will not necessarily result in zero production. In the example considered here the firm would be indifferent among all values of z in the interval $0 \leq z \leq X(c) - \lambda$. In a different example in which marginal cost was rising, the producer might have a preference for positive production. In Figure 4, suppose $\underline{X}(p) = X(p) - \min(u)$, that is $\underline{X}(p)$ is the largest amount the firm can be sure of selling at price p. Then the firm will produce and sell $\underline{z}$ at a price $\underline{p}$. These values are less than the competitive quantity and price, and they would leave an average excess demand of $X(\underline{p}) - z$, which is necessarily positive.

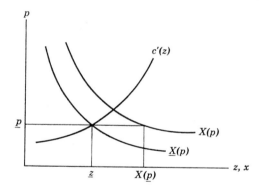

Figure 4

Chapter 6

IMPERFECT COMPETITION: MULTIPERIOD HORIZON

1. The Nature of the Multiperiod Planning Problem

The results of the previous chapter were obtained on the basis of a very strict interpretation of the assumption that the firm had a one-period planning horizon. Specifically, we assumed not only that future profits were given no weight in making current price and output decisions, but also that any excess of production over demand during the planning period was disposed of so that no inventory was carried between periods.

The assumption of a one-period planning horizon is a significant restriction in all but the most trivial decision problems. Normally, a decision has substantial effects not only in the immediate future but also in the more distant future, perhaps after further decisions of a similar nature have been taken. In spite of the fact that most economic analysis of firms' behavior has employed the one-period assumption, few economists are satisfied that it is adequate. The approximation involved is better when the future is discounted more heavily and the interval between the taking of consecutive decisions is longer. However, since production and inventory decisions are normally made at very short intervals, discounting of profits in subsequent periods can hardly be sufficiently great to make the influence of future periods on current decisions negligible. Furthermore, when the one-period assumption has been dropped in the literature it has usually been replaced by a dichotomous model which distinguishes only between "long-run" and "short-run" effects.[1] In the absence of more justification than is usually provided, this model is unsatisfactory because there is no obvious empirical counterpart to the "long-run" variables in the making of price and output decisions. The long run in this problem consists of a series of future "short-run" planning periods which may be more or less alike, and it is not generally possible to collapse these future periods into a function of any single "long-run" variable. It is argued below that approximation is often necessary, but dichotomization is neither simple nor natural for this purpose.

We pointed out in Chapter 5 that when uncertainty is taken into account there is an additional intertemporal dependence among the firm's present and future operations which is not encountered in the riskless model of imperfect competition. In both cases there is interdependence on the demand side which arises from the influence of present price on future demand. Also, in both cases there is interdependence on the supply side, arising from the possibility of reducing the cost of making available a given supply by rearranging the time pattern of production and carrying inventories. For example, if marginal production cost rises at all levels of production, it evidently pays to produce ahead to meet exceptionally high anticipated demands in order to avoid high production costs in any one period. These intertemporal supply and demand relationships are present whether there is uncertainty or not.

When uncertainty is present there is the additional consideration that rational price and output policies involve the possibility that demand will either exceed or fall short of production. In either case current operations are likely to affect future profitability. In the former case customers who are unable to make desired purchases at the announced price may shop elsewhere in the future. In the latter case, if it is possible to carry inventory between periods future production costs can be lowered by reducing output in subsequent periods and making sales from inventory. Both of these are obvious relationships to consider and they make the one-period assumption seem even more restrictive when uncertainty is present than when it is not. It is the purpose of this chapter to discuss the implications of its removal.

[1] An example of a very explicit model of this type is found in Hicks [33]. The remarks in the text above pertain only to the use of the "long-run" concept in the analysis of price and output decisions and not to its use in the analysis of fixed capital investment decisions.

Dropping the single-period horizon opens a Pandora's box of complications, and it is well to outline the general problem it introduces before making the special assumptions to be employed in this analysis.[2] The problem of taking price and output decisions when the planning horizon consists of a number of decision periods is an example of what have come to be called "multistage" or "dynamic" programming problems in decision theory.

One of the most important advances in this area in recent years has been a deeper understanding of the nature of such problems. These problems consist of a number of decisions that must be taken by the beginnings of subsequent periods, say at dates 1, 2, $\cdots$. An important innovation in the dynamic programming approach, as compared with the usual problems of simultaneous maximization in economics, is an explicit consideration of the fact that the passage of time between decision dates permits the accumulation of new relevant information.[3] Specifically, account is taken in the optimization procedure of the fact that earlier decisions must be made from a knowledge of only the distribution functions of certain random variables, the numerical values of which will be known when later decisions must be made. Time thus plays an essential role in the analysis and, in keeping with terminological tradition in economics, the time factor justifies the use of the term "dynamic" in the description of the problem. Even though we know that later decisions will be made on the basis of information not yet available, profitability (or more generally utility) is often jointly dependent on all the decisions to be made within the horizon and they must, in a sense, all be made simultaneously.

The appropriate simultaneity characteristic cannot, however, consist in joint determination of all the actual decisions. If all the decisions were made at date one either the decisions for future dates would be carried out, and the information collected meanwhile would be wasted, or the decisions would be altered in the light of this information and the earlier decisions, based on incorrect assumptions concerning later decisions, would no longer be appropriate. If, as we

---

[2] A more rigorous and general, though also more technical, outline of the structure of the problem is presented in Chapter 2 of [9].

[3] More generally, it could be said that dynamic programming utilizes information concerning the temporal structure of the decision problem in attempting to find a solution. This is not meant to imply that dynamic programming is not also useful in problems involving certainty.

assume here, what is known at date one is the distribution function of a random variable whose numerical value will be known and relevant for some future decision, what needs to be decided at date one is how different numerical values of the variable are to influence the decision in question. In other words, the simultaneity characteristic is the joint determination of a set of functions relating each decision to the information available at the time the decision has to be made. This information is dependent both on the random variables that will be known at that time and on earlier decisions.

Consider any set of functions Φ_n, $n = 1, 2, \cdots$ specifying the dependence of the nth date's decision on the information, including previous decisions and their effects, available at the nth date. At date one, Φ_1 gives the numerical value of date one's decision as a function of data known at date one. At this time each Φ_n for $n > 1$ indicates only which decision will be made on the basis of any of the sets of information that might be relevant at date n. Since, as we assume in this formulation, the distribution functions of all relevant variates within the horizon are known or estimated at date one, it is possible, at least in principle, to find the probability that any one of the possible sets of information will in fact be observed by date two. This information depends only on date one's decision, which is known, and on the values assumed by any random variables in period one, the distributions of which are known. Hence the probability that date two's decision, using Φ_2, will be any one of those possible can be calculated. Applying this procedure to date three, and using Φ_3, we obtain the probability that any particular date-two decision will be followed by any particular date-three decision. This probability is conditional on date two's decision in the same way that the probabilities of different date-two decisions are conditional on date one's decision. The total probability at date one that any particular date-three decision will be chosen is the sum of the probabilities of all date-two decisions, each weighted by the probability that it will be followed by the particular date-three decision.

In this way the probability that any particular decision will be taken at any given decision date can be found. Since the decisions taken, the random variables, the known parameters of the problem, and the initial information available at date one completely determine the profit realized each period over the horizon, it is possible to calculate the probability that each period's activity will yield any given profit level. Thus, weighting each profit level in each period by its probability, it is possible to calculate the expected value at date one of all future profits, discounted back to the present. This present value will depend on the set of functions Φ_n that is chosen, and the problem is to find the set that makes it as large as possible.

It should be emphasized that, at date one, Φ_1 determines the numerical value of date one's decision, since the information constituting its argument is known. All other Φ_n specify only a complete set of conditional or "iffy" decisions. This is all that is either possible or desirable. The only decision that must be made numerically at date one is date one's decision. Future decisions are important then only because they affect the profitability of different date-one decisions. Since the Φ_n show how date one's decision will affect future decisions they, together with the relevant distribution functions, completely represent the effect of date one's decision on expected future profits. Thus, all the information available at the time is utilized in making date one's decision. In other words, for decision purposes the appropriate relationship between the present and a future known only by its distribution functions is that current decisions affect the probability that different future decisions will be appropriate when the time comes. This means that at the present all future decisions are random variables whose distributions depend partly on the current decision.

It is easy to see that the essential characteristics of inventory holding in a world of uncertain demand give rise to problems of exactly this type. At each decision date a production, and perhaps price, decision must be made. The profitability of a given date-one production decision depends partly on the demand that materializes during period one and partly on the revenue from the sale of any inventory remaining at the end of the period. This revenue in turn depends on the price and production decisions made at date two. At the beginning of period one all future demands are random variables, only the probability distributions of which are known. The new information that becomes available at the beginning of each period consists of the realized demand of the previous period. This, together with previous production decisions, determines the initial inventory that begins the period. The Φ_n then specify the production levels of all future periods within the horizon as functions, at least, of the inventory on hand at the end of the previous period. At time one, all future production levels are random variables since the inventory levels on which they depend are themselves random variables. The problem at date one is to choose future production levels as functions of the inventory levels that will be known when each production decision has to be made.

Evidently, dynamic programming problems are often difficult to solve. At present no one knows how to solve such problems formulated in a general way, even in a relatively specialized area such as production and inventory control. Most multistage programming problems are solved in one of two ways. In many cases it is possible to discover some characteristic of the problem that can be exploited to reduce the degree of simultaneity to manageable proportions, and the problem then can often be solved using special techniques. In other cases the "true" problem can be approximated by a simpler problem, such as an analogous single-stage problem, whose solution can be found. The remainder of this section is concerned with the first possibility. The second is dealt with in Section 2. A particular single-stage approximation is chosen for the analysis of a firm in an imperfectly competitive market, and its appropriateness is discussed. In Section 3 new equilibrium conditions for the firm using this approximation are derived, and in Section 4 the firm's price and output policy is compared with that of its riskless counterpart. An example is presented in Section 5.

One special example of a characteristic that can be exploited to solve multistage programming problems has already been encountered in Chapter 4 dealing with the output and inventory policy of a firm in a perfectly competitive market. Although in principle the firm had to plan simultaneously all the output and inventory levels within its horizon as functions of expected prices, it was shown that the properties of perfect competition normally permit the firm to reduce drastically the degree of simultaneity involved, even if prices are expected to vary from period to period.

Thus, at least in cases of certainty, perfect competition seems to present intrinsically less complicated programming problems at the level of the individual firm. This is true presumably because, to some extent, a competitive market is a computing mechanism and performs some computations that the firm itself must undertake in an imperfectly competitive market. In the presence of uncertainty however, it is not so clear that this dictum holds. As we saw in Section 5 of Chapter 4, the programming problems are still essentially unsolved for a competitive firm uncertain as to future prices. Likewise, one of the main arguments of this chapter is that the interesting programming problems of an imperfectly competitive firm are unsolved when demand contains random components. In this situation, it is dangerous to say that either type of market presents simpler programming problems.

A more important characteristic that can be exploited to solve multistage planning problems, one widely utilized in published studies, arises when there is a symmetrical relationship between current and future decisions.[4] This relationship occurs when the future is expected, in a sense, to be like the present, so that each future decision will be the same function of information available when it is made as the present decision is of information presently available. Suppose, for example, that the production and inventory carrying cost functions and the distribution function of demand are all expected to remain unchanged in the future. Suppose further that the horizon consists of all future time, that price is expected to be constant over the entire horizon, and that the present value of all future expected profits, discounted in the usual way, is to be maximized. Many variants of this problem, obtained by specializing one or more of the functions in some way, have been studied extensively in the literature. The only factor relevant to the production decision that can vary from period to period is the initial inventory level with which the period begins. When an optimum production policy is followed each period, the present value of all future expected profits at date n is the same function of that date's initial inventory, regardless of the n chosen. Hence, each period's optimum decision is the same function of the period's initial inventory, and the problem reduces to that of finding a single function relating production to initial inventory each period.

Even in this special case it is not always easy, or even possible, to solve the problem. In more general cases the problem is more intractable. This fact suggests that firms faced with such problems probably approximate them with simpler versions that are easier to solve. In the next section it is argued that there exists a natural approximation of the imperfectly competitive firm's programming problem, which has often been considered implicitly or explicitly in the literature on production control. The nature of the approximation is investigated, and some evidence is presented that it corresponds to the organizational and informational procedures used in many firms.

---

[4] The first explicit formulation of this property is in [7]. Its implications for many kinds of problems have been extensively investigated by R. Bellman [13].

2. *Approximation by a Single-Stage Problem*

The preceding discussion has been intended to suggest that multistage programming problems are extremely difficult to solve in all but the simplest models. For this reason a common procedure in investigations of this type is to approximate the true problem by a simpler one which the investigator has a better chance to solve.[5]

In particular, often only the first planning period is considered explicitly in the formal optimization procedure. The effect of this period's activities on the more distant future is represented by a function of the events, such as decisions and random variables, that occur during the period. As Arrow has shown in [4], this procedure is not formally different from solving the multistage problem itself. Since all other decisions are made at points later in time than the first, and since causation cannot travel backwards in time, it follows that the first period's events can affect future profits or utility but that future events cannot affect the first period's profits. Hence the expected value of the entire horizon's profits is the first period's expected profits plus some function representing the effect of the first period's events on the expected profits of later periods. Thus, there is some function of the first period's events that collapses the multistage problem into an equivalent single-stage one. The difficulty is that this function in general depends on all future decisions (the Φ_n of Section 1) and on the distributions of all future random variables. Hence knowing the function is equivalent to solving the original problem.

The approximation arises when we suggest that this function should be estimated from intuition or experience without formally solving the multistage problem. In many cases the one-stage approximation has a strong intuitive appeal, and experience with a problem often suggests natural forms for the function representing the "carryover" effects of the current decision. Arrow, in the paper just quoted, has gone so far as to suggest this approximation as a paradigm for all operations research problems.

The natural one-stage approximation in the area of production planning, referred to above, is as follows. The basic simplification

---

[5] Of course, as has been well argued by others, there is no "natural" delineation of problems in decision theory. Life is really one big multistage decision problem, and the true problem at any point in time is to find an exhaustive set of "iffy" decisions for all possible contingencies during the remainder of one's life. Thus all decision problems are more or less arbitrary approximations of some more general problem.

is to represent the effect of current operations on future profitability by some function of the difference between total available supply and the quantity demanded in the current period. Total available supply in period n, y_n, is the sum of the nth period's production, z_n, and the inventory remaining at the end of the previous period, I_{n-1}: $y_n = z_n + I_{n-1}$. The proposal being considered is to represent the effect of the nth period's operations on the future by a function $\rho(y_n - x_n)$ of the nth period's terminal inventory (when $y_n > x_n$) or shortage (when $x_n > y_n$). This proposal argues that the firm's optimum first-period policy when it has a multiperiod horizon can be approximated by the optimum policy of the one-period model, provided that any terminal inventory or shortage for the period is evaluated according to the function ρ. Normally, one would expect ρ to have the sign of $(y_n - x_n)$. When this difference is positive ρ is the value that the firm imputes to inventory remaining at the end of the period, roughly the savings in future production cost permitted by the inventory minus the cost of storing it. When this difference is negative ρ is the cost the firm imputes to its inability to supply current demand, roughly the loss of future profits resulting from current shortages.

Clearly, in general the importance to the firm of a given terminal inventory or shortage depends on future decisions and distributions of random variables within the firm's horizon. The value of inventory on hand depends on the extra cost of producing these goods in the future, and this cost in turn depends on future production decisions. The loss of future profit from current shortage depends on the amount by which customers reduce their future demand as a result of current shortage, on the relation between future prices and costs, and so forth. Thus in general the use of the function ρ involves a genuine approximation. It is therefore important to investigate the nature and extent of the approximation involved and the appropriate form of the function.

In the first place, the ρ function can take into account only those effects of current policy on future profits that are transmitted through either inventory (when $y_n > x_n$) or shortage (when $y_n < x_n$). Specifically, the ρ function does not take into account the effect of current price on the firm's future demand and profits, referred to as the complementarity effect in Section 1 of Chapter 5. Now the reason for the complementarity effect is much the same as the reason for the effect of current shortage on future profits. Just as the frequent inability to make desired purchases from a firm induces customers to shop elsewhere in the future, so presumably does a high current price. Both effects, if they exist, arise from the presence of habit persistence in consumers' behavior.

Thus, just as it seemed plausible to represent the effect on future profit of current shortage by a function $\rho(y_n - x_n)$ of the amount of shortage, so it seems plausible to represent the similar effect of current price on future profits by a function of current price. Again, there is a genuine approximation involved in this procedure since the loss of future profit owing to a high current price depends on the extent to which the high price drives customers away and on the relation between price and costs in future periods. Although for notational simplicity this effect is not included in the model, it is easy to show that provided a high current price has an adverse effect on future profitability, all the results of this chapter are strengthened.[6]

In the second place, even considering those effects of current policies on future profits that are transmitted through inventories or shortage, in general an approximation is involved when such effects are represented by the ρ function. In this case some more precise statements can be made concerning the nature of the approximation involved. Some circumstances exist in which this approximation actually provides an exact representation of the multistage problem.[7] In other words, as often happens in programming problems, there are some cases in which current price and output policy bears only a superficial relation to events beyond the current period.

For example, take a situation where marginal production cost is constant and some production is certain to be needed next period. Here an exact valuation of inventory is possible; it is the excess of the present value of next period's marginal production cost over the cost of storing the inventory for one period. Clearly, inventory at the

---

[6] Formally, subtract from the right hand side of equation (1) in this chapter a function $\psi(p)$ representing the present value of future expected profits lost as a result of charging a current price of p. Assume $\psi'(p) > 0$, i.e., the higher the current price the greater the loss in future profits. Then (4) below becomes

$$\frac{d\bar{R}}{dp^*} \frac{1}{X'(p^*)} = c'(y^* - I) + \frac{D(y^*, p^*) + \psi'(p^*)}{X'(p^*)}$$

Thus, $\psi(p)$ has the same effect as does making $D(y, p)$ larger at given p and y. Hence the p which satisfies this equation will be smaller than it would otherwise have been.

[7] The general question of the extent and nature of the dependence of current decisions on anticipated future events appears to be ripe for thorough investigation. I have benefitted greatly from discussions on this subject with Joel Levy. See [42]. See also the Modigliani-Cohen paper [58].

end of this period is not worth less than this amount, since if it were the firm would profit by producing and storing more this period, making more of next period's sales from inventory. On the other hand, the inventory cannot be worth more than this amount, since next period's production serves the same function as this period's terminal inventory, that is, satisfying next period's demand, and more can be produced then at marginal cost.

Thus, as far as inventory valuation is concerned, in the circumstances stated the correct multiperiod decision will be made if the firm maximizes current expected profits while valuing each unit of inventory at the discounted value of marginal production cost minus storage cost. This means that if c is marginal production cost, α the discount factor, and $r(y - x)$ the total cost of storing $y - x$ units for one period, then when $y \geq x$, $\rho(y - x)$ should be $\alpha c(y - x) - r(y - x)$. This result is quite independent of the form of the carrying cost function, the prices set in the two periods, and the distribution functions of demand, except insofar as restrictions on these factors are necessary in order to ensure that some production will be necessary next period.

One would expect this to be the case if in some sense demand were expected to grow next period. For example,[8] if the probability that demand should fall short of any given amount is less next period than in this period, then a larger total supply will be necessary next period than in this period to provide a given probability of shortage. Therefore, some production must be undertaken next period, at least if some is undertaken this period. The trouble is that this condition is not independent of the prices charged in the two periods. It would be interesting to have conditions involving only the distribution functions and the cost parameters, to ensure that an optimum policy will involve positive production next period with a probability of one, but no such conditions of any great interest are at present available.[9]

Whether the one-stage model provides an approximation or an exact representation of the multistage problem when $y < x$, so that there is shortage, depends on the precise interpretation given to the cost imputed to shortage. There are two polar possibilities. On the one hand, shortage may mean that demand literally goes unsatisfied and customers must try to make their purchases elsewhere or wait until

[8] This result is due to Levy [42].

[9] The model dealt with in this chapter does not satisfy the conditions of the Simon-Theil theorem [76], pp. 507 ff.

next period. Representation of this effect by the function ρ involves a genuine approximation since the loss in this case arises from the effect of shortage on future demand. Disappointed customers may transfer future demand elsewhere and the firm may acquire a general reputation of being unreliable as a supplier. The strength of this effect depends on the frequency of shortage in competing firms. Presumably, the larger is the average shortage entailed by competitors' policies, the smaller is the loss of future demand to competitors that will result from a given amount of shortage.

There is a second possible interpretation of shortage cost. The firm's policy may be to meet shortages of its product by emergency procurement. This policy may involve production with the firm's own facilities if it possesses unused capacity, or the firm may purchase the product from another firm. Presumably, the cheapest form of emergency procurement is more costly than normal production. Otherwise, it would never pay to produce anything until demand for the period had been observed. As we pointed out in Section 2 of Chapter 5, the whole problem then becomes uninteresting. It is easy to find industrial examples of both types of emergency procurement, that is, production with the firm's own facilities and outside purchasing. Combinations of the two extremes, such as the purchase of components or partially fabricated products and internal final assembly, can also be found.

Just as emergency procurement generally involves a cost premium, it may also yield less revenue. Discounts to customers may be necessary if there is delay and inconvenience. In addition, emergency procurement may produce some deterioration in quality from the customers' viewpoint. If shortage is satisfied by emergency procurement and the procurement of v units costs $h(v)$ dollars and each unit sells for a price L, then when $y < x$, ρ should be $L(x - y) - h(x - y)$. In this case there is no approximation in using the one-stage model and ρ is an exact representation of the situation when shortage occurs.

It should be noted that a special case of emergency procurement policy is almost always considered, either explicitly or implicitly, in the literature on production and inventory planning. This literature is almost exclusively concerned with expected-cost minimization by means of the production decision. Profit maximization and the price decision are almost never investigated. If shortage is met by emergency procurement, and the price received, L, is the same as that received for normal sales, then the revenue received during the period is independent of the production level chosen at the beginning of the period though costs are not independent of this level.[10] The production decision can then be made to minimize total expected costs over the horizon, and expected profits will be maximized, at any price, with respect to output. In this case the production decision needs to be concerned only with the cost side of the firm's operations.

Even so, it is not true, as is sometimes thought, that the production decision can be made independently of the price set. It is true that for any price expected profit is maximized by minimizing expected costs with respect to output. It is not true that the output that accomplishes this is independent of the price chosen. The price influences the probability of shortage and hence of incurring the higher costs associated with emergency procurement. Thus, the output that minimizes expected costs depends on the price set. Conversely, the price that maximizes expected profit also depends on the production decision. The optimum price depends on how much production will be available for sale and how much more expensive emergency procurement is than normal production. Hence, even in this special case price and production decisions must be made jointly.

Thus, there are important circumstances in which the one-stage model provides an exact representation of the true multistage problem. Roughly, the conditions for this are that demand be growing, that marginal production cost be constant, and that any current shortages be satisfied by emergency procurement so that future demand is not affected. Even when these conditions are not fully satisfied the one-stage model probably still provides a good approximation.

It only remains in this section to argue that some decision-making procedures in firms suggest the use of the one-stage approximation in making production decisions. Since the writer is far from an expert on techniques of industrial management the evidence is of the casually empirical type. The test of the theory is of course whether it helps to understand and predict business behavior. Behavioristically, what firms do is to produce, sell, and hold inventories; the question is what theory the economist should use to describe or predict this behavior. All we suggest here is that certain procedures in the decision process

---

[10] In the notation of the previous chapter, revenue is

$$R^* = \begin{cases} px & x \leq y \\ py + L(x - y) & x \geq y \end{cases}$$

If $L = p$, this reduces to $R^* = px$, which is independent of y.

within firms are more relevant to a one-stage approximation than to a multistage model.

The first factor has to do with demand forecasts. It is reasonable to suppose that most manufacturing firms have planning horizons of at least a number of years, or that they do not discount the future so heavily that all events beyond the first year or two are irrelevant to current decisions. Yet in many such firms production decisions are made on the basis of demand forecasts extending over a period of a year or less.[11] Indeed, for these short forecasts some firms even make estimates from past sales and forecast data of the percentage of forecasts that will err by different amounts, that is, of the distribution function of demand. A concentration on very short term forecasts suggests the use of a one-stage approximation of the planning problem since a multistage model would require a forecast for each period within the horizon.

In a one-stage approximation the substitute for a multiperiod forecast is the valuation of inventory and shortage. In a sense, as was shown above, this valuation contains an implicit demand forecast for future periods since, for instance, the value of existing inventory depends in general on future prices and demands. For decision purposes, as contrasted for example to computing the firm's tax liability, the only reason for valuing inventory is to employ a one-stage approximation. In an explicit multistage formulation the optimum production and price policy depends only on the cost and revenue parameters of the model, and at no point is it necessary to put a dollar value on the stock of inventory.[12] One interpretation of the extensive accounting literature on the proper valuation of inventory is that it is concerned with finding the function ρ defined above that provides the best one-stage approximation. In any case firms do place a valuation on inventory, and to the extent that this valuation is used in making decisions there is evidence that a one-stage approximation is being employed.

---

[11] Many firms also make forecasts over a longer period, perhaps several years, for use in making fixed capital investment decisions to expand capacity. Ordinarily these forecasts are not sufficiently detailed, however, for the purposes of production and pricing decisions.

[12] This statement needs some qualification. If the planning horizon consists of a finite number of periods a rational decision requires a valuation of the random terminal inventory at the end of the horizon. However, the appropriate valuation is simply its disposal price less disposal and carrying costs. The inventory valuation controversy in accounting can hardly be over this point.

Finally, the main reason for confidence in the predictive ability of the one-period approximation is of course the difficulty of solving multistage formulations. Whatever weight is given to the inconclusive evidence concerning the internal decision-making procedures employed by firms, it requires an implausible stretch of the imagination to extend the "as if" principle (see Chapter 2, Section 3) to the solution of multistage versions of the planning problem. This would require demand and cost forecasts which do not arise naturally from business experience and are expensive to make with any useful degree of accuracy. In addition, the difference in computational complexity between a multistage model and a relatively simple one-stage version is enormous. Intuitive decision making can hardly be expected to provide a better approximation of the multistage model than is provided by the single-stage model. Thus, on the criteria presented in Chapter 2, the rational decision process for the firm may well be a one-stage approximation rather than the "correct" multistage formulation.

3. Equilibrium Conditions

This section derives the equilibrium conditions for a firm using the one-stage approximation discussed in the previous section. Actually, the model as formulated here is still very complicated to analyze in its full generality.[13] However, with relatively mild restrictions on the continuity, differentiability, and shapes of the cost and demand functions, and on the form of the distribution function, the solution is of the type obtained here by differentiation.

When the firm values inventory and shortage according to the function ρ introduced in the previous section its expected profit becomes

$$E(\Pi) = pX(p) - pD(y, p) - c(y - I) + \int_{-\infty}^{\infty} \rho(y - X(p) - u)f(u)\, du$$

$$\tag{1}$$

This equation is analogous to (4) of Chapter 5. The differences are as follows. Shortage occurs when demand exceeds total available supply, y, which is the sum of current production, z, and existing inventory, I; that is, $y = z + I$. Since we are now allowing for the possibility of

---

[13] Just how complicated is shown in the exhaustive treatment by S. Karlin in Chapter 8 of [9]. The reader is referred to this paper for a complete discussion of the types of solution possible with this model and the conditions that yield a solution of the type discussed in the text.

terminal inventory, we must also include the effect of initial inventory. This also shows up in the production cost term which, as before, depends on current production. It is written as $y - I$ because of the convenience of dealing with y rather than z. Finally, it should be noted that ρ has been added rather than subtracted so that it is positive if $y > x$ and inventory has positive value, and it is negative if $y < x$ and a positive cost is imputed to shortage.

The equilibrium price and output are obtained by equating to zero the partial derivatives of (1) with respect to p and y. This gives

$$\frac{\partial E(\Pi)}{\partial p} = \frac{d\bar{R}}{dp} - pD_p(y, p) - D(y, p)$$

$$- X'(p) \int_{-\infty}^{\infty} \rho'(y - X(p) - u)f(u)\,du = 0 \quad (2)$$

and

$$\frac{\partial E(\Pi)}{\partial y} = -pD_y(y, p) - c'(y - I) + \int_{-\infty}^{\infty} \rho'(y - X(p) - u)f(u)\,du = 0$$
$$(3)$$

Here $\rho'(v) = d\rho/dv$. In many cases, such as the example considered in Section 5, the derivative $d\rho/dv$ is not unambiguously defined at the point $v = 0$ ($u = y - X(p)$). In such cases ρ must be redefined as the sum of two functions, one representing the cost of shortage and one the value of inventory. Equations (2) and (3) are analogous respectively to the maximal conditions in the one-period horizon model (5) and (6) of Chapter 5. The joint solution of (2) and (3) yields values p^* and y^* of p and y which, provided $z^* = y^* - I \geq 0$,[14] are the equilibrium price and total supply respectively.

4. Comparison with the Riskless Model

The form that ρ assumes obviously affects the price and output policy of the firm. However, it is easy to show that the introduction of this generalization leaves unaffected all the results of Section 4 in the previous chapter. Indeed, the argument that led to (8) of Chapter 5 now gives

$$\frac{(d\bar{R}/dp^*)}{X'(p^*)} = c'(y^* - I) + \frac{D(y^*, p^*)}{X'(p^*)} \quad (4)$$

[14] This condition, which is very important and troublesome in planning applications, is of little relevance to the economist whose main interest is in explaining available price and output data, since such data are almost always sufficiently aggregative to indicate positive production each period.

This equation is of exactly the form as (8) from the previous chapter, except that y now appears in the shortage function instead of z. With this reinterpretation the theorem and corollaries proved in the previous chapter still hold. In particular, the conditions imposed on marginal production cost in the corollaries still imply the same qualitative relationship between prices in the risky and riskless models.[15]

The effect of assuming that the firm takes account of the future by evaluating inventory and shortage is to alter the emphasis in the corollaries of the previous chapter rather than to upset the qualitative results established there. These alterations can be analyzed as follows.

We assume that $\rho'(y - x)$ will be positive for all values of y and x. The assumption is true if the value imputed to inventory increases with the size of the inventory and the cost imputed to shortage increases with the amount of shortage. In this case the expected value of $\rho'(y - x)$, which appears in (2) and (3), is positive for all values of y and p. It is easy to believe that this will induce the firm to make the difference $y - X(p)$ larger, at each price, than it would otherwise have been. If value is imputed to the marginal unit of inventory and cost is imputed to the marginal unit of shortage then, at each price, it pays to make total supply larger than it would otherwise have been. This fact increases the probability that inventory will remain at the end of the period and decreases the probability of shortage, as we can see directly from (3) by writing it in the alternative form

$$F(y - X(p)) = \frac{p - c'(y - I) + \int_{-\infty}^{\infty} \rho'(y - X(p) - u)f(u)\,du}{p} \qquad (5)$$

Equation (5) differs from (6a) in the previous chapter only because of the addition of the positive integral in the numerator of the right-hand side. For each z and p the right-hand side of (5), and consequently $y - X(p)$, must be larger than it would have been if ρ had been excluded from the model. With any plausible assumption about the form of ρ it is also true that the right-hand side of (5) increases

---

[15] It should be emphasized that this is only true provided the z^* given by the solution of (2) and (3) is non-negative. If inventory is sufficiently large at the beginning of a period to make unprofitable any production, then this argument breaks down. Presumably, the firm can be induced to set an arbitrarily low price by an initial inventory that is sufficiently high. Furthermore, the argument does not contend that the holding of inventory does not affect the firm's price policy. The inventory level will influence the circumstances that determine which of the corollaries in the previous chapter is relevant.

with p. This simply reflects the fact that the higher the price the more it pays to reduce the probability of shortage by increasing total supply. It follows that the inclusion of ρ must have one or both of two effects on p^* and y^*: (i) p^* is lower with ρ included than without, or (ii) $y^* - X(p^*)$ is greater with ρ included than without. Since the presence of ρ increases the right-hand side of (5) at each y and p, either the left-hand side, and hence $y^* - X(p^*)$, must increase; or p^* must decrease, thus decreasing the right-hand side. Otherwise the equality could not continue to hold.

If (i) is true, then of course the tendency for p^* to be less than its riskless level regardless of the shape of the marginal cost curve is increased. If (ii) is true, then for any value of I the tendency for output to exceed its riskless level is increased. In Corollary C of Chapter 5 it was shown that when marginal cost is falling, an output in excess of its riskless level is precisely the condition that guarantees a price lower than its riskless level. In Corollary B it was shown that when marginal cost is rising, an output in excess of its riskless level is the condition that makes possible a price higher than its riskless level. When marginal cost is constant, it is still true that price must be less than its riskless level.

Thus, the effect of introducing a multiperiod horizon in the special way assumed here can be summarized as follows. When marginal cost is falling, the effect of long-run considerations is to strengthen the tendency for price to be less than its riskless level. When marginal cost is rising, there is a greater likelihood that price will exceed its riskless level than there is in the one-period case. When marginal cost is constant, price is necessarily less than its riskless level in both models. A somewhat crude way of putting this is to say that only if a firm is working near capacity so that marginal cost is rising is uncertainty likely to induce a firm that takes a long view of things to set its price above the riskless level. Finally, only if the long-run considerations have the effect of lowering the price can the firm's output policy make the probability of shortage greater than in the one-period case.

5. An Example

In this section the example of Section 5 of the previous chapter is extended to show the effect of the long-run considerations introduced in this chapter. The example assumed a constant marginal production cost, linear riskless demand curve, and rectangular distribution for the random term. These assumptions are retained here and in addition

ρ is assumed to have one of the simple forms discussed in the previous section. That is, when $y > x$ the firm values inventory at the difference between marginal production cost and storage cost. The latter is assumed to be proportional to the inventory on hand. Shortage cost is proportional to the number of units of shortage, and for simplicity the proportionality factor is assumed to be independent of current price. It is also assumed that the decision period is sufficiently short that the discounting of next period's marginal production cost is negligible. Thus ρ can be written

$$\rho(y - x) = \begin{cases} (c - r)(y - x) & y \geq x \\ k(y - x) & y \leq x \end{cases}$$

Shortage of one unit entails not only the current loss of one sale but also a loss of future sales the present value of the profit from which is estimated to be k dollars.

The influence of ρ on price and output policy can be investigated by obtaining results analogous to those of Section 5, Chapter 5. Insert this special form of ρ in the equilibrium conditions (2) and (3). Equation (3) can be solved, as before, to give the optimum production as a function of price and initial inventory.

$$y(p) = X(p) + 2\lambda \left(\frac{1}{2} - \frac{r}{p + k + r - c} \right) \tag{6}$$

This is the analog to (9) of Chapter 5. Evidently the firm makes y greater than $X(p)$ if the term in the final bracket on the right-hand side of (6) is positive. The condition for this reduces to $p > c + r - k$. This compares with the result in the one-period case that only if price is at least twice marginal cost does the firm make available for sale enough to clear the market on the average. In the present case the firm is normally less willing to risk shortage and more willing to risk a large inventory, because shortage is costly whereas inventory has some value. If the above condition for p is written $p > 2c - (c - r) - k$, the contrast with the one-period case is clearer. The right-hand side now consists of the minimal price in the one-period model (twice marginal cost) minus the sum of the marginal value of inventory and the marginal cost of shortage.

If $y(p)$ from (6) is substituted in $D(y, p)$ the latter becomes

$$\Phi(p) = D(y(p), p) = \frac{\lambda r^2}{(p + k + r - c)^2} \tag{7}$$

This result is analogous to (10) of Chapter 5. Comparison indicates that average shortage is likely to be much smaller in the present example than in the one-period model. In particular, if there is no carrying cost it is worthwhile to produce enough to make shortage impossible; in (7), if $r = 0$, then $\Phi = 0$ and, in (6), $y = X(p) + \lambda$. Then $p^* = \bar{p}$.

The computation of p^* and y^* is particularly simple in this example because y^*, though not z^*, is independent of I provided only $I < y(p^*)$. Inserting (6) and (7) in (4), it can be seen that p^* is a root of the cubic

$$\theta(p) = (a - 2bp + bc)(p + k + r - c)^2 - \lambda r^2 = 0 \tag{8}$$

This equation corresponds to (11) of Chapter 5, and the symbols have the meanings defined there. Equation (8) has properties precisely analogous to those deduced for (11) in the previous chapter.

Some idea of the quantitative importance of the generalization introduced in this chapter can be obtained by extending one of the numerical examples of Chapter 5, Section 5. Suppose again that $a = 20$, $b = 2$, $c = 5$, and $\lambda = 5$. Further, suppose that $r = 0.5$ and $k = 2.5$. The firm's price and output policy can be summarized as follows.

	Multiperiod Horizon	One-Period Horizon		Riskless Case
p^*	7.0	7.0	$\bar{p}$	7.5
$X(p^*)$	6.0	6.0	$x(\bar{p})$	5.0
y^*	10.0	4.0	$\bar{y} = \bar{z}$	5.0

The final two columns repeat the information tabulated in Section 5 of the previous chapter for the one-period and riskless cases respectively. The first column presents the results for the present case. In the example chosen, the long run considerations leave the price unchanged at 7.0. Total supply, however, is 2.5 times as large as in the one-period case. This reduces the probability of shortage from 0.70 to 0.10. Thus, this example suggests that the effect of the long run considerations introduced in this chapter is mainly to alter the firm's production policy rather than its price policy. It is not, however, true that ρ never affects price. If k is chosen sufficiently large, in the example, price is smaller than its riskless level of 7.5 by an arbitrarily small amount.

Chapter 7

IMPERFECT COMPETITION:
A DYNAMIC MODEL
AND SOME APPROXIMATIONS

1. Introduction

This chapter is a transition from the theoretical chapters that precede it to the applied chapters that follow. The main purpose of the first six chapters has been the formal derivation of rational price and output policies in models that included both uncertainty and inventory holding. By way of application the results have been used to investigate certain questions of interest to economists, such as the stability of a competitive market and the effect of uncertainty on prices. The main purpose of the following six chapters is to discover whether these decision rules are useful in predicting or explaining observed price and output behavior. The need for a transition arises from the complexity of the decision rules developed. The last two chapters have shown that if an imperfectly competitive firm behaves in the way postulated, its price and output policies are the simultaneous solution of two complicated equations. The observed pattern of price and output behavior of such a firm will depend on the shapes of its production, inventory, and shortage cost functions, the shape of its riskless demand curve, and the distribution of its forecasting errors.

If sufficient information were available concerning each of these factors it would be possible to test definitively whether a firm behaved consistently with this, or any other, theory. However, for the purpose of testing a theory such as this one, this information is normally not available. All that are likely to be available are ex post observations of sales, production, price, and inventory levels.[1] Hence it is important

---

[1] Usually, there is also available some qualitative information concerning the competitive and administrative structure of the industry.

to know what restrictions the theory places on the relations among these variables. Furthermore, for many purposes it is these variables that the economist is interested in predicting or explaining. In such cases, his only interest in cost functions is for use in an intermediate step to derive relations among the variables listed above. If this can be accomplished without an intervening estimate of costs, so much the better. Thus not only are cost data difficult to obtain, but also they are often largely extraneous to the economists' main interest.

For these reasons, the main purpose of this chapter is to inquire whether the theory developed in the preceding chapters implies relations among the observable market variables that can be estimated and tested. This is not, however, easy to do. Available sample sizes and statistical techniques require that great emphasis be placed on the discovery of simple relationships among the variables. Approximations must therefore be employed, which in turn make it difficult to know whether a set of observations tests the basic theory or merely the approximating procedure. Some evidence on this score will be provided by the sampling experiments reported in the next chapter, but it cannot be said that the empirical studies in Chapters 9 to 12 provide a very stringent test of the theory.

All the further investigations in this book are carried out in terms of the model of imperfect competition rather than that of perfect competition. The main reason is that most available series, and all those studied in this book, pertain to industries that are clearly not perfectly competitive. Hence, the model in Chapters 5 and 6 is the appropriate one to estimate and test. A secondary reason is that those series, mainly representing agricultural products, that pertain to competitive industries have been extensively analyzed by others (see especially Nerlove [64]).

Before we undertake the central task of this chapter, in Section 4, two preliminary sections are interposed. Section 2 presents a short survey and classification of the existing literature on the relation between price and production decisions. In Section 3, the model of the preceding chapter is altered somewhat to include a dynamic cost which arises from rapidly changing production levels.

2. Interrelated Price and Production Policies in the Literature

By way of a preliminary observation it can be stated that the traditional theory of price, from which inventories and uncertainty are excluded, is wholly inadequate to provide the type of explanation sought in this book. What we seek here is a quantitative prediction of very short-run movements, that is, monthly or quarterly, in firms' price and output levels. It is evident that, in a firm or industry in which substantial inventories are held, this prediction is not possible with a model that excludes inventories. Furthermore, this is not intended to be a criticism of the traditional theory. What should be included in a theory depends on the questions the theory is intended to answer. The traditional theory is static and can therefore be expected, at most, to answer only questions of a comparative static nature, that is, involving a comparison of static equilibria. On most definitions the behavior with which the models in this book are concerned would be called dynamic, and a static model should not be expected to explain dynamic phenomena. On the other hand, this defense leaves unclear just what is to be understood by a static equilibrium position. Some economists would say that a static equilibrium is one that can be identified with maximizing behavior on the part of those concerned. Yet, the models in this book all attempt to explain the "dynamic" behavior with which they are concerned with the aid of maximization hypotheses. Thus, on the definition suggested, the models here must be thought of as static.

Whatever position we take on this terminological question, the basic argument made here is unaffected. The traditional theory of price determination is inadequate to explain short-run movements in price and output when firms hold substantial inventories because the holding of inventories allows a richer variety of interactions between price and output policies than is consistent with the traditional theory. In the traditional theory there is only one decision to be taken. Once one of these two variables is set the other follows mechanically. If the price is set at its profit-maximizing level, the output that maximizes profits is simply the amount which can be sold at that price.

It is only dynamic considerations or risk that introduce the possibility of a non-trivial relation between price and production policies. Within the framework of dynamic analysis there is, however, a substantial literature that can be interpreted as relating the two decisions in one way or another. Furthermore, almost all this literature emphasizes one or the other of two relationships incorporated in the models presented in this book. One relationship is the effect of inventory levels on prices, and the other is the effect of inventory levels on production.

First, there is what we shall call the "price stability" literature, concerned with the stability of prices and outputs usually, but not always, in competitive markets. The assumptions employed in these investigations were described and criticized in Chapter 4. There it was stated that the usual procedure was to assume the rate of change of price to be an increasing function of the excess of demand over supply. If, as is usually the case, demand is interpreted to be for consumption purposes and supply is interpreted to be production, the difference between supply and demand is simply inventory investment or disinvestment. Hence the price formation equation just described can be written [2]

$$\Delta p_n = f(\Delta I_{n-1}) \tag{1}$$

Assuming $f'(\Delta I_{n-1}) < 0$, we see that firms raise price when demand exceeds supply and lower it when supply exceeds demand. Thus, at least on this interpretation, the price stability models assume that the only direct effect of inventory is on prices and not on production. Inventory may of course have an indirect effect on production since inventory affects price and price affects demand and therefore production. There is, however, no direct effect of this type. A high or rising inventory does not by itself cause firms to curtail production.

Second, and in contrast, there is the "inventory accelerator" literature in which the effect of inventories on production is emphasized. This literature, stemming from the work of Lundberg [43], and Metzler [50] is concerned mostly with the macro theory of inventory cycles. Here we are concerned only with the micro decision rule on which the macro model is based. This decision rule assumes that production is determined exclusively by the attempt to maintain inventory at some normal or desired level, for example, proportional to sales. Such a decision rule can be represented by a function of the type

$$z_n = \phi(I_{n-1}, I_n^d) \tag{2}$$

where I_n^d is the desired inventory. The Metzler model, for example, is the special case of (2) in which I_n^d is proportional to expected sales and ϕ indicates enough production to meet expected sales and to bring inventory to its desired level. Thus, in contrast with the price stability models, the accelerator models assume that the only effect of inventory

---

[2] See the references to the literature in Chapter 4. See p. 268 of [68] and Chapter 1 of [2] for some models in which the interpretation in terms of inventory is made explicitly. Sometimes (1) is altered to permit Δp_n to depend on the absolute inventory level, but this alteration does not affect the argument here.

is on the level of production. As in the case of the price stability models, this assumption does not preclude the existence of indirect effects on prices, but these have never been introduced into an accelerator model to the best of the writer's knowledge.

Thus, the two main strands of the dynamic literature [3] can be separated according to whether they emphasize the effect of inventory on prices or on production. The price stability literature assumes that inventory affects only prices; the inventory accelerator literature assumes that inventory affects only production. Evidently, both effects are present in a rational decision process, and both are included in the models in the preceding chapters. In these models, a high inventory will cause a firm both to lower price and to decrease production. Furthermore, these effects are independent in the sense that at any price the higher the inventory the smaller the volume of production, whereas at any volume of production, the higher the inventory the lower the price. Thus in one sense the models developed in this book can be thought of as an attempt to unify the two strands of the literature by showing the interaction between inventories, prices, and production in a model of rational decision making. It would be interesting to investigate the problem of fluctuations in business activity within a model, such as the one presented in the last chapter, that incorporates both the price and accelerator effects. However, such an investigation is outside the scope of this book. The sampling study in the next chapter suggests that the behavior of the individual firm, at least, is highly damped and that price and production rapidly converge to new stationary values in response to shifts in demand. Instability or persistent cycles could of course still result in an analogous macro model containing a feedback in the form of an expenditure function.

Granted that from a theoretical point of view a model relating price and production policies is more satisfying than the partial theories represented by (1) and (2), it still remains to discover which relationship has the greatest explanatory value. For example, does the model presented in the previous chapter provide a better explanation of empirical price and production series than does (1) or (2)? Although it is the purpose of subsequent chapters to shed light on this question, it is argued in Section 4 that with available data and statistical techniques it is extremely difficult to discriminate conclusively among competing hypotheses. Several alternative hypotheses will

---

[3] Excluding the literature concerned with fixed capital formation.

usually indicate broadly the same correlations among the different variables. For example, if (1) were the true decision rule a statistical study would still reveal that production and inventory were negatively correlated. According to (1), a high or rising inventory causes price to fall and this in turn induces the firm to reduce its production. Depending on the time lags involved the investigator might still believe that this observed correlation was evidence in favor of (2). Nevertheless, it is clear from the investigations in the rest of this book that (2) has much more explanatory power than (1). Very few of the observed movements in typical firm or industry price series can be explained by correlating price and inventory. On the other hand, a great deal of the observed movements in production can be explained by correlating production and inventory. The investigations in the following chapters also suggest that the more general model developed in this book can explain observed price and production series better than either of the partial models (1) and (2).

3. *Modification of the Model: a Dynamic Cost*

It was argued above that the models developed in previous chapters are dynamic in the sense that they describe movements in the decision variables from period to period. It has sometimes been suggested that such changes in the values of decision variables involve a cost to the decision maker that is independent of any costs associated with the value of the decision variable itself.[4] In particular it has been argued that there is a cost associated with rapid changes in the rate of production. If this cost is present it evidently affects the decision in question and should be included in a model of decision making. The purpose of this section is to explore the nature of such a cost and to modify the decision rule of the previous chapter to take it into account.

It is easy to point to particular factors that would give rise to costs associated with rapid changes in production, though it is less easy to guess the general form such a cost function should take. Partly, this is true because some of the important costs involved are not normally separated from the costs of producing at a given rate in existing accounting procedures. Rapid changes in production usually involve hiring or firing. Both of these activities involve special costs, and some firms regularly make estimates of the amounts involved. Hiring involves personnel costs that include the advertising of positions,

---

[4] See Chapters 5 and 6 of [9]. See also [35] and [53].

interviewing applicants, testing, placement, training, indoctrination, and so on. Firing may involve severance pay and other costs of an administrative and record-keeping nature. In addition, increases in production usually involve setting up new facilities, and the resulting set-up costs are partly independent of the volume of production being planned. Most of these costs could be estimated, at least in many firms, without great difficulty. However, some other, and perhaps more important, costs of changing production are more difficult to estimate. Changing the rate of production always involves some upsetting of established routines. If the change is an increase, some workers have to learn new jobs even if no hiring is required. If the change is a decrease, a similar or greater rearrangement of jobs occurs if the firm has a seniority system in which workers may "bump" each other through several stages in the hierarchy. A new rate of production almost always involves new routines, and time is required to "get the bugs out" of any such routine. The costs involved show up to some extent in learning curves in the productive process and to some extent in the "variances" recorded by the accountants when a new routine is introduced. However, it is doubtful whether either of these sources could provide a reliable estimate of the costs in question. Certainly, the stability of production and maintenance of the labor force intact appear to be factors given considerable weight by management, especially where labor is highly organized.[5]

Presumably, a similar case can be made for the introduction of a cost of changing price. A new price may have to be advertised, brochures may have to be rewritten, all of which cost money. In addition, when price is increased there may be an impact effect on demand resulting in a temporary decline in sales. Nevertheless, in order to avoid complicating the model, no such extension is attempted in this direction. In a general way, it is clear what the result would be, at least if the cost of changing price were introduced in a way analogous to the introduction below of the cost of changing production. The result would simply be to increase the importance of lagged prices in explaining current prices. In the statistical studies in the following chapters, lagged price is introduced as an explanatory variable in the price formation equations. However, for obvious reasons, the discovery that lagged price has a significant statistical effect on current price cannot be regarded as much evidence in favor of a hypothesis concerning the cost of chang-

[5] On the subject of this paragraph see [34].

ing prices. It may be that, for several reasons, price is changed less frequently than output. If the normal planning period were longer for price than for output, we would observe greater autocorrelation in price than in production series.

In the next section, specific forms for the function representing the cost of changing production are suggested. Here, this cost will simply be assumed to be a function of the difference between the rates of production in successive periods, so that in period n it can be written as

$$g(z_n - z_{n-1})$$

This way of writing the function implies that all such costs are incurred within the planning period in which the change in production occurs. Evidently, this need not be the case; the effect of a particular change may be felt long after the change is made. A more general formulation would allow for a lagged effect diminishing gradually through time. However, in the statistical series we have examined production that is lagged more than one period has no statistically discernible effect on current production.

The introduction of a cost of changing production greatly complicates the derivation of the decision rule in the true multiperiod decision problem,[6] because it introduces a further relationship between current and future production. This increases the degree of simultaneity in the problem and, indeed, solutions for such models are known only for very special cases. However, in the one-period approximation introduced and defended in the previous chapter, the formal change required is not great. All that is required is the addition of the new cost in the profit function, (1) of Chapter 6. We then obtain

$$E(\pi_n) = p_n X(p_n) - p_n D(y_n, p_n) - c(y_n - I_{n-1})$$

$$+ \int_{-\infty}^{\infty} \rho(y_n - X(p_n) - u_n) f(u_n)\, du_n - g(y_n - I_{n-1} - z_{n-1}) \quad (3)$$

It will be recalled that the firm's equilibrium price and output were those obtained by the simultaneous solutions of $\partial E(\pi_n)/\partial p_n = 0$ and $\partial E(\pi_n)/\partial y_n = 0$, (2) and (3) of Chapter 6 respectively. Since the new cost involves only production and not price, the first of these equations is unchanged, that is,

---

[6] See, for example, the models in Part II of [9], in which such a cost has been introduced, though in a somewhat different decision problem.

$$\frac{d\bar{R}}{dp_n} - D(y_n, p_n) - p_n D_{p_n}(y_n, p_n)$$
$$- X'(p_n) \int_{-\infty}^{\infty} \rho'(y_n - X(p_n) - u_n) f(u_n) \, du_n = 0 \quad (4)$$

The second equation, (3) of Chapter 6 becomes

$$-p_n D_{y_n}(y_n, p_n) - c'(y_n - I_{n-1}) + \int_{-\infty}^{\infty} \rho'(y_n - X(p_n) - u_n) f(u_n) \, du_n$$
$$- g'(y_n - I_{n-1} - z_{n-1}) = 0 \quad (5)$$

Together with the second-order and non-negativity conditions, these equations completely determine the firm's price, production, and inventory policy.[7] The studies in the rest of this book are attempts to apply and test (4) and (5). In the next section the attempt is made to discover simple price and production rules, more suitable for statistical application, which either represent or approximate the behavior implied by this model.

4. Approximating and Estimating the Decision Rules

Since y_n can be eliminated by the definition $y_n = z_n + I_{n-1}$, (4) and (5) can be regarded as two behavior relations among the four observable variables p_n, z_n, z_{n-1}, and I_{n-1}. Quite noncommitally, they might be represented by

$$h_1(p_n, z_n, z_{n-1}, I_{n-1}) = 0 \quad (4a)$$

$$h_2(p_n, z_n, z_{n-1}, I_{n-1}) = 0 \quad (5a)$$

Whenever we have two or more structural relations among the same set of variables it is important to ask whether each relation is just identified, overidentified, or underidentified. Depending on the answer one statistical estimating technique may be more appropriate than others, or there may be no technique by which estimates with desirable properties can be obtained. If (4a) and (5a) were linear and no restrictions were placed on the coefficients of any of the variables, then the model would be underdetermined and could not be estimated.[8] Then the only procedure available would be to solve the two equations jointly to obtain the reduced form of the model, that is,

---

[7] It should be noted that, with the introduction of a cost of changing production, the theorem demonstrated for the models in the last two chapters no longer holds.

[8] See [40], pp. 137–143. There are two predetermined variables in (4a) and (5a), and each appears in both equations. However, both endogenous variables

$$p_n = H_1(z_{n-1}, I_{n-1}) \tag{6}$$

$$z_n = H_2(z_{n-1}, I_{n-1}) \tag{7}$$

If (4a) and (5a) were linear, (6) and (7) would also be linear, and the parameters of these equations could be estimated. However, the parameters of the structural equations (4a) and (5a) could not be inferred from those of (6) and (7). For the purposes of prediction and testing this would not be crucial since the predictive value of the reduced form is the same as that of the structural equations. Thus, the model could still be tested by testing its ability to predict p_n and z_n from a knowledge of z_{n-1} and I_{n-1}.

In fact, the studies in subsequent chapters do not attempt to estimate the reduced form. Rather they attempt to estimate the coefficients of approximations of the behavioral equations. There are two reasons for this course of action. First, and less important, lagged production and inventories do not adequately explain observed price and output behavior in series we have examined.[9] This provides both incentive and justification for seeking other variables that provide better explanations of observed decisions.

Second, and more important, existing identification criteria provide very little help regarding the possibility of estimating (4) and (5). As was pointed out above, it is necessary to find linear approximations of (4) and (5) for purposes of estimation and testing. Therefore, it is the identifiability of the approximations that is important, and not the identifiability of (4) and (5).[10] Now the approximations derived below and estimated in subsequent chapters are identifiable, at least in some cases. Thus, the identification question is closely related to that of the adequacy of the approximations. If the approximations are close, the system is identifiable, at least in some cases. However, it is not possible to establish with certainty the adequacy of the approximations, and therefore it cannot be stated for certain whether the system is identifiable. Some evidence of the adequacy of the

appear in both equations. Thus the number of predetermined variables excluded from each equation (zero) is two less than the number of endogenous variables appearing in each equation (two). This satisfies the order condition for under-identifiability.

[9] Only some of these series are studied in this book. Some are examined in [54] and some have been studied by other writers.

[10] Almost nothing is known about the identifiability of nonlinear systems such as (4) and (5) anyway.

approximations will be reported in the next chapter but, as will be shown there, the issue cannot be settled completely.

There is a further aspect of this question. It is uncertain whether even the approximations of (4) and (5) are identifiable because they do not form a complete system in the statistical sense. Among some of the variables in the model there is a third relation, a demand equation. The inclusion of a demand equation in the model adds one new endogenous variable, quantity demanded, and several new predetermined variables, such as prices of related goods, incomes, and time. To close the model in this way would affect the identifiability of the supply side, but in a way that would depend on precisely which variables were introduced. Hence, to determine the identifiability of the supply side would require a detailed study of the demand side. Since no such study is incorporated in this book, it is not possible to say how the excluded demand relation affects the identifiability of the included supply relations. Furthermore, as was argued in Chapter 3, it is possible to estimate the decision rules on the supply side, provided they are identified, without estimating either the true demand equation or the firm's estimate of the demand equation. Hence the analysis of the demand side which would be necessary to establish identifiability is not only extensive, but also extraneous to the purpose of this book, which is to estimate relations on the supply side.

In this situation it is evidently necessary to rely somewhat on common sense, and the following discussion is partly on this footing. Some check on the conclusions reached will be provided by the sampling experiments to be presented in the next chapter, but a subjective element remains.

The argument proceeds as follows. In order to find simple approximations of (4) and (5) the linear cost functions introduced in the example of Chapter 6, Section 5 are used again:

$$c(z) = cz, \qquad c = \text{marginal production cost}$$

$$r(I) = rI, \qquad r = \text{marginal storage cost}$$

$$p(y - x) = \begin{cases} (c - r)(y - x) & y \geq x \\ k(y - x) & y < x \end{cases} \qquad k = \begin{array}{l} \text{present value of} \\ \text{profit lost per unit} \\ \text{of shortage} \end{array}$$

In addition to these linear approximations, the cost of changing production is approximated by a quadratic. Since this cost is positive whether production goes up or down, a linear function cannot be used.

Absolute values are awkward to deal with and there may be some grounds in terms or realism for assuming a rising marginal cost of changing production. The approximation is

$$g(z_n - z_{n-1}) = \frac{g}{2}(z_n - z_{n-1})^2$$

On the right-hand side, g is a number that represents the slope of the curve showing the marginal cost of changing production. The addition of constants to any of these costs does not affect the following argument. One further notational point: from here on it will be convenient to revert to the earlier notation of x_n^e rather than $X(p_n)$ for the mathematical expectation of demand. Since demand in any period depends on variables other than the current price of the product, the earlier notation is both simpler and more general in this respect. It must be remembered, however, that x_n^e is still a function of, among other things, current price.

Now introduce these special cost functions in (4) and (5). After some rearrangement, the production equation (5) becomes

$$F(y_n - x_n^e) = \frac{p_n - c + k}{p_n - c + k + r} - \frac{g(y_n - I_{n-1} - z_{n-1})}{p_n - c + k + r}$$

which is the same form as (5) in Chapter 6 except that the cost of changing production was not included there. It is still a nonlinear equation involving both decision variables and the unspecified distribution function $F(y_n - x_n^e)$. In any small vicinity this can be approximated by a linear function of its argument, which implies approximating the frequency function by a constant. Now the frequency function that is a constant is the rectangular distribution introduced in the examples in Chapters 5 and 6. In the case at hand the distribution must have a zero mean, and therefore the rectangular distribution can be represented by a single parameter, λ, equal to half the range of u. Introducing this further approximation and again rearranging terms, we obtain

$$z_n = \left[\frac{\lambda(p_n - c + k - r)}{p_n + k - c + r + 2\lambda g}\right] + \left[\frac{p_n - c + k + r}{p_n - c + k + r + 2\lambda g}\right]x_n^e$$

$$+ \left[\frac{2\lambda g}{p_n - c + k + r + 2\lambda g}\right]z_{n-1} - \left[\frac{p_n - c + k + r}{p_n - c + k + r + 2\lambda g}\right]I_{n-1}$$

$$(8)$$

In this version y_n has been removed in favor of z_n by the definition $y_n = z_n + I_{n-1}$. Equation (8) gives z_n as a linear function of x_n^e, z_{n-1}, and I_{n-1} with coefficients that depend on p_n.

The suggestion here is that these coefficients should have a high degree of temporal stability. In the first place, in each coefficient except that of z_{n-1}, p_n appears in both numerator and denominator. Thus the effects on the coefficients of changes in price will to some extent cancel themselves out. In particular, if price is large relative to the other parameters in the coefficients, the effect on the coefficients of a change in price will be negligible. In the second place, it must be recognized that the other parameters in the coefficients are not constant through time, but tend to move cyclically and secularly. In fact, movements in prices and the various costs tend to be highly correlated. Now proportionate changes in price and in all the cost parameters leave each coefficient in (8) unchanged. (Recall that λ is not a cost parameter.) Thus, there is evidently a considerable tendency to temporal stability of the coefficients of (8) even during periods of considerable cyclical fluctuation. This suggests that for statistical purposes the production rule can be approximated by

$$z_n = \beta_{10} + \beta_{11}x_n^e + \beta_{12}z_{n-1} + \beta_{13}I_{n-1} \tag{9}$$

which is the form used in all the subsequent empirical studies.

Next consider (4). Whatever is thought of the preceding argument, which led to (9), the situation is less satisfactory in the case of the price formation equation. Even if all the linear approximations suggested are introduced in (4), there still remains an important nonlinearity because $D(y_n, p_n)$, defined by (3) of Chapter 5, involves the truncated mean of u_n. Even if $f(u_n)$ is a constant, this truncated mean is still a nonlinear, in fact quadratic, function of the parameter of integration, $y_n - x_n^e$. Hence, at best, an approximation of (4) of the type used above involves a quadratic term in this difference. Furthermore, it involves terms in which p_n appears as a product with z_n, I_{n-1} and x_n^e. About all that can be said is that (4) gives p_n as a function of x_n^e, z_n, and I_{n-1}. The corresponding linear decision rule in these variables is

$$p_n = \beta_{20} + \beta_{21}x_n^e + \beta_{22}z_n + \beta_{23}I_{n-1} \tag{10}$$

There is no strong reason, though, for thinking that this is a good approximation to the true decision rule (4) even when the above linear cost functions are introduced.[11] In view of this, particular interest attaches to the results of the attempt to explain price movements by (10) in the sampling experiment in the next chapter. If (10) largely explains movements in prices that are in fact generated by (4), it is evidence that the linear approximation is a good one. If so, any inability of (10) to explain empirically observed prices would mean that it is the basic theory, or lack of identifiability, which is at fault and not the approximation. Equation (10) is the underlying form used in all the subsequent empirical analysis, though a small modification will be introduced in the next chapter.

It is important to establish the ranges within which the β_{ij} in (9) and (10) should be if (4) and (5) are the true decision rules. For (9), some fairly strong restrictions can be placed on the coefficients on the basis of the model from which it was derived. The second-order conditions for a maximum of (3), when the linear costs are inserted, require that $p_n - c - k + r$ be positive. Since λ and g are also positive, it follows from (8) that $0 < \beta_{11}, \beta_{12}, -\beta_{13} < 1$; that is, the coefficients of expected sales and of lagged production are positive and less than one, whereas the coefficient of lagged inventory is negative and greater than minus one. Furthermore, intuition concerning the relative magnitudes of price and the costs entering the β_{ij} suggests that β_{11} will be larger than β_{12}. Equation (8) has the further implications that $\beta_{11} + \beta_{12} = 1$ and $\beta_{13} = -\beta_{11}$. However, aside from sampling errors, the approximate nature of (8) itself means that these relations may not hold among empirical estimates of the coefficients.

Concerning the coefficients β_{2i} in (10) it is not possible to be so certain as to signs and magnitudes. However, a combination of intuition and calculation suggests some restrictions. Consider first β_{21}. Observed responses of p_n to changes in x_n^e are a combination of re-

---

[11] Suppose that the demand equation can be written

$$x_n^e = \beta_{30} + \beta_{31}p_n + G(n)$$

where $G(n)$ is an arbitrary function of time. In fact, for the purpose of this footnote it makes no difference if any other variables appear in $G(n)$, provided they do not also appear in (9) or (10). In this demand equation $G(n)$ is regarded as an exogenous variable. Then (9), (10) and the demand equation form a complete system in which (9) and (10) are just identified. The demand equation is overidentified.

If demand within the period is assumed to be statistically independent of that period's price, then x_n^e is exogenous and (9) and (10) form a complete system. Both (9) and (10) are then identified since the system is recursive.

sponses to shifts in the demand curve and movements along it. Depending on which of these two possibilities is predominant in any population of observations, β_{21} should assume a quite different value.

Consider first the extreme case in which the demand curve does not shift, except for random factors, and therefore all observed pairs p_n and x_n^e lie on the same riskless demand curve. In this case, there are only two reasons for p_n to change. First, the firm might be searching for the equilibrium p_n along a demand curve whose shape it does not know. This possibility is excluded from this book since we assume that the firm knows its riskless demand curve. It may of course still be important in empirical observations. Second, the firm might be responding to past extreme values of the random factor u. For example, if u_{n-1} were unusually large, I_{n-1} would be unusually small. It is argued below that this would make it worthwhile to raise p_n. However, in this case it is the value of I_{n-1} and not x_n^e that causes p_n to change. Rather, it is the change in p_n that causes the change in x_n^e, since x_n^e is functionally related to p_n. In this case x_n^e contains no information of value in predicting p_n that is not already provided by I_{n-1} or, by a similar argument, by z_n. Hence, any observed partial correlation between p_n and x_n^e in this case would represent the inverse relationship between the two variables resulting from the negative slope of the demand curve. To the extent that nonlinearities are important in the decision model, this statement requires modification.

Now consider the other extreme case in which x_n^e has a substantial exogenous component, that is, the demand curve shifts from period to period. Then x_n^e clearly has an influence on p_n that is independent of the influence of z_{n-1} and I_{n-1}. Furthermore, there is a presumption β_{21} will be positive in this case, at least if the predominant shifts in the demand curve are to the right, because a shift to the right of the demand curve necessitates either an increase in output, an increased probability of shortage, or a rise in price. In the model employed in this book, each of the first two involves a cost. Hence, one should expect that exogenous increases in demand would induce the firm to respond partly by an increase in price and partly by an increase in production, the mixture of the two depending on how costly it is to change production rapidly.

This intuitive argument suggests that β_{21} might provide information as to whether short-term price movements represent movements along the demand curve or responses to shifts in the demand curve. It suggests that if b_{21} is significantly positive, observed price changes are mainly responses to shifts in the demand curve. If b_{21} is close to zero or negative, it suggests that observed price changes are mainly movements along the demand curve induced either by fluctuations in the firm's inventory position or by the firm's search for the most profitable point on the demand curve. To some extent, these conjectures are tested by the sampling experiments reported in the next chapter. Finally, it should be remembered that this argument leaves unclear the effect of employing a proxy, such as x_n, for x_n^e. Light is also shed on this question by the sampling experiments.

Similarly, intuition strongly suggests that β_{22} and β_{23} should be negative. This is because changes in z_n and I_{n-1} are in a sense substitute policies for achieving the same end, namely changing the probability of shortage or excess inventory. If I_{n-1} is particularly small, or if x_n^e is large relative to x_{n-1}^*, then a high probability of shortage in period n can be avoided only if either price or production or both are increased. Depending on the cost of rapid changes in the rate of production, changes in price will be more or less favored relative to changes in production. Thus, since z_n appears in (10) as an independent variable, we should expect that, for fixed x_n^e and I_{n-1}, the higher is z_n (for example, because z_{n-1} was large), the lower is p_n. Likewise, for fixed x_n^e and z_n, the higher is I_{n-1}, the lower should p_n be. β_{22} and β_{23} should therefore be negative.

5. Conclusion

The model represented by the decision rules (4) and (5) shows that the price decision is essentially a more complex one than the production decision. Therefore, if the theory developed in this book provides a good approximation to firms' price and output decision making, one would expect somewhat more success in applying (9) to observed decisions than in applying (10).

On the other hand, the reverse is not true. If (9) or (10) or both are applied successfully, by any of the standard statistical criteria, they will provide relatively little evidence in favor of the theory developed in this book. Equations (9) and (10) are linear decision rules giving price and output as functions of variables that one would expect to influence these decisions on the basis of common sense and without any particular theory concerning the decisions in question. Furthermore there are many other decision theories that would lead to the determination of price and output by much the same set of independent variables contained in (9) and (10). Hence, even if (9) and (10) fit the data very well, no firm conclusions can be reached about the validity of the underlying theory.

In one sense the major difference between the empirical studies in the following chapters and other similar recent investigations is not in the set of explanatory variables employed but rather in the form of the relations used.[12] Recent studies of production and inventory policy, for example, that by Modigliani and Sauerlender [60], have employed nonlinear models involving complicated transformations of the variables included. Equations (9) and (10), on the other hand, are linear functions of untransformed observations, and involve no special seasonal considerations. Of course it may be that the simple approach has substantially less explanatory value than more complicated approaches. If so it must be discarded in their favor. On the other hand, it is obviously desirable to exploit simple approaches first, until they are shown to be inadequate. The rest of the book is an investigation of the adequacy of the model developed in this and the preceding chapters.

---

[12] Another important difference is the inclusion of a price formation equation in the model used in this book.

Chapter 8

APPLICATION
TO EXPERIMENTAL DATA

1. Introduction

The problem considered in the last chapter was that of estimating and testing the price and output decision rules developed in Chapters 5 and 6 and modified in Chapter 7, Section 3. Since the decision rules themselves are two complicated simultaneous equations, it is clear that they cannot be estimated directly with the data and techniques usually available to economists. Indeed, it was even quite difficult to establish formally some of the important qualitative properties of the system; the discussion of these properties at the end of the last chapter had to be partly intuitive. Therefore, in Section 4 of Chapter 7, two linear decision rules, intended to approximate the true, nonlinear decision rules indicated by the theory, were presented.

On two distinct grounds doubts were raised concerning the ability of the linear approximations to explain observed price and output decisions even if the basic theory is assumed to be true. In the first place, it is uncertain whether and in what circumstances (9) and (10) are good approximations to the true decision rules (5) and (4) respectively.[1] In the second place, even if (9) and (10) are good approximations it is uncertain whether they will be identifiable when embedded in a complete model containing a demand equation. We saw in Section 4 of Chapter 7 that this depends on, among other things, whether there are exogenous variables in the demand equation. The first of these considerations affects the validity of the linear approxi-

---

[1] All the equations referred to in this section are in Chapter 7.

mations; the second affects the possibility of estimating them by least squares or other techniques.

In situations of this kind, when important characteristics of a model cannot be established by theoretical considerations, approximate answers can often be obtained from sampling, or Monte Carlo,[2] experiments. The purpose of this chapter is to report a study of this kind made with the model of price and output determination in the previous chapter. Although complicated in detail, the application of the Monte Carlo technique to this model is very simple in principle. Samples of price and output decisions are generated by solving numerical specifications of the true decision model for a number of consecutive periods. In this way sample "time series" of "observed" decisions are obtained. These are then treated like any other sample of observations, and the regressions (9) and (10) are fitted to them. By repeating the calculations for different values of the cost parameters, the initial conditions, and the exogenous variables the effects of these changes can be investigated.

The Monte Carlo study should shed light on at least four issues.

First, and most important, is the extent to which the linear approximations can explain decisions generated by the nonlinear decision rules. The linear approximations will do better on this score the fewer the nonlinearities included in the decision rules and the narrower the ranges covered by the variables in the samples. In order to keep the computations within manageable limits, relatively few nonlinearities are included in the decision rules in the samples reported here. For example, linear specifications of the demand and production cost functions are used in all the samples even though it would be interesting to study the effects of nonlinearities in both these relations. On the other hand, very little extra computational complexity is introduced by allowing the variables to cover wide ranges in the samples, and this is an alternative way of bringing out the effects of nonlinearities in the model. In the experiments reported here the variables are forced to cover wide ranges by large exogenous factors introduced in the demand equations. Hence, even though relatively few nonlinearities are included in the experimental calculations, there is a presumption that the effects of those that are included will show up in the samples if they are important.

Second, the experiments should provide estimates of the ranges

---

[2] See Chapter 2, Section 4 for a brief outline of this technique.

within which the regression coefficients are likely to lie if the observed decisions are made in a manner approximated by the decision model. The β's in (9) and (10) are functions of all the parameters in the decision rules, and it is important to know how variations in the cost parameters, for example, affect the regression coefficients. Different firms or industries to which the model might be applied have different cost parameters, and one wants to know how this fact will affect the β's. In addition, it is known that within a firm or industry these parameters do not usually remain constant over the period covered by a time series sample. Thus, if the regression coefficients are very sensitive to changes in the underlying parameters, results will be poor when the regressions are estimated from empirical data even if the basic decision model is correct.

Third, at least some of the β's can be calculated directly from the decision model. For example, if (8) is the correct specification of the output decision rule then, according to the argument presented in Section 4 of the last chapter, the value of β_{12} in (9) should be approximately equal to the coefficient of z_{n-1} in (8). Direct calculation of this coefficient from the numerical values assigned to the parameters in (8) provides a nonstatistical test of the accuracy of the estimated regression coefficients. This should help to reveal inadequacies arising from lack of identifiability or multicollinearity, in the statistical estimates of the β's.

Fourth, the experiments should provide evidence as to the adequacy of the implicit expectations approach. Equations (9) and (10) both contain the expectational variable x_n^e and, as was argued in Chapter 3, economists do not usually have observations of such expectational variables among their sample data. In Section 4 of Chapter 3 the implicit expectations hypothesis was presented as a possible approach to the estimation of decision rules in which expectational variables appear without the need to make prior estimates of the expectations themselves. It will be recalled that the implicit expectations hypothesis consists essentially of the assumption that expectations, however generated, are estimators of the variable in question with statistically stable properties. This assumption permits the use of the realized value of the variable, sales in the present case, as a proxy for the expectation in estimating the parameters of the decision rule. Since, in the experimental series, the true expectations are also known, it is possible to compare the estimates of the regression coefficients when the proxy is used with those obtained when the true expectations are used. For example, one can obtain quantitative estimates of the small sample bias discussed in Chapter 3, Section 4, introduced into the regression estimates by the use of the proxy.

It was also argued in Section 4 of Chapter 3 that, in some circumstances, it is possible to estimate the expectations themselves from the implicit approach. The basis of this procedure is the association of the regression residuals with estimates of the expectational errors. In practice, use of the implicit approach to estimate the expectations is clearly a much more questionable step than its use to estimate the decision rule in which the expectation appears. Observed regression residuals result not only from expectational errors but also from misspecifications in the form of the regression, sampling errors, and errors of observation in all the variables in the regression. Although most of these sources of error do not invalidate the use of least squares to estimate the regression coefficients, they do invalidate the use of the resulting residuals to estimate the expectational errors. Each of these sources of error except the last is present in the experimental series analyzed in this chapter. For example, the nonlinearities in the decision rule imply some misspecification in the form of the regressions. To the extent that the nonlinearities are important, the regressions will yield poor estimates of the true sales expectations. However, even if the estimated expectations turn out to be poor, it may still prove possible to obtain some idea of the magnitude of expectational errors from them. A major advantage of the experimental series is that the true expectations are known, and therefore the accuracy of the estimated expectations can be ascertained.

Before presenting the sampling experiments themselves, some limitations of the Monte Carlo approach should be stated explicitly. At best, sampling experiments can yield information only about the working of the theoretical model and not about the real world. Thus, sampling experiments can never establish whether the theory is true in the sense that it can explain empirically observed decisions. All the sampling experiments can do is to suggest what properties of the regression equations should be expected if the theory is true. Furthermore, only a small number of such experiments, involving small samples based mainly on linear cost and demand functions, are presented here. Ten experiments are generated from two basic sets of cost and demand parameters by varying the initial conditions and the exogenous variables in the system. The next section argues that a judicious selection of a small number of parameters can provide considerable insight into the working of the model. Nevertheless, the number of experiments considered is very small, and other choices of parameters might yield very different results.

2. The Numerical Models

The purpose of this section is to describe in detail the numerical model from which the experimental series are generated. The series themselves are presented and discussed in Section 3. The regression estimates are presented and analyzed in Section 4. Finally, in Section 5 the estimated regressions are used to estimate the sales expectations by the implicit approach, and the estimated expectations are compared with the true expectations.

The decision model from which the experimental price and output series are generated consists of the decision rules (4) and (5) of the preceding chapter, with the linear and quadratic cost functions introduced in Section 4 of that chapter. Using these specifications, (4) and (5) become

$$x_n^e + p_n \frac{\partial x_n^e}{\partial p_n} - p_n \frac{\partial x_n^e}{\partial p_n} [1 - F(y_n - x_n^e)] - D(y_n, p_n)$$

$$- \frac{\partial x_n^e}{\partial p_n} (c - r)F(y_n - x_n^e) - k \frac{\partial x_n^e}{\partial p_n} [1 - F(y_n - x_n^e)] = 0 \quad (1)$$

and

$$p_n[1 - F(y_n - x_n^e)] - c + (c - r)F(y_n - x_n^e) + k[1 - F(y_n - x_n^e)]$$

$$- g(y_n - I_{n-1} - z_{n-1}) = 0 \quad (2)$$

Here and subsequently the symbol $X(p_n)$ is replaced by x_n^e to allow for the possibility that variables other than current price may affect demand. For the same reason, $X'(p_n)$ is replaced by the partial derivative $\partial x_n^e / \partial p_n$. The coefficients in (1) and (2) have the meanings assigned to them in the previous chapter: c, r, and k are respectively marginal production, storage, and shortage costs, and g is the slope of the marginal cost of changing production between two successive periods. The expectational error is assumed, for the purpose of this chapter, to have a rectangular distribution with parameter λ (see Chapter 5, Section 5, and Chapter 7, Section 4), so that $F(y_n - x_n^e)$ is the integral of this density function from $-\lambda$ to $y_n - x_n^e$. With this additional specification, (2) can be solved explicitly for y_n.

$$y_n = \frac{\lambda(p_n + k - c - r)}{p_n + k - c + r + 2\lambda g} + \left(\frac{p_n + k - c + r}{p_n + k - c + r + 2\lambda g}\right) x_n^e$$

$$+ \frac{2\lambda g(I_{n-1} + z_{n-1})}{p_n + k - c + r + 2\lambda g} \qquad (2a)$$

Except for some rearrangement of terms, (2a) is the same as (8) in Chapter 7. It is now possible to eliminate y_n from (1) by (2a). The result is an equation involving only p_n and the predetermined variables. This makes it possible to solve the system by first finding p_n in terms of predetermined variables. This value of p_n, and the values of the predetermined variables, can then be substituted in (2a), which can be solved for y_n. This way of avoiding the simultaneous nature of the decision rules is the central calculation in the generation of the experimental series. However, before writing out the resulting equation for p_n, it is convenient to introduce the structural specifications on the demand side.

As was stated in Section 1, it is desirable to include a substantial exogenous factor in the demand equation in order to provide a stringent test of the linear approximations of the decision rules. Furthermore, it is preferable to include not only large period-to-period changes in demand, but also large "secular" changes. This procedure ensures not only that the decision variables display large short-run adjustments, but also that these adjustments take place under several substantially different demand conditions within each sample. The obvious way to accomplish these aims is to include in the demand equation a function of time which will generate cyclical and secular movements in demand. A specification of the demand equation which does this and which also keeps the computations relatively simple is as follows:

$$x_n^e = a_1 + a_2 p_n + a_3 \sin(a_4 n) + a_{5n}. \qquad (3)$$

Equation (3) assumes that the riskless demand curve is linear in price with a slope that does not change through time, but that the curve shifts parallel to itself from period to period as a result of both cyclical and secular forces. The sine term introduces a symmetrical cycle in demand with an amplitude of $2a_3$ units and a period which depends on a_4. The last term on the right hand side of (3) introduces a trend term which, *ceteris paribus*, causes demand to grow or shrink (if a_5 is negative) a_5 units per decision period. All the a_i except a_4 are measured in units of the product; a_4 is measured in radians. Extensive use has

already been made of the assumption that actual demand and its expected value are related by an additive random variable whose distribution is independent of time and known to the decision maker. Thus, we
can write

$$x_n = x_n^e + u_n \tag{4}$$

where u_n is the expectational error, as previously stated, that is assumed to have a rectangular distribution for the purpose of this chapter. Equation (4) is the same as (3) in Chapter 3 and (1a) in Chapter
5. The foregoing assumptions imply that the decision maker knows
the values of all the a_i in (3). Furthermore, the nth period's price and
output decisions are made knowing the distribution of u_n, that is, the
value of λ, but not the value of u_n itself.

It is now possible to write the entire model in the form used to
calculate the experimental series. In doing so, it is convenient to introduce two new symbols which summarize the effects of the predetermined
variables on the model. The only exogenous variable in the model is
time, and it appears as an explicit independent variable only in the
demand equation. The only lagged endogenous variables in the model
are z_{n-1} and I_{n-1}, and they appear only as a sum in (2) and (2a).
Equations (5a) and (5b) simply introduce new symbols for these
variables, which are then used in the subsequent equations (5c) to (5h).

$$\Phi_n = a_1 + a_3 \sin (a_4 n) + a_5 n \tag{5a}$$

$$\psi_n = z_{n-1} + I_{n-1} \tag{5b}$$

$$p_n^3 + [c_1 + c_2\Phi_n + c_3\psi_n]p_n^2 + [c_4\psi_n + c_5\Phi_n + c_6]p_n$$
$$+ [c_7 + c_8\Phi_n + c_9\psi_n + c_{10}(\Phi_n - \psi_n)^2] = 0 \tag{5c}$$

$$y_n = [c_{11}p_n + c_{12} + (p_n + c_{13})(\Phi_n + c_{14}p_n)$$
$$+ c_{15}\psi_n]/(p_n + c_{16}) \tag{5d}$$

$$x_n^e = \Phi_n + a_2 p_n \tag{5e}$$

$$x_n = \Phi_n + a_2 p_n + u_n (= x_n^e + u_n) \tag{5f}$$

$$I_n = \max \{(y_n - x_n), 0\} \tag{5g}$$

$$z_n = y_n - I_{n-1} \tag{5h}$$

Equation (5c) determines p_n and is the only extensive calculation
in the model. It is the equation, referred to above, that results when

(2a), (5a), and (5b) are substituted in the price decision rule (1). Equation (5c) is a cubic in p_n, and this relatively uncomplicated form depends crucially on the use of a simple density function, such as the rectangular, for u_n. The constants c_1, c_2, $\cdots$, c_{10} in (5c) are complicated functions of the cost and demand parameters and of the parameter λ which appears in the density function. The production decision rule (2a) takes the form of (5d) when the special notation from (5a) and (5b) is introduced. The dependence of the constants c_{11}, $\cdots$, c_{16} in (5d) on the original parameters can be seen without difficulty by comparing (2a) with (5d). The riskless demand function is (5e), and (5f) generates the observed demands x_n. Equations (5g) and (5h) are the definitional relations among y_n, x_n, z_n, and I_{n-1}. In summary, we now have one exogenous variable, Φ_n, defined by (5a) and one lagged endogenous variable, ψ_n, defined by (5b). There follow six equations, (5c) to (5h), determining the six endogenous variables p_n, y_n, x_n^e, x_n, I_n, and z_n. Among these six equations there are three basic behavior relations [the two decision rules (5c) and (5d) and the demand equation, (5f)] and three identities [(5e), (5g), and (5h)].

For any n, these equations can be solved in the sequence listed. Values of Φ_n and ψ_n, calculated from a knowledge of n and the predetermined variables, can be substituted in (5c) and this equation can be solved for p_n. In all the experiments calculated, (5c) had three real roots, one positive and two negative. Hence the one positive root is the desired value of p_n. If there were two or more real, positive roots of (5c), each would have to be substituted in (3) of Chapter 7 to find out which yielded the largest expected profit. Using the value of p_n thus obtained, y_n can be calculated from (5d). It is easy to calculate x_n^e, x_n, I_n, and z_n from (5e) to (5h). The calculations require one initial condition, ψ_1, and a sample of values of u_n drawn from the appropriate rectangular distribution. The calculations for period n provide the initial condition for period $n + 1$.[3]

3. The Experimental Series

The numerical solution of the model represented by (5) depends on the choice of four cost parameters k, c, r, and g; five demand parameters a_1, $\cdots$, a_5; the parameter λ of the rectangular distribution; a sample of u's; and an initial condition. Obviously, the use of sampling

---

[3] All the experimental series were calculated on an LGP-30 computer at the Johns Hopkins University computing center.

experiments to study systematically the effects on the model of varying all these factors would require the generation and analysis of a very large number of such experiments. However, the situation is seen to be much simpler than is suggested by a list of these factors if we recall that the dynamic behavior of the system depends essentially on the parameter g, which determines the cost of changing the rate of production. Indeed, if g is put equal to zero, the dynamic behavior of the system follows easily from the example in Section 5 of Chapter 6. Changes in ϕ_n in (5a) are equivalent to changes in the parameter a in (8) of Chapter 6 and represent parallel shifts in the riskless demand curve. For $a_5 > 0$ in (5a) these shifts represent secular increases in demand and it follows easily from (8) of Chapter 6 that the result will be a secular rise in price. Furthermore, the equation for $y(p)$ on p. 118 shows that y_n will equal x_n^e plus or minus a term that is positively related to p. As price rises secularly, the risk of shortage that the firm can profitably incur decreases. Hence, y_n will increase more rapidly than x_n^e as price rises secularly. However, y_n will not depend either on z_{n-1} or on I_{n-1} if g is zero. Thus, when there is no cost of changing the rate of production the dynamic behavior of the model is trivial, and no sampling experiments are needed. The larger the value of g relative to the other cost parameters, the more important is the cost of changing production and the more important are lagged output and inventory in determining current price and output. If the cost of changing production is very large it will pay to change production only very little, and most of the firm's response to exogenous changes in demand will consist of price movements.

This argument suggests that the most important factor to investigate in the experimental series is the effect of different values of g relative to the other cost parameters. Thus, the procedure has been to generate two basic sets of experiments, one of which, A, assumes a moderate value of g and the other of which, B, assumes a large value of g. The other cost parameters are the same in all the experiments. These, and the other specifications used in the experiments, are shown in Table 1. From the top panel of the table it can be seen that in all the experiments marginal production cost and marginal shortage cost are equal, and that they are five times as large as marginal storage cost.

In group A, g is 10 per cent as large as marginal production cost. This implies that if production is reduced by one unit between two successive periods, 5 per cent of the resulting reduction in production

TABLE 1

SPECIFICATIONS FOR SAMPLING EXPERIMENTS

	A1	A2	A3	A4	A5	B1	B2	B3	B4	B5
Cost Parameters										
k	5.0	5.0	5.0	5.0	5.0	5.0	5.0	5.0	5.0	5.0
c	5.0	5.0	5.0	5.0	5.0	5.0	5.0	5.0	5.0	5.0
r	1.0	1.0	1.0	1.0	1.0	1.0	1.0	1.0	1.0	1.0
g	0.5	0.5	0.5	0.5	0.5	2.0	2.0	2.0	2.0	2.0
Demand Parameters										
a_1	30	30	30	30	30	40	40	40	40	40
a_2	-1	-1	-1	-1	-1	-2	-2	-2	-2	-2
a_3	5	5	0	0	0	4	4	0	0	0
a_4	$\Pi/8$	$\Pi/8$	0	0	0	$\Pi/8$	$\Pi/8$	0	0	0
a_5	1	1	0	0	0	1	1	0	0	0
Distribution Parameter λ	5	5	5	5	0	5	5	5	5	0
Initial Conditions										
z_0	20	10	20	10	20	21	18	21	18	21
I_0	4	4	4	4	4	4	2	4	2	4
Sample of u_n	A1	A2	A1	A2	$u_n \equiv 0$	B1	B2	B1	B2	$u_n \equiv 0$

cost is offset by the cost of making the change; if production is reduced by two units, 10 per cent is offset; if production is reduced by three units, 22.5 per cent is offset. Since production ranges from about 5 to 25 units in the sampling experiments, a change of one unit represents 4 to 20 per cent of production. In group B, g is four times as large as in group A. In this case, 20 per cent of the reduction in production cost resulting from a one-unit decrease in production is offset by the cost of making the change. If production is reduced five units, the saving in production cost is completely offset by the cost of making the change. In other words, in terms of the production levels generated by the experiments, a reduction in output of 20 per cent, for example, may be so expensive that no cost saving is realized in the period in which the reduction takes place. Thus, whatever effect the cost of changing the rate of production can have on the behavior of the model should show up in the experiments in group B.

In addition to this cost difference, somewhat different demand functions are assumed in the two groups of experiments. Demand is more responsive to price changes in group B than in group A, a_2 having a value of -2 in the former group and -1 in the latter. In both groups, the same basic cyclical pattern is built into the demand equations. A value of $\Pi/8$ radians is given to a_4, implying that a full cycle is completed every 16 periods. The samples consist of 32 observations each, or two complete cycles. However, a_3 is somewhat larger in group A than in group B, giving the cyclical term a somewhat larger weight in the former group than in the latter. The cyclical term has an amplitude of about 40 per cent of the average demand recorded in the experiments. In all experiments, a_5 has a value of one, implying an exogenous increase in demand of about five per cent per period on the average.

A value of five is given to λ in all the experiments. This fact implies that actual demand differs from the expected value of demand by 2.5 units on the average, and that the firm's average forecasting error, ignoring signs, is about 15 per cent. Each sample of values of u_n was obtained by taking the first 32 integers between zero and ten from a page of standard tables of random numbers and subtracting five from each number.

With the above information, it is possible to calculate the numerical values of the parameters in (5c) and (5d) used in the two groups of experiments. These equations then become

Group A:

$$p_n{}^3 + [8.5 - 0.6\Phi_n + 0.2\psi_n]p_n{}^2 + [2.4\psi_n - 7.2\Phi_n - 6]p_n$$
$$- [41.5 + 8.6\Phi_n + 5.8\psi_n - 0.5(\Phi_n - \psi_n)^2] = 0 \qquad (5cA)$$

$$y_n = [5p_n - 5 + (p_n + 1)(\Phi_n - p_n) + 5\psi_n]/(p_n + 6) \qquad (5dA)$$

Group B:

$$p_n{}^3 + [32.8 + 0.3\psi_n - 0.4\Phi_n]p_n{}^2 + [14.0\psi_n - 17.5\Phi_n - 91.0]p_n$$
$$- [282.1 + 25.4\Phi_n + 11.3\psi_n - 1.7(\Phi_n - \psi_n)^2] = 0 \qquad (5cB)$$

$$y_n = [5p_n - 5 + (p_n + 1)(\Phi_n - 2p_n) + 20\psi_n]/(p_n + 21) \qquad (5dB)$$

Within each group, five experiments are carried out in order to test the effects of changing the initial conditions, the sample of u's, and the exogenous demand factors. Within each group, experiments one and two assume the same values for all parameters, but employ different initial conditions and different samples of u's. Since these two factors are the only sources of sampling errors in the experimental observations, a comparison between experiments one and two provides evidence of their importance in affecting the behavior of the models. Within each group, experiment three is related to experiment one as four is related to two. In all cases, the higher numbered experiment is obtained by deleting the cyclical and trend terms from the demand equation in the lower numbered experiment, that is, by putting $a_3 = a_4 = a_5 = 0$. Thus, for example, A3 employs the same sample of u's and initial conditions as does A1, but has a purely endogenous riskless demand curve. Comparison between three and one and between four and two makes it possible to estimate the effect of the exogenous forces on the behavior of the model. Specifically, the nonlinearities in the decision rules should be much less important in three and four as compared with one and two.

Finally, in experiment five in each group, not only the trend and cyclical factors, but also the random terms, are removed from the demand equations. Thus, in five there is no exogenous factor except the initial condition, and it should be expected that the variables will quickly converge to constant values. These experiments are not intended to provide insights into the operation of the models in realistic situations, since they assume an inconsistency between anticipated and realized demand. Decisions are made on the assumption that expectational errors have a rectangular distribution with λ equal to five, whereas expectational errors are actually identically zero. The purpose of these experiments is to indicate how long the model spends searching for its new asymptotic equilibrium values once it has been disturbed by some exogenous change.

The classification of the ten experiments can be summarized as follows. The values of several parameters differ between groups A and B. Within each group, experiments one and two differ only as to their initial conditions and samples of the random term. Three differs from one, and four differs from two, only by the removal of the trend and cyclical terms in the demand function in the higher numbered experiments. Thus, three and four also differ only by their initial conditions and samples of the random term. Experiment five is even more special, having not only the trend and cyclical terms, but also the random term, removed.

The results of the ten experiments are displayed in Figures 1 to 10. The remainder of this section contains some remarks, mostly of a qualitative nature, concerning the experimental series.

Perhaps the most interesting observations are those concerning the ways the exogenous cyclical and secular terms in the demand equation are reflected in the experimental series. It should be recalled that the cyclical and secular terms are present in only four of the experiments, those numbered one and two. In each of these four experiments, the sine term generates two complete cycles. Peaks occur in periods 4 and 20, troughs in periods 12 and 28. Not surprisingly, since they are the variables most directly affected, price and the expected value of sales reflect the exogenous factors most clearly. Trend and cycle can also be perceived in the production and sales series, but the reflection is much less clear since these variables are more directly affected by the large random term. There is no apparent cyclical or secular pattern in the inventory series.

In all the experiments except A2 and A4 there is a downswing in z_n and an upswing in p_n during the first three or four periods, resulting not from the exogenous cyclical factor in the model but rather from the fact that the arbitrary initial conditions are above the equilibrium levels of production. Hence, in trying to perceive the effects of the exogenous cyclical and secular factors, the first few observations in these experiments must be ignored. In experiments A2 and A4 the initial conditions are below their equilibria, and hence there are upswings in z_n during the first few periods for the same reason.

As was pointed out above, price movements occur in this model because, when demand shifts exogenously, the cost of changing production makes it unprofitable to alter production enough to clear the market at the existing price with an inventory that is neither too large nor too small. It follows that price movements will be predominantly upward when shifts in demand are predominantly to the right. It is an interesting and generally unappreciated fact that this process alone can result in secular price rises, as it does in the experiments, even in the absence of cost functions that rise through time. Indeed, the behavior of the price series in the four experiments containing cyclical and secular factors is similar to that of post-World War II prices in the United States. Upswings are accompanied by substantial price rises, and downswings, which are mild because of the trend factor,

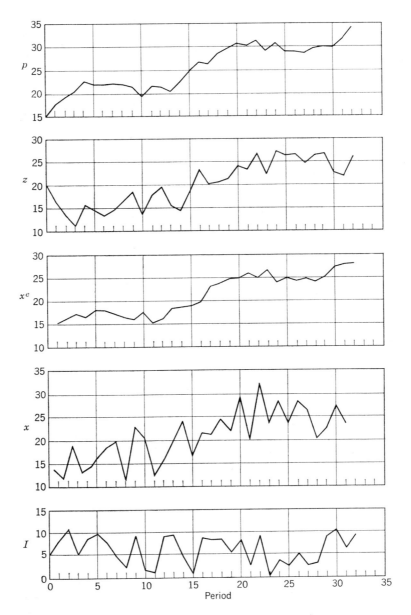

Figure 1. Data for Sampling Experiment A1.

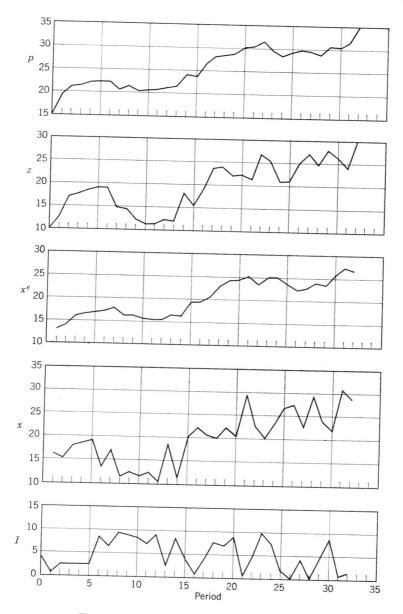

Figure 2. Data for Sampling Experiment A2.

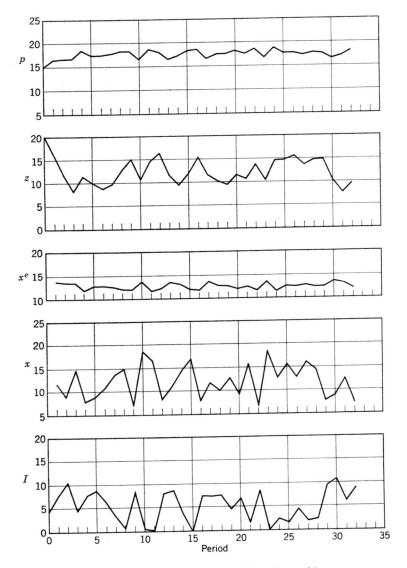

Figure 3.   Data for Sampling Experiment A3.

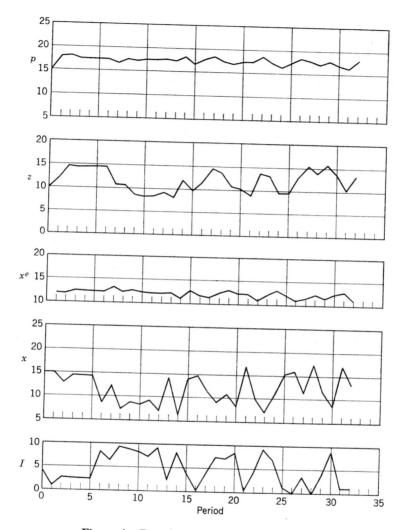

Figure 4. Data for Sampling Experiment A4.

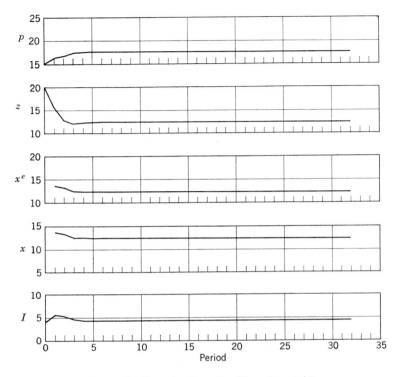

Figure 5. Data for Sampling Experiment A5.

provide only temporary interruptions of the rising trend but no significant decreases. This behavior is suggestive of an explanation of the corresponding macroeconomic phenomena, but such a topic is beyond the scope of this book.

Some differences between the cyclical and secular patterns in B1 and B2, as compared with those in A1 and A2, should also be indicated. The secular and, even more, the cyclical patterns stand out less clearly in the B group than in the A group. There are two reasons for this. First, the initial conditions in the B group are, by accident, farther from equilibrium than in the A group, forcing the model to spend relatively more periods adjusting to the initial disequilibrium than to the secular and cyclical changes in demand. Second, as was pointed out above, the cyclical term in the demand equation has a smaller coefficient in the B group than in the A group. It is also worthy of note

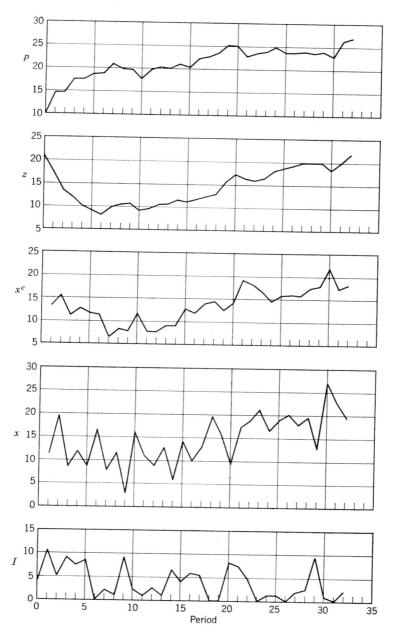

Figure 6. Data for Sampling Experiment B1.

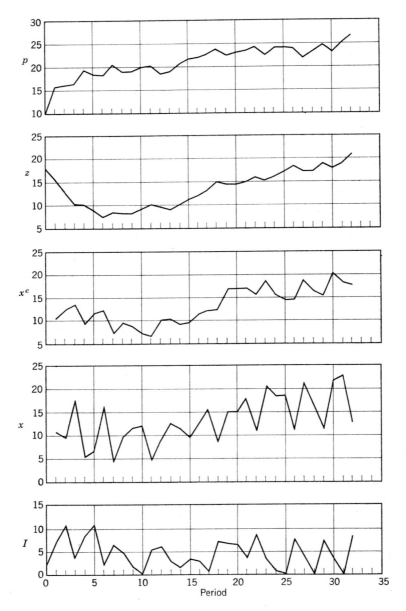

Figure 7. Data for Sampling Experiment B2.

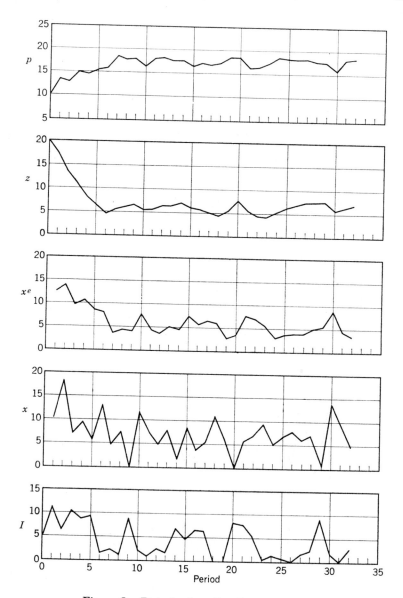

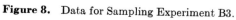

Figure 8. Data for Sampling Experiment B3.

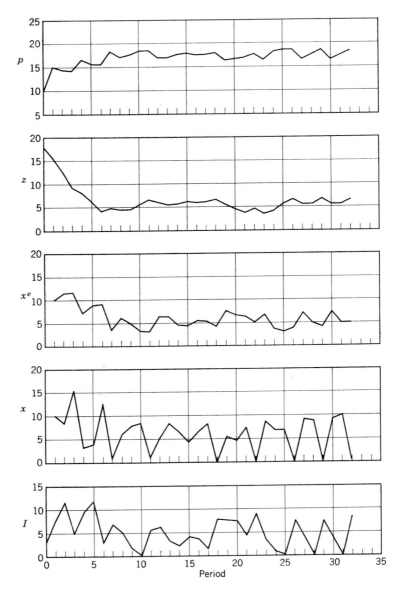

Figure 9. Data for Sampling Experiment B4.

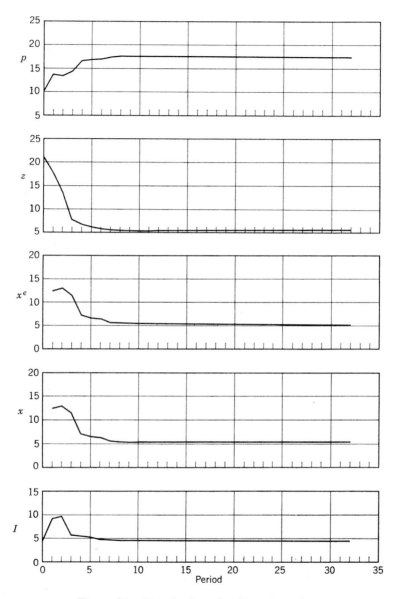

Figure 10. Data for Sampling Experiment B5.

that price fluctuations are greater relative to those in production in the group B experiments than in the group A experiments, because production changes are more costly in group B than in group A and are therefore less used relative to price changes when demand shifts.

Several comments can be made concerning the inventory series shown in the bottom panels of the figures. In principle, there should be a cyclical, and possibly a secular, pattern to inventory fluctuations. Since the distribution of forecasting errors is the same at all levels of expected demand and price, it does not pay the firm represented by the model to hold larger inventories when expected demand is high than when it is low. It is true that at high prices it is profitable to reduce the probability of shortage by carrying a large inventory, but this secular effect is probably swamped by the cyclical effect described below. Because of the cost of changing production, it pays the firm to hold less inventory when demand is rising than when it is falling. The fact that inspection of the inventory series reveals no cyclical pattern is apparently to be explained by the fact that these series are dominated by fluctuations resulting from the random term in the demand equation. There is another theoretical expectation, however, which is confirmed by the sample series. The probability of shortage that results from the firm's optimum policy depends on the circumstances in which the firm finds itself. For example, a higher probability of shortage is profitable the lower is the last period's terminal inventory. Nevertheless, it should be expected that higher probabilities of shortage would be observed on the average, the greater is the cost of changing production. The more costly it is to change production, the less it pays to increase production when a failure to do so involves a high probability of shortage. Thus, we should expect more shortages in group B experiments than in group A experiments. This expectation is confirmed since there is an average of two shortages per experiment in group A and four in group B. These observations suggest that the probability of a shortage when the optimum policy is followed is about 0.06 per period in group A on the average and 0.12 in group B.

Finally, the figures for experiments A5 and B5 show that the return of the model to equilibrium after an initial exogenous disturbance is very fast indeed. This is true even in experiment B5, in which the large cost of changing production might be expected to make the adjustment much more gradual. In principle, this adjustment must be an oscillatory process for much the same reason that oscillations appear in simple accelerator models. Suppose that the firm is in equilibrium and that demand shifts exogenously to the right. The immediate result is that the firm increases price and production and decreases inventory. Gradually, production increases, price falls, and inventory rises. When inventory and price reach their original levels, production must exceed sales since inventory has been increasing. However, it does not pay to reduce production immediately to the level of sales because of the cost of making the required change in production. Thus, the policy followed at this point is a mixture of decreased production, decreased price, and increased inventory, similar to the response to the initial disturbance. This process continues, with each variable overshooting the mark by a smaller amount at each oscillation. The oscillatory pattern does not appear in experiments A5 and B5 because the damping factor is so strong in the models that the oscillations are concealed by rounding errors in the calculations. The results of these two sampling experiments suggest that a macro model in which both price and output adjustments were included, as they are in this micro model, would be much more stable than the Metzler-type inventory cycle models in which output must make the entire adjustment.[4] However, this is no more than a conjecture, and its investigation is outside the scope of this book.

4. Regression Analysis

The next step in the analysis of the sampling experiments is to estimate from the sample data some linear regressions intended as approximations of the price and output decision rules from which the data were generated. The basic set of regressions to be estimated consists of (9) and (10) in Chapter 7. As was argued in Section 4 of that chapter, these are the best linear approximations of the decision rules in the sense that they contain the variables that appear in the decision rules. However, for purposes of comparison, estimates of several other regressions are also obtained from the data.

The more important of the additional regressions are those that test the usefulness of the implicit expectations hypothesis. As defined in Section 4 of Chapter 3 and discussed in Section 1 of the present chapter, the implicit expectations approach consists simply in the use

---

[4] See [50], [51], and [52].

of the realized value of the variable, sales in the present instance, as a proxy, on the assumption that the expectational errors have stable statistical properties. Formally, x_n^e can be eliminated from the regressions (9) and (10) of Chapter 7 by (4) of the present chapter, resulting in (6b) and (6f) to follow, which contain x_n instead of x_n^e as an independent variable. A comparison between the estimates of (6b) and (6f) on the one hand and the estimates of (9) and (10) of Chapter 7 [(6a) and (6e) below] on the other hand indicates how much explanatory power is lost by the use of the proxy instead of the correct expectational variable. Now the assumption underlying the implicit approach is correct for the sampling data, since the expectational errors u_n have the same distribution in each sample period. Therefore, it might be expected that the use of observed sales as a proxy for sales anticipations would necessarily result in less sacrifice of explanatory power in the experimental series than in empirical series, since in the latter the assumption is only approximately true at best. However, this is not so. The biases and sampling errors introduced in the b_{ij} by the use of the proxy depend on the magnitude of the random term u_n and on the size of the sample. In the experimental series, u_n has intentionally been assigned a variance that is very large relative to expected sales. Furthermore, the experimental series are much shorter than the empirical series analyzed in the next four chapters. For both these reasons, the experimental series provide a fairly stringent test of the usefulness of the implicit approach.

The set of regressions to be estimated is augmented another way, by the inclusion of lagged price in some of the price regressions. As was argued in Section 2 of Chapter 6, there is a presumption that most firms have a cost of changing price analogous to the cost of changing production that has been included in the theoretical model in this book. If this is so, lagged price should appear in the decision rules from which the empirical price series for these firms are generated. Thus, even though lagged price does not appear in the decision rules from which the experimental series were generated, it is of interest to discover the effect of including it in the regressions estimated from the experimental series. Having estimated the effects of incorrectly including lagged price should make it easier to ascertain when it is correctly included in empirical regression estimates.

The above discussion suggests that the following six regressions should be fitted to the data for each sampling experiment.

$$z_n = \beta_{10} + \beta_{11}x_n^{\ e} + \beta_{12}z_{n-1} + \beta_{13}I_{n-1} + \epsilon'_{1n} \tag{6a}$$

$$z_n = \beta_{10} + \beta_{11}x_n + \beta_{12}z_{n-1} + \beta_{13}I_{n-1} + \epsilon_{1n} \tag{6b}$$

$$p_n = \beta_{20} + \beta_{21}x_n^{\ e} + \beta_{22}z_n + \beta_{23}I_{n-1} + \beta_{24}p_{n-1} + \epsilon'_{2n} \tag{6c}$$

$$p_n = \beta_{20} + \beta_{21}x_n + \beta_{22}z_n + \beta_{23}I_{n-1} + \beta_{24}p_{n-1} + \epsilon_{2n} \tag{6d}$$

$$p_n = \beta_{30} + \beta_{31}x_n^{\ e} + \beta_{32}z_n + \beta_{33}I_{n-1} + \epsilon'_{3n} \tag{6e}$$

$$p_n = \beta_{30} + \beta_{31}x_n + \beta_{32}z_n + \beta_{33}I_{n-1} + \epsilon_{3n} \tag{6f}$$

In view of the assumption (4) underlying the implicit approach, $\epsilon'_{in} = \epsilon_{in} - \beta_{i1}u_n$ $(i = 1, 2, 3)$. Each of these regressions is estimated for each sampling experiment numbered one to four. A5 and B5 are excluded from the estimates because of their statistically degenerate nature.[5] Thus there are six regressions estimated from each of the eight sampling experiments. The estimates are presented in Table 2. The number in parentheses below each coefficient is its standard error. All estimates in this and the following chapters were obtained by standard least squares procedures. R^2's are corrected for degrees of freedom.

Before examining the estimates in Table 2 in detail, we can make three general remarks. First, the multiple correlation coefficients are very large.[6] Of the 48 R^2's in the table, only eleven are less than 0.980, and only three are less than 0.900. This demonstrates conclusively that the nonlinearities in the decision rules from which the data were generated are of only negligible importance in reducing the explanatory power of the regressions. In judging the importance of this

[5] It is quite certain that estimates of the regressions from experiments A5 and B5 would be difficult to calculate anyway, because of near singularities in the moments matrices. Even in experiments A3, A4, B3, and B4, which are much less trivial statistically than A5 and B5, near singularities occurred several times, resulting in overflows on the IBM-650 computer on which the calculations were carried out. In two cases (regression (6c) in sampling experiments A3 and A4) one unit had to be added to the last digit of the sum of squares of the dependent variable in order to make the inversion possible. This is equivalent to adding a small random term to the dependent variable. That this procedure had a negligible effect on the estimates is indicated by the fact that reestimation of the other regressions in these two experiments using the altered sum of squares affected the estimated coefficients only beyond the fourth decimal place. No such problems were encountered in experiments one and two.

[6] No d-statistics have been calculated for these regressions. Because of the large R^2's, calculated residuals would be strongly influenced by rounding errors.

TABLE 2

Regression Estimates for Sampling Experiments

Regression	Coefficient	A1	A2	A3	A4	B1	B2	B3	B4
(6a)	b_{10}	3.740 (0.089)	3.589 (0.075)	11.581 (1.841)	10.035 (3.174)	2.188 (0.091)	2.279 (0.060)	1.470 (0.214)	2.334 (0.041)
	b_{11}	0.855 (0.008)	0.856 (0.009)	0.038 (0.189)	0.123 (0.325)	0.481 (0.014)	0.500 (0.010)	1.367 (0.367)	0.021 (0.032)
	b_{12}	0.153 (0.007)	0.160 (0.007)	0.347 (0.031)	0.319 (0.053)	0.531 (0.013)	0.510 (0.010)	0.138 (0.179)	0.752 (0.015)
	b_{13}	−0.845 (0.006)	−0.847 (0.005)	−0.654 (0.030)	−0.683 (0.053)	−0.508 (0.008)	−0.516 (0.006)	−0.903 (0.167)	−0.261 (0.014)
	R^2	1.000	1.000	1.000	1.000	0.999	1.000	0.995	0.999
(6b)	b_{10}	6.755 (1.493)	7.094 (0.991)	11.211 (0.029)	11.234 (0.052)	2.418 (0.482)	2.067 (0.525)	2.199 (0.108)	2.349 (0.026)
	b_{11}	0.225 (0.080)	0.209 (0.059)	0.002 (0.002)	0.000 (0.003)	0.131 (0.032)	0.102 (0.036)	0.003 (0.015)	0.005 (0.004)
	b_{12}	0.633 (0.091)	0.629 (0.064)	0.340 (0.002)	0.339 (0.003)	0.811 (0.041)	0.876 (0.047)	0.804 (0.014)	0.760 (0.004)
	b_{13}	−0.717 (0.099)	−0.697 (0.069)	−0.660 (0.002)	−0.663 (0.003)	−0.407 (0.039)	−0.385 (0.047)	−0.284 (0.016)	−0.255 (0.004)
	R^2	0.881	0.953	1.000	1.000	0.974	0.970	0.992	0.999
(6c)	b_{20}	16.983 (0.718)	15.172 (0.541)	30.000 (0.047)	29.999 (0.021)	21.634 (1.103)	23.184 (0.768)	19.918 (0.114)	20.424 (0.111)
	b_{21}	3.743 (0.165)	3.404 (0.146)	−1.000 (0.011)	−1.000 (0.005)	2.057 (0.143)	2.285 (0.106)	−0.409 (0.032)	−0.007 (0.017)
	b_{22}	−2.632 (0.143)	−2.410 (0.138)	0.000 (0.005)	0.000 (0.002)	−1.555 (0.118)	−1.769 (0.091)	−0.053 (0.032)	−0.303 (0.012)
	b_{23}	−2.656 (0.131)	−2.441 (0.122)	0.000 (0.005)	0.000 (0.002)	−1.670 (0.104)	−1.833 (0.075)	−0.055 (0.034)	−0.308 (0.010)
	b_{24}	−0.078 (0.048)	0.049 (0.054)	0.000 (0.000)	0.000 (0.000)	0.039 (0.047)	−0.005 (0.031)	0.008 (0.005)	−0.001 (0.005)
	R^2	0.996	0.997	1.000	1.000	0.989	0.996	0.999	0.999

finding it must be remembered that these decision rules contain a number of linear relations, in the cost and demand functions and in the use of the rectangular distribution, which are not inherent in the basic model in Chapter 6 and which may not be good approximations in the real world. Second, with a few exceptions, sampling errors are very small. This is indicated by the fact that the regression estimates differ very little between sampling experiments which differ only in the samples of random terms and initial conditions. Thus, correspond-

TABLE 2 (*Continued*)

Regression	Coefficient	A1	A2	A3	A4	B1	B2	B3	B4
(6d)	b_{20}	2.187 (1.452)	4.889 (1.307)	25.752 (0.158)	25.777 (0.160)	7.574 (1.385)	7.985 (1.063)	20.067 (0.198)	20.417 (0.108)
	b_{21}	−0.034 (0.070)	0.092 (0.065)	0.001 (0.002)	0.000 (0.002)	0.052 (0.056)	0.064 (0.046)	0.000 (0.004)	0.002 (0.002)
	b_{22}	0.481 (0.194)	0.399 (0.259)	−0.485 (0.006)	−0.473 (0.008)	0.084 (0.071)	0.125 (0.062)	−0.296 (0.006)	−0.308 (0.004)
	b_{23}	0.238 (0.150)	0.112 (0.204)	−0.481 (0.005)	−0.476 (0.006)	−0.252 (0.075)	−0.298 (0.067)	−0.309 (0.004)	−0.314 (0.002)
	b_{24}	0.531 (0.182)	0.418 (0.240)	−0.004 (0.008)	−0.013 (0.009)	0.618 (0.066)	0.586 (0.056)	0.016 (0.009)	0.000 (0.005)
	R^2	0.924	0.942	0.998	0.997	0.910	0.927	0.998	0.999
(6e)	b_{30}	16.355 (0.624)	15.375 (0.489)	30.000 (0.046)	29.999 (0.021)	22.507 (0.310)	23.064 (0.214)	20.068 (0.005)	20.409 (0.020)
	b_{31}	3.596 (0.142)	3.434 (0.142)	−1.000 (0.011)	−1.000 (0.005)	2.162 (0.063)	2.269 (0.044)	−0.425 (0.054)	−0.007 (0.017)
	b_{32}	−2.567 (0.141)	−2.392 (0.136)	0.000 (0.005)	0.000 (0.002)	−1.639 (0.061)	−1.756 (0.045)	−0.048 (0.033)	−0.303 (0.011)
	b_{33}	−2.580 (0.126)	−2.431 (0.122)	0.000 (0.005)	0.000 (0.002)	−1.746 (0.046)	−1.822 (0.034)	−0.047 (0.034)	−0.308 (0.010)
	R^2	0.996	0.997	1.000	1.000	0.989	0.996	0.999	0.999
(6f)	b_{30}	2.894 (1.612)	5.743 (1.254)	25.686 (0.097)	25.615 (0.115)	18.094 (1.615)	16.429 (1.517)	20.401 (0.003)	20.411 (0.002)
	b_{31}	0.010 (0.077)	0.067 (0.066)	0.001 (0.002)	0.000 (0.002)	0.271 (0.103)	0.169 (0.099)	0.000 (0.004)	0.002 (0.002)
	b_{32}	0.986 (0.097)	0.828 (0.084)	−0.485 (0.006)	−0.478 (0.007)	0.112 (0.142)	0.329 (0.130)	−0.304 (0.004)	−0.308 (0.002)
	b_{33}	0.555 (0.117)	0.431 (0.092)	−0.481 (0.005)	−0.480 (0.006)	−0.537 (0.139)	−0.361 (0.147)	−0.312 (0.004)	−0.314 (0.002)
	R^2	0.900	0.936	0.998	0.997	0.621	0.633	0.998	0.999

ing entries are similar in A1 and A2, in A3 and A4, in B1 and B2, and in B3 and B4.[7] Third, in all the production regressions, the coefficients

[7] Further evidence that the effects of sampling errors are small is provided by an additional calculation, which is not shown. The sample of random terms for experiment B1 is an abnormal one. The last ten terms have an average value of 2.3 and are all positive except one. To test the effect of these abnormal sample values, the six regressions were fitted to only the first 22 observations in this experiment. The R^2's and coefficients estimated from this truncated sample differed surprisingly little from those presented in Table 2 for the entire sample. A few coefficients differed slightly in the second decimal place but none in the first.

of lagged production are larger relative to the other coefficients in the group B experiments than in the group A experiments. This reflects the fact that the cost of changing production is larger relative to the other costs in group B than in group A.

It is useful to classify the more detailed comments on the estimates into two groups, one referring to those experiments whose demand equations contain exogenous trend and cyclical terms and the other to those whose demand equations do not. The next four paragraphs refer to the former group, experiments A1, A2, B1, and B2; succeeding paragraphs refer to the latter group, experiments A3, A4, B3, and B4.

Consider first the estimates of the "correct" regressions, those containing the variables that appear in the decision rules from which the data were generated. These regressions are (6a) and (6e), or (9) and (10) of Chapter 7, and the estimates appear to be satisfactory in every respect. The R^2's are very large, the smallest, that for (6e) in experiment B1, having a value of 0.989. Each coefficient has the correct sign, according to the a priori restrictions imposed on them in Section 4 of Chapter 7, and is at least ten times its standard error in absolute value. Comparison between corresponding estimates in groups A and B indicates that changing the underlying cost and demand parameters has a substantial effect on some of the regression coefficients. However, aside from the effect already mentioned of the cost of changing production on the weight given to lagged production in the output regressions, it does not appear to be possible to associate differences in the regression coefficients between groups A and B with differences in the values of particular parameters between the two groups.

Another set of observations has to do with the relation between the estimated coefficients in the tables and the values of these coefficients that can be built up from a knowledge of the parameters in the decision model. Equation (8) of Chapter 7 shows the dependence of the β's in (6a) on the underlying parameters of the model. It also shows that the β's are functions of the prices generated by the decision rules; indeed, it is only for this reason that (6a) is an approximation rather than an exact representation of the production decision rule. However, if the approximation is close, the b's estimated in (6a) should not differ much from the average values of the corresponding coefficients in (8) of Chapter 7. If the average realized price and the correct cost and probability parameter values are inserted in this equation, the following values of the β's result.

	A1, A2	B1, B2
β_{11}	0.773	0.394
β_{12}	0.227	0.606
β_{13}	−0.773	−0.394

It should be emphasized that the b's in (6a) are not estimates of these β's in the usual statistical sense. Nevertheless, the similarity between corresponding b's and β's is reassuring. In each case, b_{11} and b_{13} are larger absolutely, and b_{12} smaller, than the corresponding β's.

Consider next the effects of using observed sales as a proxy for demand expectations in the regressions. This involves a comparison between (6a) and (6b), and between (6e) and (6f). The first thing to note is that, with the exception of the price regressions in experiments B1 and B2, the R^2's remain very high when the proxy is used instead of the correct anticipation. Next, as is to be expected, all the values of b_{11} and b_{31} are biased toward zero, in most cases to a substantial extent. However, in all cases these coefficients retain their correct signs. In the production regressions, the coefficients of the other variables also retain the correct signs, although they are affected by the use of the proxy. In the price regressions, however, the use of the proxy causes some of the coefficients of other variables to reverse their signs. In each of the four experiments b_{32} becomes positive and b_{33} becomes positive in two of them. The reason for the former result is that z_n and x_n^e are strongly correlated. When x_n^e is removed from the regression and x_n is used instead, z_n takes on part of the job previously done by x_n^e in the price regression. Since the coefficient of x_n^e was positive, the coefficient of z_n becomes positive. These findings suggest strongly that the price regressions are much more sensitive than the production regressions to misspecifications resulting from the use of proxies for demand anticipations.

Now consider the effect of the second misspecification, resulting from the inclusion of lagged price in the price regressions. In (6c), in which the correct expectations variable appears, the coefficient of lagged price is nonsignificant at the 5 per cent level, and the other coefficients are virtually the same as in the correct regression (6e). In (6d), in which the proxy for anticipations appears, however, the coefficients are distorted in much the same way as in (6f), in which the proxy, but not the lagged price, appears. One difference is that in (6f) one of the four values of b_{31} is significant at the 5 per cent level, whereas in (6d) none of the values of b_{21} is significant at this level. It is interesting to note that the inclusion of lagged price in the price regressions (6d) results in R^2's almost as large as those in the correct price regression (6e). Thus, the use of lagged price can make up for the inadequacies of the anticipations proxy as far as the value of R^2 is concerned. It cannot, however, remedy the distortions in the coefficients which result from the use of the proxy, although it does not appear to make them much worse.

Turn now to the regressions for the second group of experiments, A3, A4, B3, and B4, in which there are no exogenous trend and cyclical terms. The removal of these terms has important effects on the regressions, effects which can be briefly summarized.

The estimates of the production regressions for these experiments can be understood if it is recognized that z_n, p_n, and x_n^e are all completely determined once z_{n-1} and I_{n-1} have been specified. This implies that x_n^e, and hence x_n, provides no information that could help in explaining or predicting the decision variables other than the information already provided by z_{n-1} and I_{n-1}. Hence, in (6a) and (6b), these two lagged variables explain z_n almost perfectly without the assistance of x_n^e or x_n, and all but one of the coefficients of these two variables are nonsignificant at the 5 per cent level. The foregoing is simply another way of saying that, if the exogenous variables are removed from the equations for x_n^e and x_n, the production decision rule is not identified and only the reduced form, the regression of z_n on z_{n-1} and I_{n-1}, can be estimated.

Much the same situation obtains with respect to the price decision rule. There is an exact linear relationship, the riskless demand equation, between x_n^e and p_n. (Furthermore, since the exogenous variables are absent from this group of experiments, the demand equation, but not the price decision rule, is exactly identified.) In three of the four experiments in this group, (6c) and (6e) are almost exact representations of the riskless demand equation. In the fourth experiment, B4, multicollinearity resulting from the close relationship among x_n^e, z_n, and I_{n-1} has obscured this relationship. The proxy x_n is much less strongly correlated with p_n than is x_n^e and therefore in (6d) and (6f) the work is done by the other independent variables. Thus, although the price decision rule is not identified in this group of experiments, the high R^2's for the last four regressions result from the fact that p_n,

x_n^e, and z_n are all determined by the same pair of predetermined variables z_{n-1} and I_{n-1}. Furthermore, in the absence of exogenous movements in demand, the nonlinearities in the decision rules are much less important, and most of the correlations are very high.

The implications of these regression estimates for the empirical studies appear to be as follows. The second group of experiments illustrates what was shown formally in Chapter 7 and is well known, that exogenous variation on the demand side can make the supply side identifiable. Fortunately, as will be argued in the next chapter, there is good reason to think that available empirical series of the type studied in this book contain a considerable amount of exogenous variation in demand. Assuming this to be so, the sampling studies show that the correct price and output regressions could be estimated with a high degree of accuracy if accurate observations of anticipated demand were available. Since observations of anticipations are not available, some proxy variable must be used in their place. If, as in the following chapters, observed sales are used for this purpose, some small sample bias must be expected in the estimated coefficients, though not necessarily as much as has been observed in the experimental data. No sign restrictions should be violated in the production regressions, but they may be in the price regressions. Furthermore, when the proxy is used in the price regressions, the inclusion of lagged price may raise R^2 by a substantial amount even if lagged price does not appear in the decision rule.

5. *Estimates of Expectations*

It was argued in Section 4 of Chapter 3 that it is sometimes possible to estimate the expectational variable from a regression that had been calculated using the observed value of the variable as a proxy for the firm's expectation of that variable. The purpose of this section is to report some calculations of this type for the experimental series. Although the procedure did not yield very satisfactory estimates, the analysis may nevertheless be instructive.

The general procedure for calculating the implicit expectations was described in Section 4 of Chapter 3; at the cost of some repetition, it will be outlined here as it applies to the decision rules used in the sampling experiments.

It will be recalled from Chapter 3 that the general idea of the implicit approach is as follows. Suppose that we have, as in (6b), (6d),

and (6f), an estimate of a decision rule obtained without prior estimation of the expectational variable that appears in the true decision rule.
Then the implicit expectation is the value of the variable such that, if
it were the firm's expectation, it would have led the firm to make the
decision it was observed to make. If, for example, we observe that in
period n production exceeds the level predicted by an estimate of (6b),
we assume that it happened because the firm expected a larger demand
than materialized in that period and therefore produced more than
was justified by the realized demand. The implicit expectation is the
amount such that, if inserted in (6b) instead of observed sales, it would
yield an estimated production $\hat{z}_n$ equal to realized production z_n.

Continuing with the example of the production regression, the
formal procedure is as follows. Clearly, the implicit expectation is a
better estimate of the true expectation the less important are residuals
from sources other than expectational errors. To take the extreme
case, suppose that residuals in the true regression arise only from expectational errors, so that

$$\epsilon'_{1n} \equiv 0 \text{ in (6a)} \quad \text{and} \quad \epsilon_{1n} = -\beta_{11}u_n \text{ in (6b)}$$

Now suppose that we have an estimate of (6b) whose residuals are

$$e_{1n} = z_n - \hat{z}_n$$

where $\hat{z}_n$ is the value of z_n calculated from the regression. Then

$$e_{1n} = \text{est } \epsilon_{1n} = \text{est } (-\beta_{11} u_n)$$

Using the estimate b_{11} of β_{11}, we derive the estimate $\hat{u}_{1n}$ of u_n by

$$e_{1n} = -b_{11}\hat{u}_{1n}$$

or

$$\hat{u}_{1n} = -e_{1n}/b_{11} \tag{7}$$

Then the implicit expectation is

$$\hat{x}^e_{1n} = x_n - \hat{u}_{1n} \tag{8}$$

which is analogous to (4).

In principle there are three estimating equations like (8); one from
each regression containing x_n, one for each sampling experiment, and
the theoretically best estimate would presumably be obtained by
pooling them in some way. However, the optimum pooling procedure
would not be easy to find and no attempt has been made to do so.

Since division by b_{i1} is involved in the calculation, no regression should be used in which b_{i1} is not significantly different from zero. This criterion precludes the use of the price regressions (6d) and (6e) and it precludes estimation from experiments A3, A4, B3, and B4 altogether. There remains one regression (6b) from which to estimate expectations in each of the four sampling experiments A1, A2, B1, and B2. Thus, (8) is the only formula actually used to calculate implicit expectations.

The next step is to compare the implicit expectations $\hat{x}_{1n}^{e}$ with the true expectations x_n^{e}. The difference $\hat{x}_{1n}^{e} - x_n^{e}$ is the error made in estimating the expectation and these errors should be small if the implicit approach is to be useful. Of course, smallness must be measured in relation to errors made in estimating expectations by other means and some standard of comparison is needed. The obvious standard to use is the error made in estimating the expectation by the naive estimate x_n. The proposal is to use the observed sales as a naive estimate of the firm's demand expectation and to judge a more sophisticated estimate of the firm's demand expectation by the extent to which it involves smaller errors of estimation than the naive estimate. The error of estimation of the naive estimate is $x_n - x_n^{e} = u_n$, the economist's error in using x_n to estimate x_n^{e} is simply minus the firm's error in using x_n^{e} to estimate x_n.

The accuracy of the implicit and naive estimates of expectations can be measured in several ways, two of which are presented here. One measure is the average absolute percentage error, and the other is the standard deviation S of the error of estimate. The results are presented in Table 3. As can be seen from the table, in each of the

TABLE 3

ACCURACY OF ESTIMATES OF EXPECTATIONS

Sampling Experiment	$\dfrac{100}{32} \sum \dfrac{\lvert \hat{x}_{1n}^{e} - x_n^{e} \rvert}{x_n^{e}}$	$\dfrac{100}{32} \sum \dfrac{\lvert x_n - x_n^{e} \rvert}{x_n^{e}}$	$S(\hat{x}_{1n}^{e} - x_n^{e})$	$S(x_n - x_n^{e})$
A1	24.6	16.0	6.21	3.50
A2	20.4	14.5	5.22	3.28
B1	27.5	23.1	4.64	3.19
B2	32.5	22.8	6.20	3.28

four experiments the naive estimate does better by both measures. This is a discouraging result and it suggests that it would be unwise to attach much value to estimates of expectations obtained by the implicit approach from empirical series. It does not of course imply that the use of observed sales as a proxy for anticipations will result either in poor estimates of the decision rules or in poor forecasts of the decisions taken.

It is not hard to discover why the implicit expectations are such poor estimates of the true expectations in the experimental series. The implicit expectations may be poor estimates either because b_{11} is a poor estimate of β_{11} or because there are important sources of residuals other than expectational errors in the regressions. It is clear from the figures in Table 2 that the former rather than the latter is at work in the experimental series. The R^2's for (6a) show that other sources of residuals are negligible, and the comparison between (6a) and (6b) shows that b_{11} is biased downward in (6b). Thus, b_{11} is too small, and when it is divided into the regression residual the result is an estimate of u_n that is too large in absolute value. Although u_n and $\hat{u}_{1n}$ are strongly correlated, the latter is a larger error of estimate than the former.

It seems quite likely that the relative importance of the two sources of error in estimating expectations will be the reverse in empirical series of what was found in the experimental series. It is likely that b_{11} will be less biased when estimated from empirical data,[8] both because the samples are larger and because expectational errors are in practice less than the average of almost 20 per cent recorded in Table 3 for the experimental series. However, it is almost inevitable that specification errors will be more important in applications of the regressions to empirical data than they were in the applications to experimental data. If this is so, the empirical regressions will also yield poor estimates of anticipations, though for a different reason than in the experimental regressions. The moral seems to be that residuals make poor estimators.

In conclusion, it might be mentioned that an attempt was made to rescue the implicit expectations by omitting the first few observations. The rationale for this procedure is that the initial conditions in the experimental series are arbitrary, rather than generated by the system itself as would be true of initial values in empirical samples. Therefore, the first few regression residuals in the experimental series are strongly affected by the model's search for equilibrium. It would not, however,

[8] Unfortunately, this does not imply that the bias in $1/b_{11}$ will also be small.

be justifiable to omit many observations on this basis since, as we saw in experiments A5 and B5, the decision model converges rapidly. The alternative calculation therefore omitted only the first two observations of $\hat{u}_{1n}$ and u_n in each experiment. The result is to bring the implicit expectations much closer to the naive estimates by the measures in Table 3, but the implicit expectations are still inferior in each case.

Chapter 9

APPLICATION TO INDUSTRY DATA: SOUTHERN PINE LUMBER

1. Introduction

This chapter presents the first of four empirical studies utilizing the models of price and output determination which have been developed in the preceding chapters. The other empirical studies will be presented in the three succeeding chapters.

In no sense can these studies be said to provide exhaustive or systematic tests and estimates of the model. The most we can hope is that they will provide insight into the feasibility of using models of the type developed in this book to explain observed short-run price and output policies. Exhaustive testing and estimation would be very difficult, and are precluded by lack of data, computational facilities, time, energy, and patience. Aside from the basic question whether these models generally represent the decision processes employed by firms, there are many factors, none of which can be systematically explored in this book, that might limit or extend the range of empirical applicability of the models. Among these are: the degree of durability and storeability of the product; the extent of seasonal fluctuations on both supply and demand sides; the amount of aggregation over products, firms, and time that the series employ; the precise market structure within which the decisions are made; changes through time in the nature of the product; and exogenous changes in costs. The last factor, in particular, would have to be taken into account in a complete study of short-run price determination, but is ignored here in order to focus attention on the explanatory power of the decision rule itself. Although the series studied in these chapters display considerable variation with respect to many of these factors, no systematic study of their effect has been made. For example, one would like to be able to make separate studies of data for firms, industries, and even more aggregate groups, to make it possible to test the effect of more or less aggregation on the applicability of the model. In fact, all four applications in this book are to data representing industry totals, largely because of the virtual absence of series on a less aggregative basis.[1] Although some attempt has been made to choose data for these studies on the basis of the diversity of the material covered, the overriding criterion has been the availability of easily accessible series. The minimum data requirements are the availability of monthly or quarterly price, output, sales, and inventory series recorded consecutively for several years. Although the relevant quantity series are now available for many products, corresponding price series are still very hard to obtain and this has limited the choice greatly.

The data chosen for study in this chapter are monthly sales, production, inventory, and price series for the southern pine lumber industry covering most of the decade of the 1930's. There are several reasons for the choice of this data for study. First and foremost, as intimated above, is the availability of long, unbroken, relevant monthly series which have a high degree of coverage and reliability. It is also to be noted that the physical volume data in these series are direct estimates rather than deflated dollar value figures. In a study in which the price itself appears as a variable it is probably an advantage if other variables in the system are not deflated by the same price data.

A second reason for interest in this industry is that the data display substantial movements that appear to be rather typical of movements in a wide class of products for which data are available. The basic evidence on this score is the definitive study by Abramovitz [1] of all the available data on inventory movements up to 1940. The reader is referred particularly to Chapter 11 of this major work for a summary and analysis of production, sales, and inventory fluctuations in southern pine lumber and for a comparison with inventory behavior in other industries. Although the evidence presented by Abramovitz does not imply that any conclusions reached in the study presented here can automatically be applied to other products, it does provide some con-

---

[1] I have included in [54] studies of the output, but not price, policies of several English manufacturing firms.

fidence that the model would have similar degrees of success in explaining other series studied.

The presence of a considerable amount of cyclical and secular fluctuation in both price and physical volume series for southern pine lumber is evident from the data in Table 1, on which this study is based. At the high point in 1940, monthly sales were 500 per cent of their volume at the lowest point in 1933. For price, the figure is 250 per cent. In addition, the price and sales figures roughly follow the cyclical pattern typical of the 1930's, some of which presumably originates in the instability of the construction industry.

In addition to this large cyclical and secular movement there is evidence in the series in Table 1 of some seasonal movement, although it does not appear to be nearly as pronounced as the seasonal movements in the data for some of the other industries, particularly cement, presented in later chapters. Since the significance of seasonal movements for models of the type developed in this book will be discussed in some detail in the next chapter, a few remarks related specifically to the series at hand will suffice here. Seasonal movements in much of the lumber industry originate at least partly on the supply side, owing to the influence of weather conditions on lumbering operations. This does not, however, appear to be a significant factor in the case of southern pine. The fact that winters are relatively moderate in most areas where southern pine is cut, and the fact that by the 1930's all-weather roads were available in most of the important producing areas, mean that operations in this industry take place on a substantially year-round basis.[2] Seasonal fluctuations evidently originate largely on the demand side and presumably reflect the seasonal nature of construction activity. It will be suggested in the next chapter that the application of models of the type developed in this book is more plausible when seasonal movements originate on the demand rather than on the supply side.

In summary, we can say that these series display substantial fluctuations of a secular, cyclical, and seasonal nature. Furthermore, these movements show up in both the price and the physical volume series. Finally, according to Abramovitz's evidence, the cyclical behavior of inventories in this industry is more or less typical of the pattern in other industries for which data are available. In view of all this there is some reason to think that the success of the theoretical model in

_____

[2] For descriptive information pertaining to this industry the reader is referred to [14], [20], and [73].

TABLE 1

Price, Output, Sales, and Inventory
Series for Southern Pine Lumber

n	x_n	p_n	z_n	I_n	n	x_n	p_n	z_n	I_n
1933					**1936**				
J	232	13.55	232	2,250	J	513	23.04	515	1,929
F	218	13.43	208	2,240	F	493	23.16	480	1,916
M	282	13.73	242	2,201	M	587	24.13	540	1,869
A	311	14.26	247	2,136	A	585	24.65	571	1,855
M	418	14.93	310	2,028	M	579	25.71	582	1,858
J	456	18.98	341	1,913	J	552	25.88	578	1,884
J	540	22.85	511	1,884	J	574	24.97	625	1,935
A	514	23.46	522	1,892	A	648	24.01	619	1,906
S	430	25.76	449	1,911	S	661	24.13	630	1,875
O	441	26.73	478	1,949	O	699	24.69	661	1,837
N	464	25.85	474	1,959	N	643	23.61	651	1,845
D	378	27.17	430	2,002	D	701	25.81	661	1,805
1934					**1937**				
J	316	27.38	379	2,065	J	687	27.97	612	1,730
F	333	26.81	366	2,098	F	712	32.45	624	1,642
M	383	28.05	422	2,136	M	658	31.98	708	1,692
A	398	28.34	413	2,151	A	623	31.77	709	1,778
M	444	27.07	435	2,142	M	594	32.43	698	1,882
J	372	27.47	390	2,160	J	531	28.70	675	2,026
J	336	25.41	351	2,175	J	629	27.18	655	2,052
A	399	24.95	369	2,145	A	668	27.13	655	2,039
S	377	23.71	343	2,111	S	610	27.44	630	2,059
O	405	23.61	349	2,055	O	591	25.44	583	2,051
N	389	23.45	339	2,006	N	502	24.47	577	2,126
D	323	23.25	317	2,000	D	426	23.77	566	2,266
1935					**1938**				
J	398	21.85	413	2,015	J	576	23.28	543	2,234
F	385	20.99	405	2,035	F	537	24.50	540	2,241
M	441	21.27	437	2,031	M	620	23.87	635	2,256
A	482	21.37	456	2,005	A	515	23.48	543	2,284
M	630	22.10	477	1,852	M	554	23.17	585	2,315
J	576	23.23	499	1,775	J	558	21.33	541	2,298
J	545	24.39	553	1,783	J	691	21.55	594	2,201
A	543	23.99	550	1,790	A	701	22.52	670	2,170
S	515	22.61	529	1,804	S	666	22.70	685	2,189
O	569	22.18	579	1,814	O	722	22.56	658	2,125
N	503	21.18	540	1,851	N	655	25.37	605	2,075
D	446	21.63	522	1,927	D	578	25.64	597	2,094

TABLE 1 (*Continued*)

n	x_n	p_n	z_n	I_n	n	x_n	p_n	z_n	I_n
1939					1940				
J	599	25.08	605	2,100	J	639	28.69	669	1,949
F	550	25.13	551	2,101	F	643	27.86	708	2,014
M	669	24.84	660	2,092	M	784	27.95	807	2,037
A	616	25.13	623	2,099	A	835	27.36	826	2,028
M	705	24.77	697	2,091	M	893	27.14	856	1,991
J	687	24.91	652	2,056	J	758	26.86	763	1,996
J	625	24.39	641	2,052	J	877	26.61	793	1,912
A	739	24.68	705	2,068	A	1,012	27.75	914	1,814
S	751	27.08	640	1,907	S	1,070	31.42	937	1,681
O	782	31.15	686	1,811	O	1,174	34.02	1,049	1,556
N	649	30.47	663	1,825	N	1,010	35.55	931	1,477
D	532	27.94	626	1,919	D	884	34.80	910	1,503

explaining price and output behavior in this industry will be indicative of its potential success with other industry data.

2. Sources of Data

The data employed in this study are the 96 monthly estimates of each of the variables from January 1933 to December 1940. All the data are presented in Table 1. The series in the table were originally compiled by the Southern Pine Association and have been published by the Department of Commerce [78]. The price data, however, were generously furnished directly by the Southern Pine Association. These prices represent those of average southern pine sales f.o.b. mill, per 1,000 board feet, all grades and dimensions.

As was mentioned in the previous section, Abramovitz has included in his study the output sales and inventory data on which this chapter is based. The reader is referred to his work for a detailed discription of the compilation and coverage of these series.[3] The physical volume figures in the table are in millions of board feet.

All the series in the table are available before 1933 and after 1940. The reason for starting this study with 1933 is that the coverage of the physical volume series is much more complete and reliable commencing with that year than it was earlier. The reason for stopping with

[3] See [1], especially pp. 590–2.

1940 is of course that the effects of the United States defense program and World War II became considerable after that date.

3. Regression Analysis

In this section the model of price and output determination derived in Chapters 5, 6, and 7 is estimated from the data in Table 1 and the results are analyzed. It will be recalled that in Chapter 7 linear approximations of the price and output decision rules were derived which would be suitable for statistical estimation. These approximations are (9) and (10) of Chapter 7. Then in Section 3 of Chapter 7 it was argued that, although excluded from the model, a cost of changing price analogous to the cost of changing production might be present in the real world. If this were true, a lagged price term should appear in the price regression (10) of Chapter 7. Such a regression was included among those fitted to the data from the sampling experiments in Chapter 8, even though the decision rule from which the series were generated did not involve lagged price. In this and subsequent empirical applications price regressions with and without the lagged price term are also presented. Hence, there are three basic regressions to be estimated from the series for each industry, one involving production and the other two involving price as dependent variable.

In the sampling experiments in Chapter 8, the true expectations $x_n{}^e$ were known and hence could be included in the regressions as independent variables. With the exception of cement, considered in the next chapter, there are no recorded sales expectations for any of the industries studied in this book. Hence, it is necessary to use proxies of some kind for the expectation variables that appear in the regressions. In Section 4 of Chapter 3 one such proxy, which was designated the implicit expectations approach, was presented and discussed. This approach led to the use of the regressions (6b), (6d), and (6f) of Chapter 8, and these, as well as the regressions containing the true expectations, were fitted to the experimental data. Since these regressions are also to be used in this and subsequent chapters they are repeated here for easy reference.

$$z_n = \beta_{10} + \beta_{11}x_n + \beta_{12}z_{n-1} + \beta_{13}I_{n-1} + \epsilon_{1n} \tag{1}$$

$$p_n = \beta_{20} + \beta_{21}x_n + \beta_{22}z_n + \beta_{23}I_{n-1} + \beta_{24}p_{n-1} + \epsilon_{2n} \tag{2}$$

$$p_n = \beta_{30} + \beta_{31}x_n + \beta_{32}z_n + \beta_{33}I_{n-1} + \epsilon_{3n} \tag{3}$$

The least squares estimates of these equations from the data in Table 1 are

$$\hat{z}_n = 14.683 + 0.594x_n + 0.343z_{n-1} + 0.009I_{n-1} \tag{4}$$

$$(1.802) \quad (0.086) \qquad (0.095) \qquad (0.034)$$

$$R^2 = 0.769 \qquad\qquad d = 1.33$$

$$\hat{p}_n = 6.971 + 0.764x_n - 0.572z_n - 0.286I_{n-1} + 0.910p_{n-1} \tag{5}$$

$$(0.651) \quad (0.062) \qquad (0.063) \qquad (0.021) \qquad (0.034)$$

$$R^2 = 0.980 \qquad\qquad d = 1.57$$

$$\hat{p}_n = 21.354 + 0.525x_n + 0.900z_n - 0.224I_{n-1} \tag{6}$$

$$(8.720) \quad (0.354) \qquad (0.352) \qquad (0.120)$$

$$R^2 = 0.403$$

Before discussing the economic implications of these estimates we should make a few remarks of a statistical nature. First, each of the coefficients in (4), (5), and (6) except one is larger in absolute value than its standard error, shown in brackets below the coefficient to which it refers. Excluding the last equation (6) each coefficient except one is larger in absolute value than three times its standard error. Second, the residuals in each of the three equations show strong evidence of positive autocorrelation.[4] The d-statistic for (4) is significant at the 1 per cent level, and that for (5) is significant at the 5 per cent level. Although not computed, the d-statistic for (6) is almost certainly at least as significant as is that for (5). These tests suggest that it might be desirable to refit (1) to (3) using some transformation of the variables such as first differences. Although some experimental calculations of this sort have been made for these data, and for the data used in subsequent chapters, the results are not sufficiently satisfactory to warrant systematic recalculation. In the first place, some of the coefficients are implausible and unstable. For example, it is easy to show that taking first differences biases downward the estimates

---

[4] The statistic by which residuals from least squares regression equations are tested for first-order autocorrelation is the "d-statistic," due to Durbin and Watson. Tables of significance are presented in [21]. It is a test of the null hypothesis that $\rho = 0$ when the true residuals ϵ_n are generated by $\epsilon_n = \rho\epsilon_{n-1} + \eta_n$, where η_n is nonautocorrelated.

of the coefficients in (1) and (2) of those variables that are lagged values of the dependent variables. Furthermore, taking first differences of (1) to (3) does not always eliminate the autocorrelation of residuals, since the d-statistics sometimes still show significant positive autocorrelation among residuals even when the estimates and residuals are obtained from first differences. All of this undoubtedly results from the fact that, when the period of observation is as short as a month, a great deal of autocorrelation is certain to be present among residuals as well as among the variables included in the analysis. Furthermore, the fact that the autocorrelation is not always removed by taking first differences shows that higher-order autocorrelation is present.

To what extent do the estimated equations (4) to (6) verify the decision models developed in earlier chapters? Consider first the production equation (4). The coefficients of x_n and z_{n-1} are positive and significant. This is what would be expected intuitively and what is predicted by the theoretical model. It is also what was found in the sampling experiments, at least when x_n had an exogenous component. That x_n has a large exogenous component [5] in these data seems clear. Presumably the large movements in x_n during the sample period are mostly to be explained by cyclical and secular movements in the economy as a whole rather than by movements in the price of southern pine lumber. Furthermore, the coefficient of x_n is larger than that found for x_n in the sampling experiments, but smaller than that found for x_n^e. This fact suggests that x_n may be a better proxy for expected sales in this series than was true in the sampling experiments. The coefficient of I_{n-1}, however, is nonsignificant and positive. This contradicts both intuition and the implications of the theoretical model. To say that a large value of I_{n-1} should not, for fixed x_n and z_{n-1}, persuade firms to reduce z_n, violates common sense.

Within the context of the industry there are two probable reasons for this finding. One is that, as Abramovitz found,[6] durable inventories generally, and those in southern pine particularly, tend to conform inversely to cycles in production and shipments. Abramovitz points out that this is because the costs arising from deterioration and obsolescence are relatively small for inventories of basic durables, which makes it relatively unimportant for firms to adjust inventories quickly

---

[5] Exogenous here and elsewhere in this book means exogenous to the industry and not necessarily to the economy as a whole.

[6] See Chapter 11 of [1].

when sales change. Although the argument has some force and should persuade us to believe that in these circumstances the effect of inventory on production may be small, it is not completely convincing. Reference to equation (8) of Chapter 7 shows that even if there is no inventory carrying cost, that is, $r = 0$ in that equation, the coefficient of I_{n-1} is not zero. The size of this coefficient depends not only on carrying cost, which is the cost of a high inventory, but also on shortage cost, the cost of a low inventory, k in the equation. Indeed, as can easily be seen from the equation, if there were no carrying cost, no shortage cost, and no cost of changing production, β_{13} would be minus one. It is interesting to note here that the inventory fluctuations recorded in Table 1 are surprisingly small. The largest value of I in the sample exceeds the smallest value by only 50 per cent, suggesting that in this industry it may be rather costly to let inventory get far out of line, contrary to Abramovitz's conjecture. However, this is inconclusive. The observed amplitude of inventory fluctuations depends on other parameters of the model, such as the cost of changing production, as well as on storage cost and on the pattern of expectational errors.

The second likely explanation has to do with the vertical structure of the southern pine industry during the 1930's. In Table 1, x_n and p_n refer to quantities and prices of sales by lumber mills to lumber wholesalers or to final users of lumber. Likewise, I_n refers to inventory held by the mills. Frequently, however, the mills did not own the standing timber and the decision to cut was made by the owner of the land on which the timber stood. Therefore z_n refers to a decision made by the owner of the trees, whereas x_n, I_n, and p_n refer to decisions, or results of decisions, made one stage further up in the vertical structure, by the lumber mill. The effect of a large I_{n-1} is presumably that the mill lowers the price it is willing to pay to the owner of the land on which it cuts timber. The effect of I_{n-1} on z_n is indirect, working through an intermediate market rather than through a single integrated firm, and it is likely that the partial correlation between these two variables over a period as short as a month is very small. Although these intermediate prices are not available, they are presumably closely related to the prices, recorded in Table 1, at which mills sold their lumber. In this connection it is interesting to note that I_{n-1} has a small but significant effect on p_n in (5) and (6). The possibility that recorded values of the four variables p_n, x_n, z_n, and I_n do not all refer to decisions, or consequences of decisions, made by the same group of firms, plagues the user of such series. Fortunately, it does not, to the best of my knowledge, arise again in the three succeeding studies.

Turn now to the price equations (5) and (6). Whereas (4) explained just over three-quarters of the observed variance in z_n, (5) explains 98 per cent of the observed variance of p_n. Furthermore, a large part of this explanation is lost if the term in lagged price is excluded from the regression. Equation (6) explains less than half as much of the variance of p_n as does (5). This fact contrasts with the results found in the sampling experiments and strongly suggests that lagged price appears in the true decision rule in this industry, in contrast with the decision rule from which the sampling experiments were generated. If it is accepted that (5) contains the correct independent variables, then it can be said that each coefficient has the right sign. It was argued in Section 4 of Chapter 7 that when x_n^e contains an exogenous component, its coefficient should be positive. Furthermore, this was found to be the case in the experimental data in Chapter 8. No significance can be attached to the absolute magnitude of b_{21} because p_n and x_n are measured in different units. However, the fact that b_{21} is more than ten times as large as its standard error suggests that x_n is a better proxy for x_n^e in these data than was true in the sampling data. Likewise, it was predicted in Section 4 of Chapter 7, on the basis of the theoretical model, that large values of z_n and I_{n-1} would have a depressing effect on p_n; this was found in the sampling experiments when the correct variables were included in the price regressions. Hence, the fact that z_n and I_{n-1}, have negative coefficients in (5) is in accord with a priori expectations. Of course, the fact that lagged price has a positive and large coefficient accords with expectations based either on intuition or on theoretical considerations of the role of lagged price in a decision model with a cost of changing price.

Some further insights into the processes at work in these series can be obtained by considering the raw, that is, zero-order, correlations between the variables. These are presented in Table 2.

Turning first to Table 2a, we see that current production is strongly correlated with both current sales and lagged production. Current sales and lagged production, however, are themselves strongly correlated, and this multicollinearity reduces the effectiveness of the calculations in discriminating between the effects of x_n and z_{n-1} on z_n. Nevertheless, the coefficients of x_n and z_{n-1} in (4) exceed their respective standard errors by factors of three or more. Current pro-

TABLE 2

ZERO-ORDER CORRELATIONS FOR SOUTHERN PINE LUMBER DATA

2a Production Equation				
	z_n	x_n	z_{n-1}	I_{n-1}
z_n	..	0.857	0.805	−0.124
x_n	..	..	0.813	−0.114
z_{n-1}	..	..	..	−0.239
I_{n-1}	..	..	..	..

2b Price Equations					
	p_n	x_n	z_n	I_{n-1}	p_{n-1}
p_n	..	0.583	0.599	−0.226	0.956
x_n	..	..	0.857	−0.114	0.472
z_n	..	..	..	−0.124	0.575
I_{n-1}	..	..	..	..	−0.032
p_{n-1}	..	..	..	..	..

duction is negatively and much less strongly correlated with lagged inventory. Furthermore, this correlation is of the same sign and roughly the same order of magnitude as the correlation between lagged inventories and the other two explanatory variables in (4), current sales and lagged production. In this case, the correlation between I_{n-1} and z_n is accounted for by the fact that I_{n-1} is correlated with x_n and z_{n-1}, and these two in turn are correlated with z_n. The partial correlation of z_n and I_{n-1}, and hence the coefficient b_{13}, therefore becomes nonsignificant.

Turning to Table 2b, we see that current price is positively and rather strongly correlated with current sales and current production. As we saw in Table 2a, however, the fact that these two explanatory variables are themselves positively and strongly correlated introduces substantial multicollinearity into (5) and (6). Nevertheless, b_{21} and b_{22} are on the order of ten times their respective standard errors. Current price and lagged inventory are correlated negatively, though in this case the correlation of I_{n-1} with the other explanatory variables does not reduce to nonsignificance, even at the 1 per cent level in (5), its partial correlation with the dependent variable. Current and lagged prices are of course strongly and positively correlated. Indeed, lagged price explains 91.4 per cent of the variance of current price. Depending on what one wants to emphasize one can either say that the other variables in (5) improve this explanation by less than 10 per cent or that the other variables reduce the variance left unexplained by lagged price by nearly 80 per cent. Nevertheless, it is clear that a large part of the work in (5) is done by lagged price. It is also clear from this table that in (6), z_n is doing part of the job done by p_{n-1} in (5). We see that z_n and p_{n-1} are positively correlated, and z_n is also positively correlated with p_n. Hence, when p_{n-1} is excluded from the regression, as in (6), the coefficient of z_n becomes positive to explain some of the variation in p_n that is otherwise explained by p_{n-1}.

As a final source of insight into the forces at work in these series, consider Figures 1a and 1b. These figures portray the contribution of each of the explanatory variables to the prediction of the dependent variables in (4) and (5). Specifically, the top panel in each graph shows the observed value of the dependent variable (solid line) and the value calculated from the regression (dotted line). The panels below show the contribution of each independent variable to the calculated or predicted value of the dependent variable. For example, the second panel from the top in Figure 1a shows the value $0.594x_n$ for each n from February 1933 until December 1940. The bottom panel shows the error made in predicting the dependent variable and is therefore the difference between the two lines in the top panel. For example, $e_{1n} = z_n - \hat{z}_n$. All the vertical scales are the same within each figure. In the top panel in Figure 1a the errors made in predicting production do not seem to follow any simple pattern. There is no consistent tendency to underpredict peaks or troughs or to underpredict in general the absolute magnitudes of changes in z_n. Furthermore, although some peaks and troughs are predicted wrongly, there is no consistent tendency for predictions to lag observed turning points. The second and third panels from the top in Figure 1a show that x_n and z_{n-1} both make substantial contributions to $\hat{z}_n$, although x_n appears to do somewhat more of the work than does z_{n-1}. No discernible contribution is made by I_{n-1}.

Figure 1b shows a different pattern. Although (5) has a substantially higher multiple correlation coefficient than does (4), $\hat{p}_n$ shows a persistent tendency to underpredict in absolute magnitude the changes in p_n and to lag behind the turning points in p_n by one period. These facts are explained by the predominant role played by p_{n-1} in predicting p_n. That p_{n-1} makes the largest contribution to $\hat{p}_n$ is clearly indicated by the lower panels in Figure 1b. After p_{n-1}, the contributions of x_n, z_n, and I_{n-1} to $\hat{p}_n$ rank in that order in importance. There are four periods of rapid price rise in the data: starting in mid-1933, late 1936, late 1939, and mid-1940. The model fails to predict the spurt in prices in all four cases. That is, there is nothing in the behavior of current sales, current production, or lagged inventory that would suggest the imminence of a substantial price movement in any of these four periods. This suggests that in these series a variable of major importance in explaining price movements has been left out of the regressions. On the

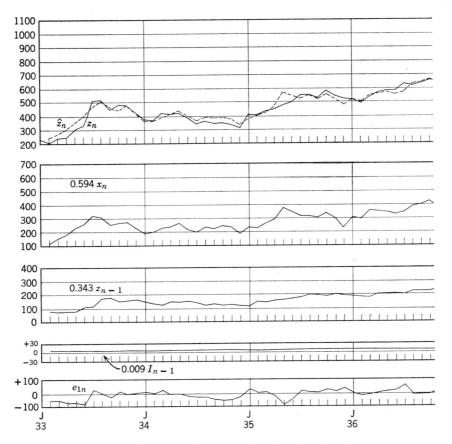

Figure 1a. Production Equation. Southern Pine Lumber.

basis of available evidence it is not possible to say what this excluded variable is. It may pertain to costs, to expectations, to the administrative process of price formation in the industry, to the length of the unit period covered by the data, to inaccuracies in the price series, or to other factors.

4. Comparison with Naive Forecasts

Independently of any theory of price and output determination, one cannot be very surprised that regressions such as (4) and (5) yield high multiple correlation coefficients. When a time period as short as a month is considered, price and output are bound to be

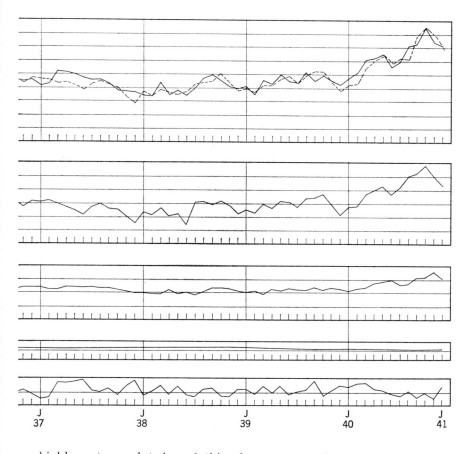

highly autocorrelated, and this alone ensures that (1) and (2) will provide good "fits." On the other hand, the fact that a large part of the explanations of z_n and p_n come from z_{n-1} and p_{n-1} respectively does not imply that the theory is wrong or unhelpful. In fact, one of the implications of the theory is that price and output should be autocorrelated. The model simply interprets this autocorrelation as arising from, among other things, the cost involved in changing these variables rapidly.

Nevertheless, one feels intuitively that if a theory is to be very useful it should have more predictive power than some simple method, involving no elaborate calculations, to explain or forecast the variable in question. For this reason the comparison is frequently made [7] between

[7] See [26] and [60] for examples.

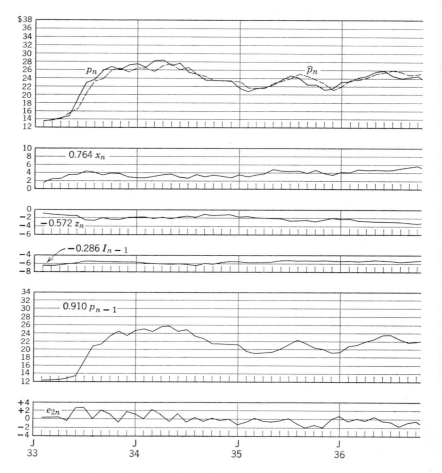

Figure 1b. Price Equation. Southern Pine Lumber.

the predictive power of the theory and that of some naive forecast of the variable the theory is intended to explain. For this purpose, the most commonly used naive forecast is the last previously observed value of the variable in question. In the present context, this means using z_{n-1} and p_{n-1} as naive forecasts of z_n and p_n respectively. In the case of z_n, a second variable that suggests itself as a basis for a naive forecast is x_n. Roughly, we might say that we need a separate theory of output adjustment only to the extent that changes in output are not the same

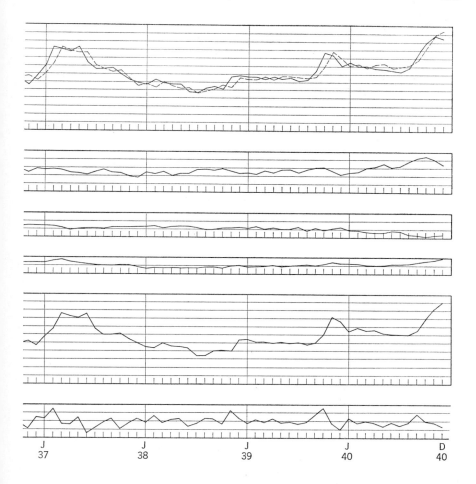

J
37
J
38
J
39
J
40
D
40

as changes in sales. The accuracy of the naive forecasts can then be compared with the accuracy of the values $\hat{z}_n$ and $\hat{p}_n$ calculated from the regressions.

Within this framework, there are still several ways in which one can use x_n and the lagged values of z_n and p_n to forecast z_n and p_n themselves. One natural procedure is to choose the linear function of z_{n-1} or x_n that provides the best forecast of z_n and the linear function of p_{n-1} that provides the best forecast of p_n. For these forecasts, the natural measure of accuracy of the forecast would be the percentage of the variance of z_n explained by this function of z_{n-1} or x_n and the percentage of the variance of p_n explained by this function of p_{n-1}. These percentages are of course just the squares of the relevant correlation coefficients in Tables 2a and 2b. Similarly, the percentages of the variances of z_n and p_n explained respectively by $\hat{z}_n$ and $\hat{p}_n$ are the R^2's from (4) and (5). Hence, this comparison can easily be made with calculations already presented and the results can be summarized as follows:

TABLE 3

COMPARISON BETWEEN REGRESSION FORECASTS AND NAIVE FORECASTS

	Naive Forecast	Naive Forecast	Regression Forecast
Production	$\mathrm{corr}^2(z_n, z_{n-1})$ = 0.648	$\mathrm{corr}^2(z_n, x_n)$ = 0.734	R^2[from (4)] = 0.769
Price	$\mathrm{corr}^2(p_n, p_{n-1})$ = 0.914		R^2[from (5)] = 0.980

Looking at the top line we can say that, of the part of the variance of z_n not explained by z_{n-1}, about one-third is explained by the regression (4); of the part of the variance of z_n not explained by x_n, about 15 per cent is explained by (4). Looking at the bottom line we can say that, of the part of the variance of p_n not explained by p_{n-1}, about three-quarters is explained by (5). Of course, on both lines all the naive forecasts explain large parts of the variances of the dependent variables.

For many purposes these naive forecasts are not naive enough. A much simpler forecast, which can be made with no calculation at all, is to take z_{n-1}, or x_n, itself as the forecast of z_n and p_{n-1} itself as the forecast of p_n. Using z_{n-1} and p_{n-1} involves forecasting "no change" for each variable and saying that the regressions are an improvement to the extent that they can forecast changes in the variables. Using x_n as a naive forecast of z_n is motivated as follows. Instead of predicting no change in production, this naive forecast predicts no change in inventory since, when production equals sales, inventory is constant. x_n is the value that z_n would assume if there were no inventory fluctuations, as in the case of the traditional static theory. Thus, $z_n - x_n$, or ΔI_n, measures the maximum scope that inventories or other variables not included in the static theory have for influencing z_n.

The commonly used measure of accuracy for these forecasts is the average absolute percentage error observed during the sample period. It should be noted that, in contrast with the correlation measure discussed above, there is no guarantee that, by this measure, the regressions provide better forecasts than the naive forecasts. The regressions minimize the unexplained variance of the dependent variable, whereas this measure of forecasting accuracy is concerned with absolute rather than with squared deviations and uses weights proportional to the reciprocal of the dependent variable. For the southern pine lumber data, these comparisons can be summarized as follows.

TABLE 4

COMPARISON BETWEEN REGRESSION FORECASTS AND NAIVE FORECASTS

	Naive Forecast	Naive Forecast	Regression Forecast
Production	$\frac{100}{N} \sum \frac{|z_n - z_{n-1}|}{z_n}$	$\frac{100}{n} \sum \frac{|z_n - x_n|}{z_n}$	$\frac{100}{n} \sum \frac{|z_n - \hat{z}_n|}{z_n}$
	$= 6.78$	$= 8.14$	$= 5.41$
Price	$\frac{100}{N} \sum \frac{|p_n - p_{n-1}|}{p_n}$		$\frac{100}{n} \sum \frac{|p_n - \hat{p}_n|}{p_n}$
	$= 3.98$		$= 3.36$

Looking first at the top line, we see that the average monthly change in production was 6.78 per cent, whereas on the average monthly sales differed from monthly production by 8.14 per cent. The use of the regression reduces the forecasting errors of the naive forecast z_{n-1} by about one-fifth; it reduces the forecasting errors of the naive forecast x_n by about one-third. Looking at the second line, we see that the average monthly change in price during the sample period was almost 4 per cent. Considering that the sample period starts in 1933, after the largest price declines resulting from the depression, this represents a substantial amount of price fluctuation. It does not suggest the degree of price rigidity displayed by many price series during this period. However, the regression (5) explains only about 15 per cent of this variation.

We can summarize the results presented in this section as follows:

In all cases, the naive forecasts predict quite well. This is to be expected since most economic variables do not change much from month to month. In most cases, the regressions reduce substantially the forecasting errors of the naive forecasts. For the price variable in the first comparison, involving unexplained variances, the regression does better relative to the naive forecast than it does in the second comparison, involving absolute percentage deviations.

Chapter 10

APPLICATION TO INDUSTRY DATA: CEMENT

1. Introduction

As a second empirical application of the model developed in Chapters 5, 6, and 7, this chapter presents a study of price, production and inventory fluctuations in the United States cement industry during a part of the interwar period.[1] Several factors have motivated the choice of this industry for study.

(i) Most important is the availability of long, unbroken series of price, production, sales, and inventory estimates for a homogeneous product whose physical characteristics remained virtually unchanged during the sample period. Because some of the relevant data are available only on a quarterly basis, the study in this chapter is conducted using a time period of a quarter of a year. Since the other three empirical studies reported in this book all employ a one-month time period, a comparison between the results in this chapter and those in the other empirical chapters provides some insight into the effects of temporal aggregation on the models employed in these studies.

(ii) There is also available for this industry an equally long series of quarterly published expectations, purporting to record the industry's aggregated sales forecast for each quarter. These make it possible

---

[1] The output, sales, inventory, and expectations (but not the price) data employed in this chapter are also the subject of an extensive investigation by Modigliani and Sauerlender, reported in [60]. Although the approach here is quite different from the one in their paper, this chapter has benefited greatly from their work. Reference is frequently made here to their paper for background material.

to test whether the published expectations provide a better explanation of the observed price and output decisions than do alternative
approaches, such as the implicit expectations hypothesis. The result
of this test provides some evidence as to which series, the published
or implicit expectations, provides the better estimate of the true expectations, those on which decisions are based.

(iii) There is a strong seasonal pattern in the production, sales,
and inventory series for cement. Now models designed to explain
seasonal fluctuations in production and inventories are usually quite
complicated. The model in the Modigliani-Sauerlender study, to take
the best example, is nonlinear, involves complicated transformations of
the variables, and employs a different decision rule for each season.
From a decision theory point of view, it is not clear why the presence
of seasonal fluctuations should require special treatment.[2] The only
apparent argument for special treatment is that seasonal movements
are relatively easy to predict in many series, such as sales, as compared
with other components of observed movements in the series. If this
is not true, then seasonal fluctuations are on the same footing as fluctuations resulting from other factors, such as inventory cycles, and no
one suggests that the presence of these factors requires the use of special kinds of decision rules.[3]

It is certainly true that the presence or absence of considerable
uncertainty makes an important difference in the analysis of price
and production decisions. All the models in this book are based on
this assumption. But what is important is the predictability of the
variable itself, not of particular components of the variable, such as
seasonal factors. It is by no means clear, at least to the writer, that
variables with strong seasonal patterns are in any sense easier to pre-

[2] One should distinguish between seasonal influences on the supply and demand
sides. A seasonal effect on the supply side would show up in one or more of the
costs entering the profit function. For example, the cost of shipping on Lake
Superior becomes prohibitive during the winter months. This means that the form
of the cost function varies with the season. The remarks in the text are intended
to apply exclusively to seasonal influences on the demand side.

[3] Of course the presence of seasonal movements in sales will affect expectations,
and therefore the price and output decisions taken, even in the models used in this
book. The question at issue is whether the form of the decision rule should be
changed if seasonal movements are present. As Modigliani and Hohn have
shown [59], seasonality considerations, among others, may determine the effective
planning horizon. In this sense they clearly affect the form of the decision rule,
but not in a way that is different from the effect of any other cyclical movement
in the series.

dict than nonseasonal variables. This might be the case if seasonality consisted of a simple symmetrical, additive sinusoidal function with a period of 12 months, but there is little evidence that this is so. Furthermore, although seasonality was not introduced explicitly, the decision model developed in Chapters 5 and 6 suggests that this is not a major influence in the making of price and output decisions. For example, the demonstration in Section 2 of Chapter 6 that under certain conditions all expectations more than one period in advance are irrelevant to current decisions shows that, at least in these circumstances, seasonal considerations are irrelevant. In summary, the most that can be said is that the matter is unclear. It is therefore extremely important to discover whether the simple nonseasonal model (represented by (9) and (10) of Chapter 7) provides noticeably poorer explanations of decisions in seasonal industries than do more complicated models that take explicit account of seasonal factors. If not, the gain in simplicity is considerable. Unless there is an important seasonal variation in the form of the decision rule, the attempt to treat each of, for instance, four seasons separately throws away a considerable amount of information.

All the data employed in this chapter are presented in Table 1. The published expectations are denoted by $\bar{x}_n^e$. (See also Figures 1 and 2 in Section 3.) The output, sales, expectations, and inventory series show clearly the seasonal pattern discussed in the last paragraph. This seasonal movement is very large, shipments in the best quarter of the year typically being about 100 per cent larger than shipments in the worst quarter of the year. The same series also show the cyclical pattern typical of the 1930's. The peak sales year covered by the series was 1928, after which sales fell off steadily except for seasonal movements until they reached a trough in 1933. Sales in 1933 were about one-third of their 1928 volume. After 1933 there was a gradual recovery, interrupted somewhat in 1938. By 1941, however, sales were still somewhat short of their 1928 volume. The inventory data in Table 1 also display cyclical movements broadly typical of those in durable goods during the period covered. Again, the basic reference is Chapter 11 of Abramovitz's study [1], where inventory movements in cement are compared with those in other major durable commodities.

The price series, which covers only the shorter period 1933 to 1941, tells a quite different story. Here there is no discernible seasonal pattern and no reflection of the cyclical movements that dominated the 1930's. Furthermore, the series displays very little price variation

TABLE 1

CEMENT INDUSTRY DATA

		$\bar{x}_n{}^e$	x_n	z_n	I_n	p_n
1927	III	642	602	532	140	
	IV	432	399	436	225	
1928	I	260	232	288	274	
	II	556	507	483	250	
	III	639	623	541	168	
	IV	392	392	448	228	
1929	I	240	213	284	297	
	II	568	490	467	275	
	III	682	633	531	173	
	IV	439	359	420	237	
1930	I	247	208	279	306	
	II	556	493	480	294	
	III	646	585	510	219	
	IV	351	301	340	258	
1931	I	194	170	208	297	
	II	472	415	394	276	
	III	538	444	395	227	
	IV	246	237	249	243	
1932	I	156	105	138	275	
	II	366	238	203	241	
	III	328	299	237	179	
	IV	181	164	186	204	
1933	I	99	83	94	213	83.5
	II	187	196	182	199	83.6
	III	242	212	225	212	92.6
	IV	136	150	133	196	92.9
1934	I	94	113	132	214	93.4
	II	236	238	239	216	92.7
	III	233	235	237	217	93.2
	IV	145	172	169	215	93.2
1935	I	111	107	106	213	92.8
	II	235	213	231	231	93.1
	III	257	237	224	218	92.8
	IV	173	193	204	229	92.3
1936	I	124	143	124	211	92.4
	II	244	329	311	193	92.4
	III	281	371	364	187	92.4
	IV	220	283	324	226	91.6

TABLE 1 (*Continued*)

		$\bar{x}_n{}^e$	x_n	z_n	I_n	p_n
1937	I	155	177	209	256	89.2
	II	377	348	332	240	89.1
	III	430	373	347	214	88.8
	IV	311	242	277	249	88.9
1938	I	149	162	143	230	89.8
	II	329	294	289	225	90.0
	III	364	337	325	214	90.9
	IV	257	272	298	239	90.6
1939	I	180	192	190	238	91.1
	II	327	351	328	215	91.5
	III	362	383	370	202	91.4
	IV	285	298	331	234	91.3
1940	I	201	165	192	261	91.3
	II	382	373	352	240	90.5
	III	424	422	381	199	90.6
	IV	343	343	379	234	90.8
1941	I	203	254	280	260	90.8
	II	450	463	422	219	91.5
	III	553	528	485	176	92.1
	IV	412	431	454	199	93.1

of any kind during this period, the average quarterly change, ignoring sign, being about 0.7 per cent. Indeed, there is only one substantial price movement recorded during the eight years covered by the series, a rise of about 10 per cent in the third quarter of 1933. It is interesting to note that each of the four empirical price series studied in this book displays a sharp rise about the second and third quarters of 1933. A sharp upward spurt during the early days of the New Deal is indeed typical of almost all recorded price indexes, whether wholesale or retail. Apparently, this price movement is to be explained generally by the policies and attitudes of the administration at that time. At least, there is nothing in the sales, inventory, or production data for the firms studied in this book that would permit one to predict this rise in prices.

2. Sources of Data

The data used in this chapter are quarterly estimates of production, sales, inventory, sales expectations, and price in the United States cement industry during part of the interwar period. The physical volume data cover the period from the third quarter of 1927 to the end of 1941, inclusive, with 58 observations in each series.

The production, sales, and inventory series are taken from [78] and [79] for the relevant years. The figures are given there on a monthly basis in thousands of barrels of cement. However, since the expectations data described below are available only on a quarterly basis, the other series are aggregated to a comparable basis and the entire study is carried out using quarterly totals. The inventory series of course represents end-of-quarter levels. For computational purposes all the physical volume data are rounded to the nearest hundred thousand barrels to give the three-digit figures in Table 1. That there are some slight discrepancies in these figures is indicated by the failure of the identity $z_n - x_n = \Delta I_n$ to hold in every period. However, the discrepancies are small, and when the figures are rounded to the extent of those in the table they are negligible. Therefore the original uncorrected data are used in the computations. All the physical volume figures are direct estimates and do not involve deflation by the price index.

Somewhat more detailed comment is required concerning the series of published sales expectations in the first column of Table 1. The forecasts on which this series is based were originally compiled by the Regional Shippers Advisory Boards and published by the Car Service Division of the Association of American Railroads in a quarterly publication entitled "National Forecast of the Regional Shippers Advisory Boards." The forecasts were, and are, made primarily by transportation managers of producing firms, to assist railroads in allocating freight cars to meet the shipping requirements of firms in different regions of the country. These "carloading forecasts," and the number of carloads actually shipped, have been studied extensively elsewhere (see [28], [60] and particularly the thorough study by Ferber [26], from which the carloadings data for this study were taken). Therefore the nature, accuracy, and limitations of these forecasts need not be reviewed extensively here. The main interest in this study, however, is not in the accuracy of the forecasts, but rather in testing whether the forecasts provide better explanations of the observed price and production decisions than does the implicit expectations hypothesis. In order to do this the carloadings forecasts must be placed on a comparable basis with the data in columns 2 to 4 of Table 1.

As pointed out by Modigliani and Sauerlender, discrepancies between the carloadings forecasts and actual shipments can result from three sources: (a) An error in predicting the fraction of sales that go by rail; (b) An error in predicting the number of barrels per carload; (c) An error in predicting shipments themselves. The procedure followed here is the conservative one of assuming error types (a) and (b) to be zero. If this is true then the shipments forecast is the carloadings forecast multiplied by the ratio of actual shipments to actual carloadings. In symbols, if $\bar{x}_n{}^e$ is the shipments forecast derived from the carloadings forecasts, then

$$\bar{x}_n{}^e = (\text{carloadings forecast in } n) \frac{(\text{actual shipments in } n)}{(\text{actual carloadings in } n)}$$

The figures in column 1 are the values of $\bar{x}_n{}^e$ computed in this way. This differs slightly from the procedure followed by Modigliani and Sauerlender.

One of the purposes of this chapter is to discover the relative explanatory value of published and implicit expectations. Why might the published expectations not be the true expectations? Several reasons have been, or can be, suggested (see the discussion by Modigliani and Sauerlender).

(i) The carloadings forecast for each quarter is normally made about six weeks before the end of the preceeding quarter. If the firm makes its production plans at a different time, these plans may be made on the basis of different forecasts. For example, if production plans are made nearer the beginning of the quarter to which they apply, more information and better forecasts may be available for decision purposes than those which have been recorded.

(ii) If the period of time during which production plans are normally unchanged is less than a quarter of a year, the forecasts relevant to production plans would be for this shorter period. Of course the whole idea of a fixed production period is an approximation, since a sufficiently drastic change in circumstances induces firms to alter production at almost any time. Aside from this, three months is a long time, and many firms normally vary production at much shorter intervals.

(iii) It has been suggested that transportation managers, who normally make the carloadings forecasts, may not have available all the information concerning future sales that is accessible to those who actually make production decisions in the firms. It is frequently true, as we argued in Chapter 3, that forecasts that firms record are partly intended as goals to stimulate personnel to improved performance. When production decisions are made by production executives the

official forecasts are sometimes corrected, at least informally, to allow
for this bias.   There is evidently a possibility that transportation
managers might rely heavily on the official forecasts, not having the
information necessary to make the needed corrections.   In addition
to this, the shipping firms evidently have a certain incentive to bias
their forecasts in an upward direction.   The cost of an overforecast
is mainly borne by the railroads in the form of unused freight cars.
The cost of an underforecast may be borne by the shipping firm itself
in the form of an inability to make desired shipments.   If either of
these factors is present, it should show up in the recorded expectations
in a tendency to overforecast shipments.   In the forecasts recorded in
Table 1 there is in fact an optimistic bias amounting to an average
overforecast of 5 per cent.

(iv) Finally, some doubts are raised by the fact that published
forecasts of this type are frequently less accurate on the average than
various naive forecasts.   This fact has been observed for virtually
all industries included in the carloadings forecasts before World War
II, and to a smaller extent in more recent years (see Ferber [26], pp.
57–64).   The naive forecast employed in this comparison is usually
the realized value of the shipments variable in the previous period,
possibly corrected in some mechanical way for seasonal movements.
The argument, as developed in Chapter 3, is that the naive forecast
is available at virtually no cost, and therefore no rational decision
maker would employ a more costly forecasting procedure unless it
yielded more accurate forecasts on the average.   Thus, if the published
forecasts are less accurate on the average than the naive forecasts,
we have evidence that the published forecasts are not the true expectations on which decisions are based.   In practice, this argument is not
conclusive, because the naive forecast is not available when the
production decision must normally be made.   Normally production
decisions must be taken somewhat before the beginning of the
period to which they apply, and therefore some of the information
utilized in the naive forecast is not available when the decision is made.
Hence the fact that the naive forecast is more accurate than the published forecast does not necessarily mean that it is irrational to use
the latter for decision purposes.

For all these reasons there is doubt about whether the recorded
forecasts adequately represent the true expectations.   It is therefore
of interest to see whether the published expectations provide better
explanations of observed decisions than do other estimates of expected
sales.   If so, there is evidence that the published expectations are good

estimates of the true expectations. If not, the suspicion that the published expectations are not those utilized for decision purposes is strengthened.

The price series used in this study consists of index numbers of wholesale prices of portland cement, compiled by the Bureau of Labor Statistics as a component of the United States Wholesale Price Index. The index is published in [81]. Its compilation and coverage are described in detail in [80]. This index is available on a monthly basis since 1933; it was computed only annually before that time. Therefore the price equations reported in the next section are computed from data for the period from 1933 to 1941, inclusive, with thirty-six observations in all. Thus, the sample for the price equations is slightly less than two-thirds the size of the sample for the production equations. For the purposes of this study, the monthly price index is converted to quarterly averages. The price quotations on which the index is based represent delivered prices to dealers of portland cement as reported by a sample of manufacturers throughout the country. There appears to be no significant difference between the coverage of the price and sales data reported in Table 1. Portland cement constitutes 99 per cent of cement volume and value. Furthermore, both price and sales series represent estimates for the country as a whole, taking into account regional variations. Finally, the price series represents prices reported by manufacturers, and it is the shipments by manufacturers that are represented by the sales figures. Questions can of course be raised concerning the accuracy of the reported prices. For example, it is often suggested that many official indexes underestimate the extent of price decreases during the 1930's because they do not take sufficient account of price discounts and hidden price concessions during periods of depression. The extreme inflexibility of the prices in Table 1 creates a strong suspicion that this is the case for the cement price index. It is not, however, possible to make any corrections for this or other sources of inaccuracy.

3. Regression Analysis

The regression estimates and analysis presented in this section for the cement industry data in Table 1 are basically the same as those presented in Section 3 of the last chapter for the southern pine lumber industry. The difference is that for this industry, but not for the other three industries considered, we have available a second specification of the regression models using the shippers' forecasts as an index of expectations. We therefore have the following two sets of regression

equations to be estimated from the data in Table 1. Using the implicit
expectations approach

$$z_n = \beta_{10} + \beta_{11}x_n + \beta_{12}z_{n-1} + \beta_{13}I_{n-1} + \epsilon_{1n} \tag{1}$$

$$p_n = \beta_{20} + \beta_{21}x_n + \beta_{22}z_n + \beta_{23}I_{n-1} + \beta_{24}p_{n-1} + \epsilon_{2n} \tag{2}$$

$$p_n = \beta_{30} + \beta_{31}x_n + \beta_{32}z_n + \beta_{33}I_{n-1} + \epsilon_{3n} \tag{3}$$

Using the published expectations

$$z_n = \beta'_{10} + \beta'_{11}\bar{x}_n^e + \beta'_{12}z_{n-1} + \beta'_{13}I_{n-1} + \epsilon'_{1n} \tag{4}$$

$$p_n = \beta'_{20} + \beta'_{21}\bar{x}_n^e + \beta'_{22}z_n + \beta'_{23}I_{n-1} + \beta'_{24}p_{n-1} + \epsilon'_{2n} \tag{5}$$

$$p_n = \beta'_{30} + \beta'_{31}\bar{x}_n^e + \beta'_{32}z_n + \beta'_{33}I_{n-1} + \epsilon'_{3n} \tag{6}$$

The least squares estimates of these equations are

$$\hat{z}_n = 68.8 \quad + 0.791\ x_n + 0.156\ z_{n-1} - 0.234\ I_{n-1} \tag{7}$$

$$(6.179) \quad (0.068) \qquad (0.026) \qquad (0.068)$$

$$R^2 = 0.964 \qquad d = 1.98$$

$$\hat{p}_n = 47.7 \quad + 0.015\ x_n - 0.016\ z_n - 0.032\ I_{n-1} + 0.560\ p_{n-1} \tag{8}$$

$$(9.988) \quad (0.012) \qquad (0.013) \qquad (0.014) \qquad (0.100)$$

$$R^2 = 0.571 \qquad d = 2.27$$

$$\hat{p}_n = 100.6 \quad + 0.015\ x_n - 0.017\ z_n - 0.040\ I_{n-1} \tag{9}$$

$$(4.531) \quad (0.017) \qquad (0.018) \qquad (0.019)$$

$$R^2 = 0.124$$

and

$$\hat{z}_n = -48.8 \quad + 0.255\ \bar{x}_n^e + 0.478\ z_{n-1} + 0.553\ I_{n-1} \tag{10}$$

$$(20.273) \quad (0.102) \qquad (0.121) \qquad (0.132)$$

$$R^2 = 0.531 \qquad d = 1.82$$

$$\hat{p}_n = 43.9 \quad + 0.008\ \bar{x}_n^e - 0.010\ z_n - 0.031\ I_{n-1} + 0.601\ p_{n-1}$$

$$(9.850) \quad (0.007) \qquad (0.007) \qquad (0.014) \qquad (0.105) \quad (11)$$

$$R^2 = 0.572 \qquad d = 2.22$$

$$\hat{p}_n = 97.1 \quad - 0.003\ \bar{x}_n^e + 0.002\ z_n - 0.025\ I_{n-1} \tag{12}$$

$$(4.523) \quad (0.009) \qquad (0.010) \qquad (0.020)$$

$$R^2 = 0.105$$

Some statistical remarks can be made before discussing the substantive implications of these estimates. In the two production equations (7) and (10), each coefficient is significant at the 5 per cent level and most exceed their standard errors by at least five times. In the price equations, the coefficients of x_n, $\bar{x}_n^e$, and z_n are about the same absolute size as their standard errors and none is significant at the 5 per cent level. The inventory terms in the price equations are all significant at the 5 per cent level, except in the last equation in which the inventory term is just slightly larger than its standard error. The terms in lagged price are both significant at the 1 per cent level. All four d-statistics are nonsignificant at the 5 per cent level. The fact that the d-statistics are typically very significant in the other empirical chapters in this book, but nonsignificant in this chapter, suggests that autocorrelated residuals are much less common among quarterly data than among monthly data. Probably, a quarter of a year is about the shortest time interval that can be employed with economic data without incurring a serious risk of finding autocorrelated residuals.

Turning first to equations (10), (11), and (12), employing the published expectations, we see that there are several unsatisfactory results. In the production equation (10) the coefficients of $\bar{x}_n^e$ and z_{n-1} have the correct signs and are significant, the former at the 5 per cent level and the latter at the 1 per cent level, although the coefficient of $\bar{x}_n^e$ is smaller than any of the coefficients of current sales estimated in this or the other empirical chapters. However, b_{13} is positive and significant at the 1 per cent level. Since this contradicts not only the theory presented here, but also one's intuition about the effect of inventory on production, it strongly suggests that (10) misspecifies the production decision in a critical way. This is discussed further below. It should also be noted that (10) has the smallest multiple correlation coefficient of any of the empirical production equations presented in this book, explaining just over half of the observed variance in production. Turning to the price equations, (11) and (12), there are again some unsatisfactory results. All the coefficients in (11) have the correct signs, although only that of lagged price is as much as three times as large as its standard error. However, (11) explains only a little more than half of the variance of p_n and of this more than 80 per cent is accounted for by the lagged price term, since (12), which excludes p_{n-1}, has an R^2 less than one-fifth as large as has (11). In (12), the coefficients of $\bar{x}_n^e$ and z_n have signs opposite to the corresponding terms in (11), but in (12) these coefficients are definitely nonsignificant at the 5 per cent level. In summary, it must be said that the regressions containing the published expectations perform very unimpressively and clearly exclude one or more major factors in the determination of prices and outputs.

In the first set of estimates (7), (8), and (9), employing current sales as a proxy for expectations, most but not all of the results are satisfactory. The production equation (7) is better in every respect than (10). All the coefficients have the correct signs and are significant at the one per cent level. Furthermore, (7) explains 96.4 per cent of the variance of z_n, almost 40 per cent more than is explained by (10). A comparison between (7) and (10) strongly suggests that the deficiency in (10) is that the shippers' forecasts are poor indexes of sales expectations. Their use explains production decisions much less adequately than does the implicit expectations approach and leads to less plausible estimates of the coefficients in the production equation. On the other hand, the fact that (7) does well by the usual tests is only limited evidence in favor of the model on which it is based. It is clear that if a sufficiently long unit period is adopted, the correlation between current sales and current production can be made almost arbitrarily close to one. Thus, if the high R^2 in (7) results mainly from a high correlation between z_n and x_n, (7) is somewhat less impressive evidence in favor of the approach advocated in this book. However, in the absence of more information as to the correct unit period, it is not possible to know how much weight should be given to this argument. One more factor concerning (7) should be noted. It is clear from equation (8) of Chapter 7 that the more stable price is, the better is (1) as an approximation of the true production decision rule. Thus, the fact that the price series included in this study shows only very small movements may help to explain why (7) has such a large R^2. It cannot, however, explain why (7) has so much larger an R^2 than has (10).

Inspection of the price equations (8) and (9) indicates that, in contrast with the production regressions, the implicit approach provides very little improvement over the use of the published expectations in explaining price movements. In fact, (8) is remarkably similar to (11). Corresponding coefficients have the same sign, are of similar magnitude, and are significant at about the same levels. Furthermore, (8) and (11) have almost exactly the same R^2's. The effect of estimating the price equation without the term in lagged price (9) is almost exactly the same as it is in the regression using the published expectations. As was true of (12) in comparison with (11), (9) has an R^2 about one-fifth the size of the R^2 for (8). In slight contrast with (12), the coefficients in (9) retain their correct signs and one, that of lagged inventory, is significant at the 5 per cent level. This investigation suggests very strongly that lagged price appears in the true price decision rule in the cement industry, a conclusion also reached in the other industry studies presented in this book. The distressing thing is that it fails to show that any of the other included variables have much influence on price. The conclusion seems practically inescapable that there is almost no information in the sales, production, or inventory data for the cement industry that would permit one to explain or predict the rather small price movements in the cement industry during the 1930's. To what extent the reason lies in inadequacies in the price series and to what extent in the absence from the model of important price-determining factors, is hard to say. The fact that the price movements recorded during the sample period are not only hard to explain but also are very small suggests that a major factor missing from the model must be the administrative procedure by which prices were set. It is well known that a basing point system of delivered price quotations was employed effectively in the cement industry during the 1930's.[4] The use of such administered price schemes presumably has the effect of reducing or removing the influence of short-run movements in sales, inventories, and so on, on price. Thus, to the extent that such collusive agreements are effective these variables should be expected to have little effect on price and in this sense the model is consistent with the observed behavior of price in this industry.

Consider next the following tables of raw correlations between the variables employed in the regressions (7) to (12).

Looking first at Table 2a, we see that z_n is much more strongly correlated with x_n than with $\bar{x}_n^e$. Indeed, the square of the raw correlation between z_n and x_n, 0.935, is only about three percentage points smaller than R^2 in (7). This confirms the suspicion stated above that the high R^2 in (7) is largely accounted for by the strong correlation between production and sales. Table 2a also makes it clear why the inventory coefficient is positive in (10), but has the correct negative sign in (7). Lagged inventory is more strongly correlated with $\bar{x}_n^e$ than with x_n and, since $\bar{x}_n^e$ is less strongly correlated with z_n than is

---

[4] See [45].

TABLE 2

ZERO-ORDER CORRELATIONS FOR CEMENT DATA

	2a Production Equations						2b Price Equations				
	z_n	x_n	$\bar{x}_n^e$	z_{n-1}	I_{n-1}		p_n	x_n	$\bar{x}_n^e$	z_n	I_{n-1}	p_{n-1}
z_n	..	0.967	0.626	0.616	0.209	p_n	..	−0.078	−0.138	−0.061	−0.324	0.690
x_n	..	..	..	0.492	0.329	x_n	..	..	..	0.967	0.329	−0.047
$\bar{x}_n^e$	..	..	..	0.492	0.414	$\bar{x}_n^e$	..	..	..	0.626	0.414	−0.147
z_{n-1}	..	..	..	..	−0.165	z_n	..	..	..	..	0.209	−0.028
I_{n-1}	..	..	..	..	..	I_{n-1}	..	..	..	..	..	−0.114
						p_{n-1}	..	..	..	..	..	..

x_n, lagged inventory does part of the job in (10) which is done by x_n in (7).

Turning to Table 2b, we see that the correlations between p_n on the one hand and x_n, $\bar{x}_n^e$, and z_n on the other hand, are all negative and nearly zero. Aside from p_{n-1}, only I_{n-1} has any substantial correlation with p_n. In spite of these generally small correlations, the R^2's in (8) and (11) exceed the squared correlation between p_n and p_{n-1} by almost ten percentage points (0.571 and 0.572 as compared with 0.476). The almost perfect correlation between z_n and x_n means that almost no reliability can be placed on the coefficients of these variables in (8) in sorting out the partial effects of z_n and x_n on p_n. It is interesting to note that $\bar{x}_n^e$ has a substantially stronger correlation with p_{n-1} than has x_n. This suggests that those who formulated the shippers' forecasts may have overestimated the extent to which a change in price would affect the demand for cement.

Figures 1 and 2 confirm several of the above observations and provide some new insights into the processes involved in these series. Figure 1a, portraying the production equation based on the published expectations, confirms the impression that equation (10) provides only a moderately good explanation of the observed production levels. In the early part of the sample period, $\hat{z}_n$ shows a tendency to underpredict z_n at seasonal peaks in z_n and to overpredict z_n at seasonal troughs in z_n. Later in the sample period, $\hat{z}_n$ predicts several seasonal turning points one period after they occur, and it fails altogether to predict one or two of them. Looking at the lower panels of Figure 1a, we see that both $\bar{x}_n^e$ and z_{n-1} make substantial contributions to $\hat{z}_n$ and that these contributions reinforce each other on the whole. It is interesting to note that, in spite of the obvious seasonal pattern in the error terms in the bottom panel of Figure 1a, the d-statistic for equation (10) fails to provide any evidence of first-order autocorrelation.

An inspection of Figure 2a, portraying the production equation based on implicit expectations, strengthens the impression that (7) is much more satisfactory than (10). A comparison between the top panels in Figures 1a and 2a shows that (7) provides much more accurate predictions of z_n than does (10). Equation (7) also predicts the seasonal turning points better than does (10). No turning points are missed, no false ones are predicted, and each is predicted in its correct quarter. The tendency found in (10) for $\hat{z}_n$ to underpredict the absolute changes in z_n at peaks and troughs of z_n is also absent from (7). Indeed, in the early years of the sample period there appears to

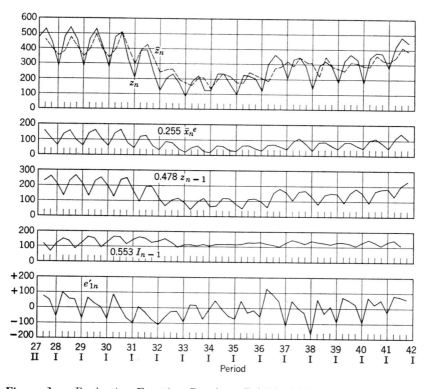

Figure 1a. Production Equation Based on Published Expectations. Cement.

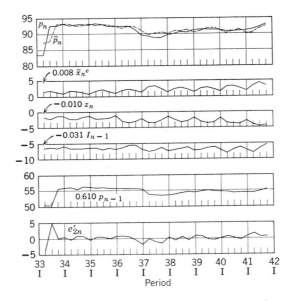

Figure 1b. Price Equation Based on Published Expectations. Cement.

be some tendency for $\hat{z}_n$ to overpredict z_n at peaks and to underpredict z_n at troughs; this is commented on below in Section 5. This tendency is absent during the later years of the sample period. The lower panels in Figure 2a confirm the finding that x_n plays a much more important role in (7) than does $\bar{x}_n^e$ in (10). These panels, when compared with corresponding panels in Figure 1a, show graphically that $\hat{z}_n$ in (7) is dominated by movements in x_n to a much greater extent than any term dominates $\hat{z}_n$ in (10). Finally, the error terms in Figure 2a, although on the average much smaller in absolute size than those in Figure 1a, again display a fairly clear seasonal pattern, particularly during the early years of the period. That neither of the d-statistics computed for (7) and (10) indicate autocorrelation among the regression residuals suggests that this statistic is quite insensitive to the presence of other kinds of autocorrelation among regression residuals than the simple first-order pattern for which it explicitly tests.

Figures 1b and 2b show clearly that the two price equations (8) and (11) have the same virtues and the same defects. Indeed, the graphs of the two equations are almost identical because each of these equations is dominated by its term in p_{n-1}. It is obviously for this reason that changes in $\hat{p}_n$ tend to lag changes in p_n by one period in both graphs. It is also clear from these graphs that the contribution of z_n to $\hat{p}_n$ tends to be offset by the contributions of x_n and $\bar{x}_n{}^e$. This is because, as can be seen from Table 2, z_n is positively correlated with both x_n and $\bar{x}_n{}^e$, whereas the coefficients of z_n on the one hand and of x_n and $\bar{x}_n{}^e$ on the other hand have opposite signs.

4. Comparison with Naive Forecasts

As in the previous chapter, the predictive accuracy of some of the regressions in the previous section is compared with that of several naive forecasts of the variable in question. Again, two sets of comparisons are made, one employing correlations among the variables and the other employing average absolute percentage differences between forecasts and realized values of the variables. The only difference between the comparisons made in this section and those made

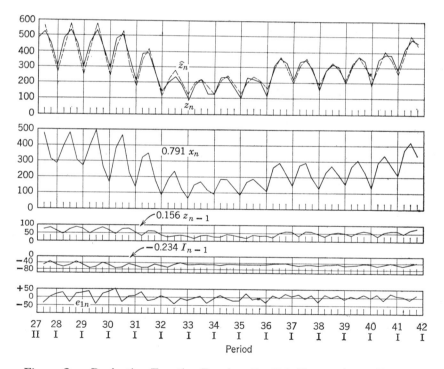

Figure 2a. Production Equation Based on Implicit Expectations. Cement.

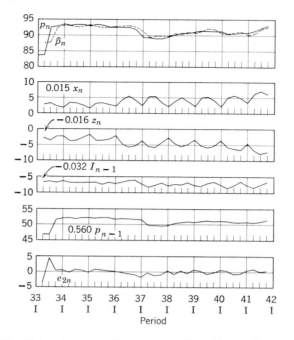

Figure 2b.   Price Equation Based on Implicit Expectations.   Cement.

in the previous chapter is that here we have available a new set of forecasts based on the published expectations.   In addition to x_n and z_{n-1}, we also have $\bar{x}_n^e$ from which to derive a naive forecast of z_n. Likewise, we have second regression forecasts for z_n and p_n, based on $\bar{x}_n^e$.   The naive forecasts of p_n are exactly the same as those in the previous chapter.   Aside from alterations resulting from these extra comparisons the following discussion parallels that of Chapter 9, Section 4, and the reader is referred there for a description and discussion of the measures used.

The first set of comparisons, based on the correlation coefficients, is summarized in Table 3.   From the top part of the table it is clear that the regression equation (7) provides a much better forecast of z_n than do any of the naive forecasts except possibly x_n.   We see that z_{n-1} is a very poor forecasting variable for z_n, explaining less than 40 per cent of the variance of z_n.   Equation (7) explains more than twice as much of the variance of z_n as does z_{n-1}.   The large seasonal movement in z_n is the obvious cause of the poor forecasting performance of z_{n-1}. Likewise, $\bar{x}_n^e$ explains only a little more of the variance of z_n than does z_{n-1}. However, x_n explains 93.5 per cent of the variance of z_n, and R^2 in (7) exceeds this by only three percentage points. Alternatively, one can say that (7) explains 30 per cent of the variance of z_n that is left unexplained by x_n. Turning to the bottom part of the table it can be seen that p_{n-1} explains somewhat more of the variance of p_n than does z_{n-1} of z_n (48 per cent as compared with 38 per cent). The two price regressions, however, represent only a small improvement on this naive forecast, explaining just less than 20 per cent of the part of the variance of p_n that is left unexplained by p_{n-1}.

Table 4 summarizes the second comparison between naive forecasts and regression forecasts. Here the naive forecasts are simply the values assumed by the forecasting variables themselves, and the measure of forecasting error is the average absolute percentage forecasting error.

From the top of Table 4 we see that this comparison ranks the naive forecasts of z_n in the same order as do the data in Table 3. In both tables, z_{n-1} yields the worst naive forecast, $\bar{x}_n^e$ a better one, and x_n the best. Likewise, in both tables the regression forecast in (7),

TABLE 3

Comparison of Regression Forecasts with Naive Forecasts

Variable	Forecast Based on	Naive Forecast	Naive Forecast	Regression Forecast
Production	Published Expectations	$\mathrm{corr}^2(z_n, z_{n-1})$ $= 0.379$	$\mathrm{corr}^2(z_n, \bar{x}_n^e)$ $= 0.392$	R^2[from (10)] $= 0.531$
	Implicit Expectations		$\mathrm{corr}^2(z_n, x_n)$ $= 0.935$	R^2[from (7)] $= 0.964$
Price	Published Expectations	$\mathrm{corr}^2(p_n, p_{n-1})$ $= 0.476$		R^2[from (11)] $= 0.572$
	Implicit Expectations			R^2[from (8)] $= 0.571$

TABLE 4

COMPARISON OF REGRESSION FORECASTS WITH NAIVE FORECASTS

Variable	Forecast Based on	Naive Forecast	Naive Forecast	Regression Forecast
Production	Published Expectations	$\dfrac{100}{N}\sum \dfrac{\lvert z_n - z_{n-1}\rvert}{z_n}$ $= 34.22$	$\dfrac{100}{N}\sum \dfrac{\lvert z_n - \bar{x}_n^e\rvert}{z_n}$ $= 14.00$	$\dfrac{100}{N}\sum \dfrac{\lvert z_n - \hat{z}_n\rvert}{z_n}$ $= 23.46$
	Implicit Expectations		$\dfrac{100}{N}\sum \dfrac{\lvert z_n - x_n\rvert}{z_n}$ $= 10.09$	$\dfrac{100}{N}\sum \dfrac{\lvert z_n - \hat{z}_n\rvert}{z_n}$ $= 7.33$
Price	Published Expectations	$\dfrac{100}{N}\sum \dfrac{\lvert p_n - p_{n-1}\rvert}{p_n}$ $= 0.71$		$\dfrac{100}{N}\sum \dfrac{\lvert p_n - \hat{p}_n\rvert}{p_n}$ $= 0.78$
	Implicit Expectations			$\dfrac{100}{N}\sum \dfrac{\lvert p_n - \hat{p}_n\rvert}{p_n}$ $= 0.73$

using implicit expectations, is much more accurate than the regression forecast from (10), using the published expectations. The regression forecasts of production based on (7) have an average error less than one-fourth of the average error of the naive forecast z_{n-1}, about half of the average error of the naive forecast $\bar{x}_n^e$, and about 70 per cent of the average error of the naive forecast x_n. The only striking thing about the table is that, by this measure, the regression forecast using (10), based on the published expectations, is much less accurate than the naive forecast $\bar{x}_n^e$. This means that $\bar{x}_n^e$ itself forms a better forecast of z_n than does the regression in which $\bar{x}_n^e$ appears. The explanation of this paradoxical result can be seen in the top panel of Figure 1a. There it appears that the largest forecasting errors in (10) occur in the periods in which z_n is smallest. Since the measure of accuracy employed in Table 4 weights forecasting errors by the reciprocal of z_n, this measure gives greater weight than does the regression to precisely those errors that were largest in (10).

The bottom of Table 4 provides no way of choosing between the naive forecast p_{n-1} of p_n and either of the regression forecasts (11) and (8). The measure of accuracy fails to indicate even the slight measure of superiority of the price regressions over the naive forecast shown in Table 3. The basic reason that the regressions give results so similar to the naive forecast is the one stated above, that the regressions are dominated by p_{n-1}, which is also the source of the naive forecast. The bottom of Table 4 also provides striking confirmation of the assertion that cement prices changed very little during the sample period, the average absolute percentage change per quarter being only 0.71 per cent.

The results of this and the previous section can be briefly summarized as follows. By every standard, the implicit expectations approach provides a more satisfactory explanation of the production variable and a more satisfactory basis for forecasting than do the published expectations. This fact strongly suggests that there are important differences between the shippers' forecasts and the expectations on which decisions are based. Neither approach, however, provides a satisfactory explanation or forecast of the price variable. The evidence appears to be strong that the few substantial changes observed in the cement price index during the sample period were not mainly based on current market conditions.

5. Estimates of Expectations

The purpose of this section is to present and analyze the implicit expectations for the cement industry. These estimates of expectations were defined and discussed generally in Section 4 of Chapter 3. In Section 5 of Chapter 8 the calculation of the implicit demand expectations from estimates of the price and production regressions (1) to (3) was discussed in detail. In that section, the implicit expectations for the data from the sampling experiments were presented and analyzed. It was shown that, at least for the experimental data, the implicit expectations were poor estimates of the true expectations. Because of this discouraging result, the implicit expectations are not presented for the other three empirical studies in this book. However, for the cement industry the shippers' forecasts are available as an alternative estimate of demand expectations, and it is interesting to compare the implicit expectations with them. Although both are likely to be rather inaccurate estimates of the true expectations, the comparison may suggest that one is a more plausible estimate than the other. In any case, it is worthwhile to analyze the implicit expectations for one set of empirical series simply to illustrate the kind of series they yield.

The implicit expectations for the cement industry are calculated exactly as they were for the experimental data, and the reader is referred to Section 5 of Chapter 8 for details of the procedure. Again, only the production regression (7) is used in the calculations even though other estimates are in principle available from (8) and (9). The reason is the same as it was for the experimental data, that the coefficients of current sales in the price regressions, b_{21} and b_{31}, are not significant at the 5 per cent level.

The observed sales, the implicit expectations, and the shippers' forecasts are shown in Figure 3. As in Chapter 8, $\hat{x}_{1n}^e$ is the implicit expectation calculated from the production regression in period n. There are a number of interesting differences between the implicit expectations and the shippers' forecasts, most of which lend plausibility to the implicit expectations.

First, the implicit expectations are somewhat more accurate forecasts of actual sales than are the shippers' forecasts. Measuring the

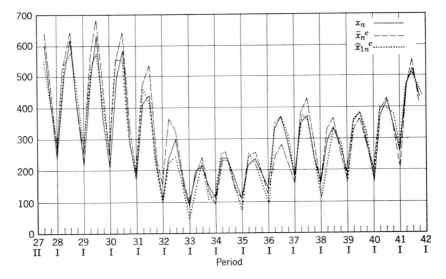

Figure 3. Sales and Expectations: Cement.

accuracy of the estimates by the average absolute percentage forecasting error, we have

$$\frac{100}{N} \sum \frac{|\bar{x}_n^e - x_n|}{x_n} = 10.72 \quad \text{and} \quad \frac{100}{N} \sum \frac{|\hat{x}_{1n}^e - x_n|}{x_n} = 9.38$$

Thus, the implicit expectations involve about 10 per cent smaller forecasting errors on the average than the shippers' forecasts. It must be emphasized that these measures show the average difference between the estimated expectations and the observed sales, not the average difference between the estimated expectations and the actual expectations, since the last variable is unknown. Therefore, the smaller value of this measure does not necessarily indicate the better estimate of expectations. All that can be said is that, if either $\hat{x}_{1n}^e$ or $\bar{x}_n^e$ is a good estimate of expectations, then for that variable this measure should be neither very small nor very large, since a good estimate of expectations should have an average forecasting error approximately equal to that of the true expectations. Intuitively, the above estimates of an average forecasting error of about 10 per cent seem plausible, although the two estimates are so close together that it is not possible to say that one is more plausible than the other. Given the difficulties in forecasting economic phenomena of this type three or more months in advance, one should probably be suspicious of estimates of expectations that are much more accurate forecasts of sales than are these.

Second, the two estimates display different temporal patterns in their forecasting errors, and this difference adds some plausibility to the implicit expectations. Since the forecasting errors of the implicit expectations are proportional to the observed regression residuals [from (7) of Chapter 8], the two have the same autoregressive structure. In particular, if the regression residuals are nonautocorrelated, so are the forecasting errors of the implicit expectations. Therefore the evidence that the former are not autocorrelated, from the significance test of the d-statistic for (7), is evidence that the latter are not either. Indeed, the first-order autocorrelation coefficient for the regression residuals, and hence for the forecasting errors of the implicit expectations, is only 0.09. This result is in keeping with the argument in Chapter 3, Section 3, that a rational decision maker who can calculate his own expectational errors will use whatever information they contain to make better forecasts, and therefore observed forecasting errors should be nonautocorrelated. However, not much can be made of this finding since, as will be concluded in Chapter 13, the absence of autocorrelation among the regression residuals in this chapter is probably mainly the result of the use of quarterly rather than monthly data and not of basic structural properties of the decision process. Nevertheless, it is interesting to note that the absence of autocorrelation is not a property of the forecasting errors of the shippers' forecasts. The first-order autocorrelation coefficient for these forecasting errors is 0.50, which is significant at the 5 per cent level.[5]

The final remarks in this section have to do with the cyclical patterns of the implicit expectations and the shippers' forecasts. As can be seen in Figure 3, both forecast seasonal turning points fairly well. A difference between the two is that the shippers' forecasts overpredict sales for the entire year in very bad years and underpredict sales for the year in very good years, whereas the implicit expectations display no such pattern. Thus, the implicit expectations suggest a much more rapid adjustment of expectations to major cyclical movements in sales than is suggested by the shippers' forecasts.

There is, however, a more interesting difference. Whereas the shippers' forecasts reveal an optimistic bias at seasonal peaks and troughs during most of the sample period, the implicit expectations undergo a change during the period. During the early years, until about 1931, there is a tendency for the implicit expectations to underpredict both the heights of peaks and the depths of troughs. This is a commonly observed phenomenon, sometimes called the regressive nature of expectations. It reflects the fact, shown in Figure 1a, that the production regression (7) overpredicts the heights of peaks and the depths of troughs during this period. The interpretation that the implicit approach gives to this observation is that the regression predicts the production $\hat{z}_n$ justified by the actual sales; $\hat{z}_n$ is (an estimate of) what would have been produced if realized sales had been correctly anticipated. If actual production z_n falls short of the predicted level

---

[5] Since the forecasting errors of the implicit expectations are calculated from the regression residuals, the d-statistic is the appropriate statistic for testing the significance of their autocorrelation, the autocorrelation coefficient for regression residuals being biased toward zero. However, the forecasting errors for the shippers' forecasts are not estimated from regression residuals and therefore the usual significance test of the autocorrelation coefficient can be used.

$\hat{z}_n$, it is interpreted to happen because firms forecast a smaller volume of sales than materializes. This is what happened at the peaks of sales during the early part of the sample period. At the troughs, the reverse occurred. Firms forecast more sales than materialized and therefore produced more than was justified by actual sales.

After the onset of the worst of the depression this pattern changed. After about 1932, there is a tendency for the implicit expectations to overpredict the heights of peaks and the depths of troughs in sales. Particularly at the troughs, expectations tend to be more pessimistic than events warranted. This fact is reflected by observed production levels that are less than the levels predicted by the regression, particularly at troughs, during the later period. The interpretation is that at this time firms expected sales to fall further than they did and therefore produced less than events justified. The suggestion here is that events had a destabilizing effect on expectations. From having been slightly optimistic about the seasonal declines in sales during the prosperous 1920's, firms became more pessimistic on this score during the depressed 1930's. These calculations suggest that expectations tend to be stabilizing during periods of prosperity and stability but destabilizing during periods of depression and instability. Having been caught once in a cataclysmic downturn they did not anticipate, firms came to expect worse disasters and cut back production accordingly. This idea of a "boom and bust" psychology is not new of course. Some older business cycle theories were based on it,[6] and it is sometimes suggested that one of the reasons for the stability of the post-World War II United States economy is that a period of stability induces firms to anticipate further stability, which in turn induces them to follow policies that promote stability. What is new is the idea that the boom and bust psychology can be directly observed in statistical series.

Of course, there are many other factors that might account for the cyclical behavior of the implicit expectations, including such possibilities as the cyclical behavior of components of regression residuals from sources quite different from expectational errors. Nevertheless, the fact that there are undoubtedly major components of regression residuals from sources other than expectational errors does not invalidate the interpretation given in the preceding paragraph. What has

[6] See [29].

to be shown is that components of residuals from other sources underwent the peculiar cyclical change observed above. It is rather striking that, according to the estimates in Figure 3, no seasonal trough in cement sales was higher than anticipated by firms before 1933, whereas every seasonal trough was higher than anticipated for all the very bad years of the depression, 1933, 1934, 1935, 1936, and 1938.

Chapter 11

APPLICATION TO INDUSTRY DATA: PNEUMATIC TIRES

1. Introduction

This chapter presents the third of four empirical studies employing the model of price and output determination developed in Chapters 5 to 8. The data selected for study in this chapter are monthly series of sales, output, inventory, and price for the United States rubber tire industry covering the period 1929 to 1940 inclusive. As in the other empirical chapters in this book, the primary reason for selecting this industry is the availability of long, comprehensive, reliable series of the relevant statistics. Aside from this, however, the tire industry is an interesting subject of study. Rubber tires were a major durable commodity in the 1930's, produced by a highly oligopolistic industry whose market structure changed little during the period, and sold in part to another oligopolistic industry, the automobile manufacturers. In addition, the commodity is unusually well defined, making the problems of market delineation and coverage negligible, and it has a natural unit of measurement and relatively unchanging physical characteristics and technology during the sample period.

The data analyzed in this chapter are presented in Table 1 (see also Figure 1 in Section 3). As was also true of the data for the southern pine lumber and cement industries, the physical volume series in Table 1 are included in the Abramovitz study to which reference has already been made several times (see [1], Chapter 11). Again, the reader is referred there for a comparison of the pattern of inventory fluctuations in the tire industry with that of inventory fluctuations in other major durable items during the 1930's. Here, only a few general

TABLE I

Date	x_n	z_n	I_n	p_n
J 29	621	630	1286	58.0
F	495	662	1453	56.0
M	629	709	1533	55.8
A	684	738	1587	55.8
M	674	760	1673	55.2
J	680	657	1650	55.2
J	736	589	1503	55.2
A	735	566	1334	55.2
S	562	435	1207	55.2
O	465	462	1204	55.1
N	334	342	1213	54.9
D	324	295	1184	55.2
J 30	441	449	1192	50.1
F	420	469	1241	50.1
M	472	482	1251	50.1
A	509	566	1308	50.1
M	522	557	1343	49.9
J	529	514	1328	47.2
J	545	398	1181	46.9
A	518	422	1085	46.9
S	441	337	981	46.9
O	350	349	980	46.9
N	283	263	960	46.4
D	336	276	900	46.4
J 31	374	370	896	45.4
F	340	398	954	44.9
M	412	459	1001	44.9
A	493	495	1003	44.9
M	542	570	1031	44.9
J	557	571	1045	43.6
J	546	493	992	43.6
A	496	394	890	43.6
S	393	319	816	43.6
O	285	299	830	43.6
N	289	251	792	43.6
D	278	264	778	39.8
J 32	325	338	791	38.5
F	255	381	917	38.5
M	295	366	988	38.5
A	370	367	985	38.5
M	426	379	938	38.5
J	1007	569	500	39.1
J	240	360	620	39.7
A	266	312	666	39.7
S	308	252	610	41.5
O	180	258	688	43.2
N	171	228	745	43.2
D	182	201	764	43.2

TABLE I (*Continued*)

Date	x_n	z_n	I_n	p_n
J 33	260	220	724	43.2
F	229	243	739	48.3
M	209	200	729	39.7
A	365	313	677	34.9
M	518	517	676	35.8
J	631	617	662	38.1
J	550	572	684	39.4
A	471	494	707	41.5
S	350	403	760	41.5
O	254	340	846	41.5
N	220	299	925	41.5
D	353	317	889	41.5
J 34	322	401	968	41.5
F	329	434	1073	42.0
M	422	514	1165	42.7
A	444	477	1198	42.7
M	533	448	1113	42.7
J	523	432	1022	42.7
J	416	338	944	42.7
A	431	357	870	42.7
S	318	290	842	42.7
O	301	325	866	42.7
N	319	331	878	45.6
D	311	379	946	45.6
J 35	366	460	1040	45.6
F	329	442	1153	45.6
M	420	435	1168	44.4
A	514	446	1100	44.0
M	407	420	1113	42.5
J	426	389	1076	42.5
J	545	354	885	42.5
A	474	370	781	42.5
S	330	378	829	42.5
O	406	406	829	42.5
N	393	389	825	42.5
D	408	403	820	42.5
J 36	374	414	860	42.6
F	310	343	893	42.6
M	372	355	876	42.6
A	473	468	871	42.6
M	563	481	789	45.6
J	559	526	756	45.6
J	554	545	747	45.7
A	480	485	752	45.7
S	370	487	869	45.7
O	394	499	974	45.7
N	408	478	1044	48.3
D	484	512	1072	48.3

TABLE I (*Continued*)

Date	x_n	z_n	I_n	p_n
J 37	435	460	1097	49.7
F	422	512	1187	51.1
M	558	571	1200	53.1
A	536	554	1218	54.4
M	518	514	1214	54.4
J	520	514	1208	54.4
J	501	417	1124	54.4
A	471	390	1043	54.4
S	339	416	1120	54.4
O	381	384	1123	54.4
N	364	298	1057	56.2
D	305	286	1038	56.2
J 38	250	293	1081	56.2
F	234	209	1056	56.2
M	286	282	1052	56.2
A	321	283	1014	56.2
M	335	273	952	56.2
J	398	293	847	56.2
J	391	348	804	56.2
A	401	419	822	56.2
S	394	374	802	56.2
O	422	444	824	56.2
N	454	422	792	57.8
D	428	498	862	57.8
J 39	415	439	886	
F	373	435	948	
M	457	505	996	
A	446	431	981	
M	480	453	954	
J	585	494	863	
J	514	461	810	59.5
A	499	558	869	59.5
S	566	505	808	59.5
O	516	546	838	59.5
N	428	482	892	55.7
D	473	448	867	55.7
J 40	427	495	935	
F	414	493	1014	
M	437	502	1079	
A	504	512	1087	
M	576	541	1052	
J	680	515	887	
J	432	480	935	59.4
A	412	468	991	59.4
S	446	439	984	59.4
O	553	510	941	59.4
N	497	472	916	59.2
D	499	496	913	59.2

remarks are included to indicate the overall outline of fluctuations in the tire industry during the sample period. To begin with, a considerable amount of seasonal movement is evident in the production, sales, and inventory data in the table, particularly during the first half of the sample period. The seasonal trough in production occurs near the end of the year, and the seasonal peak usually occurs about mid-spring. Turning points in inventories roughly coincide with those in production, and turning points in sales usually lag those in production by a month or so. Production in the month of the seasonal peak is typically about twice its volume in the month of the seasonal trough. These seasonal movements are substantial and roughly similar to those found in the cement industry, although they are considerably less extreme in the present case. However, during the second half of the sample period the seasonal pattern becomes much more confused, and seasonal turning points are much harder to identify. It is of some importance to note here that the seasonal pattern becomes confused not only in the production and inventory series, but also in the sales series. This fact suggests that the changed seasonal pattern in production represents at least partly a response to a changed seasonal pattern in sales instead of a basic change in the form of the response of production to the seasonal movement of sales. The significance of this distinction is that a change in the form of the response implies a change in the parameters of the production decision rule itself, whereas a change in the pattern of production in response to a change in the pattern of sales is consistent with a decision rule with unchanged parameters. As was also true of the price series for southern pine lumber and cement, the price series in Table 1 displays no noticeable seasonal movement.

The overall cyclical fluctuations of the 1930's stand out clearly in these series. The largest calendar-year sales volume during the sample period occurred in 1929. By 1933 sales had fallen to about two-thirds of their 1929 volume. There followed a gradual, sustained rise in sales, except for seasonal fluctuations, until the 1937 to 1938 recession when annual sales again fell substantially. Another gradual rise continued until the end of the sample period in 1940. By 1940 sales were still 15 per cent below their 1929 volume. The production series followed the same general cyclical pattern as did the sales series, though with somewhat diminished amplitude, indicating that inventories were allowed to act as a buffer and absorb some of the fluctuations in sales. The average monthly change in production, ignoring signs, is 11.6 per cent.

The price series in Table 1 displays a pattern somewhat distinct from that displayed by either of the empirical price series previously analyzed. On the whole, tire prices fluctuated less than southern pine lumber prices, but more than cement prices. The average monthly price change in the series in Table 1, ignoring sign, is 1.1 per cent. More striking is the fact that, from its peak in January 1929 the index of tire prices fell nearly 40 per cent to its trough in April 1933. By the end of the sample period the index was slightly above its initial level. Thus, this price series cannot be said to display the stickiness found in cement prices. The salient feature of this price index is not that it moved very little, but rather that the movements took place in large, infrequent, irregular jumps. In more than half of the periods included in the sample of prices there was no change in the index at all. Furthermore, more than half of the absolute amount by which the price index changed during the sample period was recorded in less than 10 per cent of the periods. In the early years of the sample there was some tendency for these large changes to occur at about the beginning of the calendar year. However, this was by no means always true and was hardly even a tendency in the later years of the sample. Thus, the explanation for the discrete nature of the observed price movements cannot be simply that the price decision period extended over several months. The presumption created by price series of this type is that major price changes were coordinated among the large producers of tires and that this fact accounts for the discrete nature of the price movements. It should be emphasized, however, that this is not the only hypothesis consistent with the evidence furnished by this index.

In any case, the presence or absence of coordination or collusion is indirectly relevant to this study. The model used here consists of a set of rules for optimum price and output policy in a monopolistic or imperfectly competitive firm. The relevance of collusive price setting, if any is present, is that such arrangements are frequently unresponsive to short run changes in sales, inventories, and so on. This fact may result from irrationality or from the difficulty of renegotiating such an agreement once it has been made. If unresponsiveness is present it strongly suggests that the model employed here, which relies for its explanatory power on such responsiveness, will explain or predict price changes badly.

2. Sources of Data

The data in Table 1 are all obtained from published sources. As was stated previously the sales, output, and inventory series are included in the Abramovitz study, and the reader is referred to [1], pp. 597–8 for a detailed description of the sources and coverage of these series. They were originally collected by the Rubber Manufacturers Association and have been published by the Department of Commerce.[1] The original data contain some internal inconsistencies since the identity $z_n - x_n = \Delta I_n$ fails to hold exactly. However, these discrepancies are small, averaging less than 1 per cent of shipments, and for the purpose of this study they were removed by redefining z_n from the above identity. The production column in Table 1 gives the redefined figures. The physical volume figures in the table are given in units of ten thousand tires. The coverage includes estimated industry totals of pneumatic automotive casings for cars, trucks, and buses. Excluded are tubes, solid tires, and pneumatic tires for motorcycles, bicycles and aviation, industrial and agricultural equipment. The data include tires both for original equipment and replacement purposes. Shipments of the latter category average two or three times those of the former. The physical volume series are all direct estimates rather than deflated value figures.

As was true of the price series used in the previous chapter, the price data in Table 1 are a component of the United States Wholesale Price Index.[2] In the present case, the data constitute the index for balloon tires (1926 = 100).

Several questions should be raised concerning the accuracy and coverage of this price index. In the first place, it is not known whether or not this index underestimates the extent of price decreases during

---

[1] Specific sources are as follows: 1929–1935, [78], May 1939, pp. 16–18; 1936–1937, [77], 1940, p. 149; 1938, furnished directly by the Office of Business Economics, Department of Commerce; 1939–1940, [77], 1942, p. 161.

[2] The entries are taken from [81]. Unfortunately the index is not available for the first six months of 1939 and the first six months of 1940. Therefore the price regressions in the next section are computed from a sample of 132 observations for each variable, 12 less than the full 144 observations on which the production regression is based.

the depression by failing to take adequate account of discounts and so on from "official" prices during periods of falling demand. This was suggested as probable in the case of the cement price index in the last chapter. However, in view of the substantial decline of almost 40 per cent recorded in the balloon tire index from 1929 to 1933 it seems unlikely to be a major factor here. In the second place, there are several small discrepancies and one major discrepancy between the coverage of the price series and the physical volume series in Table 1. The small discrepancies result from the fact that certain nonautomotive pneumatic tires, such as those for tractors and other farm equipment, are included in the price series but excluded from the physical volume series. Of course, to the extent that prices of tires for agricultural equipment bear a simple relationship, for example, linear or proportional, to prices of tires for automotive equipment, this fact has no importance. The major discrepancy results from the fact that the price index includes only tires sold to dealers for replacement purposes whereas, as we pointed out above, the physical volume series includes tires sold to automobile manufacturers for original equipment. It is known that shipments for replacement purposes were about three-quarters of total shipments covered by the series in Table 1 during the sample period. Therefore the available price index does represent the class of shipments that was quantitatively most important. Nevertheless, the price index excludes a major sales category that is included in the quantity series. Furthermore, this category is known to have prices systematically different from those of the sales included in the index, since tires are sold to automobile manufacturers for original equipment more cheaply than they are sold to dealers for replacement purposes. Again, to the extent that prices of original and replacement equipment bear a simple relationship to each other, the difference in coverage is irrelevant. It is not known to what extent this is true.

3. Regression Analysis

The three regressions to be estimated from the data in Table 1 are the same as those estimated from the data in the previous two chapters:

$$z_n = \beta_{10} + \beta_{11}x_n + \beta_{12}z_{n-1} + \beta_{13}I_{n-1} + \epsilon_{1n} \tag{1}$$

$$p_n = \beta_{20} + \beta_{21}x_n + \beta_{22}z_n + \beta_{23}I_{n-1} + \beta_{24}p_{n-1} + \epsilon_{2n} \tag{2}$$

$$p_n = \beta_{30} + \beta_{31}x_n + \beta_{32}z_n + \beta_{33}I_{n-1} + \epsilon_{3n} \tag{3}$$

The least squares estimates of these equations are

$$\hat{z}_n = 52.489 + 0.389\ x_n + 0.559\ z_{n-1} - 0.033\ I_{n-1} \tag{4}$$

$$(20.650)\quad (0.047)\qquad (0.053)\qquad\quad (0.023)$$

$$R^2 = 0.808 \qquad d = 1.39$$

$$\hat{p}_n = 0.157 + 0.001\ x_n + 0.001\ z_n - 0.001\ I_{n-1} + 1.005\ p_{n-1}$$

$$(0.837)\quad (0.001)\qquad (0.002)\qquad\quad (0.001)\qquad\quad (0.021) \tag{5}$$

$$R^2 = 0.968 \qquad d = 1.65$$

$$\hat{p}_n = 31.983 - 0.010\ x_n + 0.003\ z_n + 0.018\ I_{n-1} \tag{6}$$

$$(2.186)\quad (0.006)\qquad (0.006)\qquad\quad (0.002)$$

$$R^2 = 0.353$$

In these equations each coefficient except two, one in (5) and one in (6), is at least as large in absolute value as its standard error. The d-statistics strongly support the hypothesis of positive autocorrelation among the regression residuals. The d-statistic for (4) is significant at the 1 per cent level, and that for (5) is in the range of indeterminacy at the 5 per cent level.[3]

Each coefficient in the production equation (4) has the correct sign according to the theoretical arguments in Chapter 7 and the evidence of the sampling experiments in Chapter 8. The coefficients of current sales and lagged production are significant at the 5 per cent level, but that of lagged inventory is not significant at the 5 per cent level. As was true in the two preceding chapters, the coefficients of x_n and z_{n-1} sum to nearly one, and this is in accord with the a priori expectations established in Chapters 7 and 8. The relative magnitudes of b_{11} and b_{12} are, however, reversed in this chapter as compared with the other empirical chapters. In the other empirical estimates, b_{11} is substantially larger than b_{12}, reflecting the fact that x_n provides the major contribution to $\hat{z}_n$. In this case, however, b_{12} exceeds b_{11}, suggesting that z_{n-1} plays a more important role in this regression than in the production regressions estimated in the other empirical chapters. As was shown in Chapters 7 and 8, this fact is consistent with a relatively

---

[3] The tables provided by Durbin and Watson in [21] provide a range of values of d, on one side of which d is significant and on the other side of which d is not significant, but within which significance is not ascertained.

large cost of changing the rate of production. It was also found in Chapter 8 that b_{12} becomes large relative to b_{11} when x_n is a poor proxy for sales expectations. When this happens, b_{11} is biased downward, since there are then large errors of observation in the sales expectations variable, and z_{n-1} does part of the job done by the expectations variable when it can be estimated accurately. Thus, a second possible explanation for the unusually small value of b_{11} relative to b_{12} is that x_n is a relatively poor proxy for sales expectations in this industry. The small absolute value of b_{13} suggests that inventory is not a major factor in determining the rate of production in this industry. Finally, it should be noted that R^2, although substantial, is the next to smallest of the R^2's calculated for the four empirical production regressions like (4) in this book. It leaves unexplained 20 per cent of the variance of z_n. In summary, although (4) is fairly satisfactory, it appears that a factor of some importance, possibly having to do with sales expectations, has been omitted.

The price equations (5) and (6) are in many ways similar to those found in the last chapter for the cement industry. The coefficients of sales, production and lagged inventory in (5) are nonsignificant at the 5 per cent level. All except that of production have the correct sign, however. Again referring to (5), the coefficient of p_{n-1} is large, significant at the 1 per cent level and positive, as it should be. Furthermore (5) explains almost 97 per cent of the variance of p_n, an amount much greater than is explained by any of the price equations for the cement industry. As the smallness of the other coefficients suggests, most of this explanation is provided by the term in lagged price. In (6), which omits the lagged price term, R^2 falls by more than 60 percentage points to 0.353. In summary, although the price equation has a very large R^2 there appears to be relatively little information in the sales, output, and inventory variables that is useful in explaining or forecasting the substantial price movements recorded for the tire industry in Table 1. Indeed, since the coefficient of p_{n-1} in (5) is nearly one, this regression consists of little more than a naive extrapolation of the previous month's price. This suggests that (5) does badly at predicting turning points in price, an idea confirmed below. That price should be changed in large, discrete jumps at irregular intervals in an administered industry is not surprising. It is at least disappointing that these price changes do not to an important extent appear to result from cumulative movements in sales, inventories, and so on.

Table 2, showing the raw correlations between pairs of variables

TABLE 2 [4]

Zero-Order Correlations for Pneumatic Tire Data

	2a Production Equation					2b Price Equations			
	z_n	x_n	z_{n-1}	I_{n-1}		p_n	x_n	z_n	I_{n-1}	p_{n-1}.
z_n	..	0.814	0.847	0.438	p_n	..	0.211	0.215	0.500	0.976
x_n	..	..	0.702	0.514	x_n	..	..	0.809	0.531	0.187
z_{n-1}	..	..	..	0.531	z_n	..	..	..	0.464	0.200
I_{n-1}	..	..	..	..	I_{n-1}	..	..	..	..	0.429
					p_{n-1}	..	..	..	..	..

in equations (4) to (6), confirms and extends the assertions in the above paragraphs.

Table 2a confirms the impression obtained from (4) that z_{n-1} plays a larger role relative to x_n in the explanation of z_n here than it did in the two previous chapters. This is the only industry considered so far in which the correlation between z_n and z_{n-1} has exceeded that between z_n and x_n. Furthermore, the correlation between z_n and I_{n-1} is the strongest so far observed in the industry studies. The fact that, in spite of this, I_{n-1} has a small coefficient in absolute size in (4) is explained by the strong correlation between I_{n-1} and the other two explanatory variables.

Table 2b confirms the finding from (5) and (6) that p_{n-1} dominates the price regressions. Indeed, the squared correlation between p_n and p_{n-1} is almost as large as R^2 in (5). Not only is p_{n-1} much more strongly correlated with p_n than are x_n, z_n, and I_{n-1}, but also the correlations between p_{n-1} and the other explanatory variables in (5) are smaller than the correlations between pairs of the other explanatory variables themselves. This is shown by the fact that the entries in the last column of 2b are small compared with the entries in the interior positions of the table. For example, p_n is rather strongly correlated with I_{n-1} (0.500), but I_{n-1} is also strongly correlated with z_n and x_n, the result being that the partial correlation between p_n and I_{n-1}, and hence the sign of b_{23}, is negative. Likewise, the correlation between

---

[4] Small differences between correlations that are common to 2a and 2b result from the fact the correlations in 2b omit for all variables the 12 observations corresponding to those unavailable for p_n.

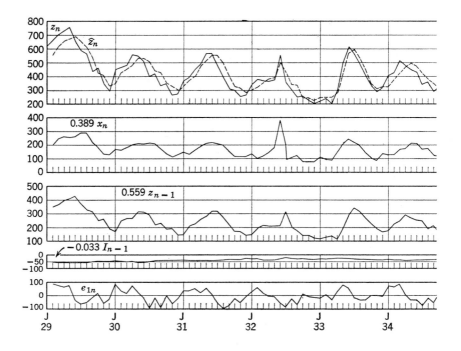

x_n and z_n is much larger than the correlation between either of these and p_n. All this means that a large part of the correlations between x_n, z_n, and I_{n-1} on the one hand and p_n on the other hand is to be explained by the large correlations among the former set of variables.

As in the previous empirical chapters, this section concludes with an examination of a set of graphs showing various components of the output and price regressions.

Figure 1a portrays this information for the production equation (4). Inspection of its panels supports the assertion that both x_n and z_{n-1} make major contributions to $\hat{z}_n$, whereas I_{n-1} makes only a negligible contribution. Comparison with analogous panels in the two preceding chapters attests to the fact that z_{n-1} is a more important factor in this production regression, relative to x_n, than it has been in the previously reported production regressions. The importance of z_{n-1} in the production regression is also indicated by the tendency for $\hat{z}_n$ to

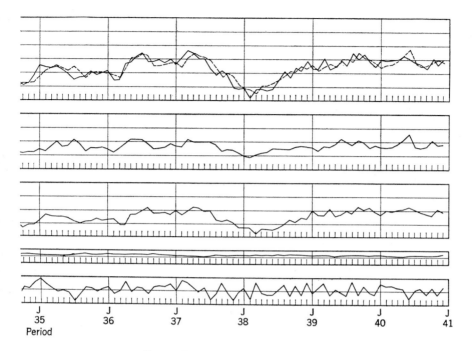

Figure 1a. Production Equation. Tires.

lag one period behind z_n, particularly during the first half of the sample period. Statistically, this tendency results from the high partial correlation between z_n and z_{n-1}. Economically, it suggests that some factor of importance in production planning in this industry may have been excluded from the regression.

One possibility is that production planning may have a seasonal component that is excluded from the decision model. The presence of such a seasonal component would mean that during seasonal troughs and upturns more would be produced than could be predicted on the basis of current sales and inventory because firms were adding to inventory in anticipation of rising future sales. Likewise, during periods of peak and declining sales, firms would produce less than would be predicted on the basis of current sales and inventory levels because firms were working off inventory in anticipation of seasonally declining sales. An inspection of Figure 1a shows that the results are consistent

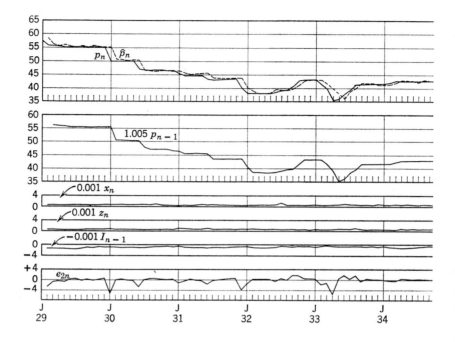

with this interpretation. There, $\hat{z}_n$ underpredicts z_n during seasonal upturns and $\hat{z}_n$ overpredicts z_n during seasonal downturns. One is tempted to conclude that the model employed here is not capable of accounting for seasonal movements in production, at least of the type encountered in this industry. However, this is not necessarily so. The seasonal pattern just described is of course no more than the policy of production smoothing in the face of fluctuations in sales and has been encountered in some degree in all the nonprice series analyzed in this book. Yet this is the first occasion on which this factor has resulted in a systematic misprediction of production by the regression model (1). The question arises of why the model has trouble with seasonal movements in this industry, but not in the others. The answer may be contained in the fact, pointed out in Section 1, that the seasonal pattern in this industry changed drastically in the second half of the sample period. Furthermore, not only the seasonal pattern of sales, but also those of production, inventory, and the regression

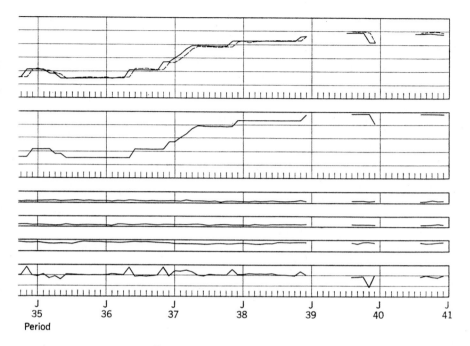

Figure 1b. Price Equation. Tires.

errors changed. This fact suggests that some of the parameters of the true decision rule may have changed around the middle of the sample period. If so, the regression calculations would choose some average values for the relevant parameters, and these values might account for the altered pattern of regression errors between the earlier and later years. In any case, it is certainly true that the pattern of regression errors observed during the early years of the sample would be much more convincing evidence of a basic inability of the model to account for seasonal movements if the pattern had persisted throughout.

The panels of Figure 1b show clearly the domination of the price regression (5) by p_{n-1}, to which reference has already been made. It is not only that the panels showing the contributions of x_n, z_n, and I_{n-1} to $\hat{p}_n$ show almost no visible change. In addition to this, the graph of $\hat{p}_n$ is almost an exact replica of the graph of p_{n-1}. Furthermore, $\hat{p}_n$ lags one period behind p_n at each major change in p_n in either direction. All this is of course no more than a reflection of the fact that $\hat{p}_n$ in (5) is almost exactly a simple extrapolation of p_{n-1}. Indeed, the evidence presented in this section suggests that tire prices during these years can be approximated by a "random walk" in which the month-to-month change in price is a random variable with a zero mean. Viewed in this way, perhaps the surprising thing about (5) is that it explains such a large part of the variance of p_n.

4. Comparison with Naive Forecasts

As in the previous empirical chapters, the forecasting ability of the regressions (4) and (5) is compared with that of two sets of naive forecasts of the output and price variables.

The first set of comparisons is between the percentage of the variance of the dependent variable explainable by the regressions and the percentage explainable by some naive forecasting variables. The results are summarized in Table 3.

The top line of Table 3 shows that by the correlation measure, (4) yields a substantially better forecast of production than do the naive forecasts obtained from current sales and lagged production. We see that z_{n-1} explains 71.7 per cent of the variance of z_n, and of the unexplained variance about one-third is explained by the regression. Similarly, x_n explains 66.3 per cent of the variance of z_n, and of the unexplained variance of this naive forecast the regression explains nearly 45 per cent. Thus, in spite of the fact that (4) leaves nearly 20 per cent of the variance of z_n unexplained, it does considerably better than does either of its two component variables z_{n-1} and x_n by itself.

In the case of the price variable the comparison, shown at the bottom of Table 3, is somewhat different. In this case the naive fore-

TABLE 3

COMPARISON BETWEEN REGRESSION FORECASTS AND NAIVE FORECASTS

	Naive Forecast	Naive Forecast	Regression Forecast
Production	$\mathrm{corr}^2(z_n, z_{n-1})$ = 0.717	$\mathrm{corr}^2(z_n, x_n)$ = 0.663	R^2[from (4)] = 0.808
Price	$\mathrm{corr}^2(p_n, p_{n-1})$ = 0.953		R^2[from (5)] = 0.968

cast variable p_{n-1} explains 95.3 per cent of the variance of p_n. Although the regression (5) explains almost a third of the part of the variance of p_n that is not explained by p_{n-1}, this amounts to only 1.5 more percentage points of the variance of p_n. Thus, in this case the naive forecast does so well that relatively little improvement is possible from the regressions.

The second set of naive forecasts consists in simply using the value of the forecasting variable itself as a naive forecast. A comparison between the average forecasting errors of these forecasts and those of the regressions is shown in Table 4.

Looking at the top line of Table 4, we see that using last month's production as a forecast of the current month's production involves an average forecasting error of 11.52 per cent. The forecast that each month's production will be the same as that month's sales, the best forecast possible on the basis of the static theory of output determination that does not take inventory holding into account, involves an average forecasting error of 12.78 per cent. The forecasting errors of the production equation (4) are smaller, on the average, than the forecasting errors of these two naive forecasts by about one-fifth and one-fourth respectively. Inevitably, both naive forecasts provide fairly accurate forecasts of monthly production. This is simply another way of saying that neither production nor inventories change very much from month to month. Given this fact, it can be said that the regression provides a substantial reduction in the errors of these naive forecasts.

TABLE 4

COMPARISON BETWEEN REGRESSION FORECASTS AND NAIVE FORECASTS

	Naive Forecast	Naive Forecast	Regression Forecast
Production	$\dfrac{100}{N} \sum \dfrac{\lvert z_n - z_{n-1}\rvert}{z_n}$	$\dfrac{100}{N} \sum \dfrac{\lvert z_n - x_n \rvert}{z_n}$	$\dfrac{100}{N} \sum \dfrac{\lvert z_n - \hat{z}_n \rvert}{z_n}$
	$= 11.52$	$= 12.78$	$= 9.49$
Price	$\dfrac{100}{N} \sum \dfrac{\lvert p_n - p_{n-1}\rvert}{p_n}$		$\dfrac{100}{N} \sum \dfrac{\lvert p_n - \hat{p}_n \rvert}{p_n}$
	$= 1.14$		$= 1.26$

Looking at the bottom of Table 4, we see that both the naive forecast, involving a simple extrapolation of lagged price, and the price regression (5) involve very small forecasting errors. These two forecasts are certain to yield similar patterns of forecasting errors since, as was pointed out in the last section, the price regression differs only slightly from a simple extrapolation of lagged price. Not only are the forecasting errors small, but also the average forecasting error of the price regression is about 10 per cent greater than the average forecasting error of the naive forecast. By the correlation criterion employed in Table 3 it is not possible for a naive forecast to do better than a regression involving the naive forecasting variable, since the multiple correlation cannot be less than the largest raw correlation between the dependent and independent variables. The naive forecast can do better by the criterion employed in Table 4 because the regression minimizes the average squared forecasting error rather than the average percentage forecasting error. In any case, the difference recorded in the table between the average forecasting error of the naive price forecast and that of the price regression is so small that it can hardly be considered significant. All we can say is that, according to the criterion of average percentage forecasting error, there is no evidence that the regression provides better forecasts of tire prices than does the naive forecast.

Chapter 12

APPLICATION TO INDUSTRY DATA: DEPARTMENT STORE SHOES

1. Introduction

The final industry study presented consists of an analysis of data relevant to the price, output, and inventory decisions of shoe departments in United States department stores during the nine-year period 1932 to 1940. The choice of these data for analysis was motivated by a reading of Ruth P. Mack's thorough and detailed description and analysis of the shoe-leather-hide industry sequence.[1] No attempt is made here to repeat or summarize Mrs. Mack's analysis and insights except to the extent that they bear directly on the estimates presented in this chapter. The reader is referred to her book not only for background and descriptive material but also for extensive analysis of these and other series relevant to the retail shoe industry.

This is the only one of the four empirical studies in which the "industry" is a branch of retail trade. Although there appears to be no important a priori reason for the model of price and output decisions to apply less well to retail than to industrial activities, it is neverthe-

---

[1] See [46]. All the data employed in this chapter were kindly furnished by Mrs. Mack. Many of Mrs. Mack's series, but not those studied here, have also been analyzed in [17]. There are several sets of series, referring to different stages in the shoe-leather-hide sequence, in Mrs. Mack's study to which a model of price, output, and inventory determination could be applied. The reason for the choice of the department store data is that they have an unusually high degree of uniformity and consistency. A relatively unchanging segment of the shoe industry is covered throughout the period, and the series all refer to the same set of decision-making units. For example, the price index is designed specifically to cover the kinds of shoes sold by department stores.

less true that the model was formulated with considerations in mind that are mainly relevant to manufacturing. It should therefore be interesting to contrast the estimates and tests of the decision rules in a retail trade with those in the other industries studied. One of the principal differences between retailing and manufacturing is that in retail trade "production" usually consists of the receipt of orders by the retailer from either a wholesaler or a manufacturer rather than in the physical or chemical transformation of materials. Thus, the production series used in this chapter refers to receipts of shoes by department stores.[2] One implication is that the distinction between raw material, in-process, and finished goods inventories has no meaning in retail trade. A second implication is that the pattern of production in retailing is much more closely associated with the relations with wholesalers than with considerations related to internal efficiency in the retail firm. Lead times required for delivery, transportation costs, ordering costs, et cetera, tend to replace considerations such as smoothing production in order to stabilize factory routines.

Another set of differences between retailing and manufacturing concerns the factors that are important for inventory policy.[3] As with the manufacturer, the retailer must also be concerned with the buffer and speculative functions of inventory. In retailing, however, inventories are often also valuable for display purposes, a factor that is not usually important in manufacturing. To the extent that inventories are for display purposes, their influence on production may be weakened, and β_{13} would be nearly zero in the production regression (1) to come. In addition, the production-smoothing function of inventories is much less important in retailing than in manufacturing. The smoothing of production is important in manufacturing and many other operations because it helps to avoid disruption of established routines. There is no close analogy in retailing. Indeed, in retailing there is often an incentive, resulting from the presence of economies in placing large orders, to receive goods in large discrete shipments. On the basis of this argument, lagged production should have a relatively small effect on current production, and β_{12} should therefore be close to zero in the production regression in this chapter.

Another factor often relevant to inventory policy in retail trade

[2] It might be noted that Mrs. Mack does not always use the term production in this way. In Chart 1 on p. 23 of [46], she measures the "output" of the retail shoe industry by its sales to final consumers.

[3] On this, see Chapters 8 and 9 of [46].

is the occurrence of style changes. From an economic point of view, style changes are a form of obsolescence and should not, therefore, require treatment that is qualitatively different from other forms of obsolescence. However, the other three industry studies in this book have been concerned with products for which there is relatively little depreciation of any kind. Hence, the extent to which rapid depreciation of inventory affects the validity of the model employed in these industry studies has not yet been ascertained. Although shoes (women's in particular) are obviously subject to rapid style changes,[4] their effect is probably relatively small in the data studied in this chapter, since department stores tended, during the period studied, to sell mainly staple shoes rather than style shoes. However, even if the effect of style changes is small, there is a seasonal pattern in the kinds of shoes bought in department stores, and this presumably has much the same effect as style changes. In concluding this discussion we must say that it is not clear what effect the occurrence of style changes should be expected to have on the regression coefficients estimated in this book. In an extreme case in which inventory periodically becomes worthless, it is clear that last month's terminal inventory should have no effect at all on this month's price or purchase decisions. Hence the coefficients of lagged inventory in the regressions would be zero. In more realistic cases, several factors confuse the picture. Some of the goods represented in the indexes of price, output, sales, and inventory are more subject to style changes than others; style changes occur at irregular intervals; some of the retailers' purchases are of old styles and some are of new styles; and prices can be lowered in order to stimulate demand for out-of-style lines. Depending on the relative importance of these factors, the effect of style changes may or may not be to make the coefficients of lagged inventory and production small.

Table 1 presents all the data used in the calculations in this chapter (see also Figure 1 in Section 3). Except for the price series, all the data are seasonally adjusted (see Section 2 below), and none of the series displays any apparent seasonal pattern. Qualitatively, these data follow the cyclical movements characteristic of the years 1932 to 1940. Quantitatively, however, the movements are on the whole somewhat smaller than those observed in the series used in the preceding chapters. Sales declined about 5 per cent between 1932 and 1933.

4 See Chapters 8 and 9 of [46].

TABLE 1

PRICE, OUTPUT, SALES, AND INVENTORY DATA
FOR DEPARTMENT STORE SHOES

n	x_n	p_n	z_n	I_n	n	x_n	p_n	z_n	I_n
1932					**1935**				
J	66.69	132.4	69.62	318.14	J	68.94	136.2	64.28	286.22
F	70.48	130.1	65.49	313.15	F	66.20	135.5	68.31	288.34
M	64.36	128.5	69.98	318.77	M	69.28	135.4	69.04	288.10
A	66.22	126.7	64.97	317.52	A	67.53	134.9	79.77	300.34
M	64.39	124.7	60.50	313.63	M	63.58	134.8	62.66	299.42
J	66.67	123.6	55.97	302.93	J	67.63	134.4	68.31	300.10
J	59.57	122.2	59.14	302.50	J	68.88	134.3	62.25	293.47
A	57.91	120.7	48.93	293.52	A	69.83	133.9	68.10	291.74
S	65.33	119.7	57.65	285.84	S	67.31	134.0	70.19	294.62
O	61.07	119.2	59.87	284.64	O	67.34	134.1	75.94	303.22
N	62.22	117.8	69.40	291.84	N	70.86	134.2	75.90	308.26
D	61.85	116.9	63.72	293.71	D	68.62	134.5	76.97	316.61
1933					**1936**				
J	57.76	116.0	59.25	295.20	J	69.98	134.9	76.31	322.94
F	61.93	114.8	59.72	292.99	F	75.07	135.2	69.03	316.90
M	62.57	113.8	45.72	276.14	M	69.42	135.7	64.95	312.43
A	61.78	113.3	63.94	278.30	A	72.10	136.2	72.25	312.58
M	67.40	113.2	66.97	277.87	M	73.66	136.3	77.40	316.32
J	67.84	114.1	67.17	277.20	J	69.85	136.0	71.10	317.57
J	60.51	117.5	68.05	284.74	J	73.88	135.9	74.02	317.71
A	64.38	125.5	69.47	289.82	A	69.62	136.6	75.77	323.86
S	63.48	132.8	67.18	293.52	S	73.78	136.9	75.65	325.73
O	54.82	134.8	55.92	294.62	O	78.57	137.2	77.56	324.72
N	56.10	135.3	54.28	292.80	N	73.27	137.3	85.46	336.91
D	56.61	135.3	47.87	284.06	D	75.15	137.6	79.90	341.66
1934					**1937**				
J	61.69	135.2	63.57	285.94	J	76.72	137.9	75.00	339.94
F	63.84	135.5	71.23	293.33	F	76.12	139.0	77.12	340.94
M	66.10	136.0	62.16	289.39	M	71.56	140.3	90.09	359.47
A	63.26	136.1	57.16	283.30	A	75.92	141.6	73.71	357.26
M	69.23	136.5	62.36	276.43	M	78.45	143.4	70.87	349.68
J	64.66	136.4	64.81	276.58	J	75.33	144.3	76.91	351.26
J	60.64	136.7	64.76	280.70	J	76.49	145.5	72.94	347.71
A	70.45	136.7	70.07	280.32	A	67.77	148.6	75.40	355.34
S	61.00	136.4	61.24	280.56	S	71.02	150.1	76.11	360.43
O	61.41	136.3	63.57	282.72	O	72.30	150.9	66.97	355.10
N	59.84	136.2	63.68	286.56	N	66.20	150.6	58.24	347.14
D	64.10	136.2	68.42	290.88	D	66.82	150.1	55.78	336.10

TABLE 1 (*Continued*)

n	x_n	p_n	z_n	I_n	n	x_n	p_n	z_n	I_n
1938					1940				
J	66.08	148.9	59.55	329.57	J	71.07	146.2	74.76	344.78
F	65.54	148.0	55.84	319.87	F	68.33	146.5	82.40	358.85
M	66.35	147.4	65.54	319.06	M	66.01	146.8	65.19	358.03
A	70.56	147.1	74.49	322.99	A	71.32	146.8	62.59	349.30
M	59.92	146.2	70.34	333.41	M	68.60	146.8	59.28	339.98
J	65.77	145.2	62.70	330.34	J	72.82	146.8	65.62	332.78
J	66.16	145.1	65.68	329.86	J	71.19	146.8	66.20	327.79
A	63.99	144.7	62.50	328.37	A	78.61	146.8	77.60	326.78
S	69.10	144.0	61.66	320.93	S	70.98	146.8	71.90	327.70
O	68.75	143.7	68.94	321.12	O	69.93	147.0	79.29	337.06
N	69.47	143.8	68.41	320.06	N	79.39	147.0	76.94	334.61
D	69.24	143.7	72.08	322.90	D	72.48	146.8	75.31	337.44
1939									
J	66.60	143.4	69.38	325.68					
F	68.41	143.4	68.79	326.06					
M	71.64	143.5	74.76	329.18					
A	69.54	143.8	71.65	331.30					
M	70.70	143.7	63.83	324.43					
J	69.33	143.8	71.78	326.88					
J	67.66	143.8	72.41	331.63					
A	68.57	143.8	70.69	333.84					
S	71.55	144.1	77.79	340.08					
O	67.82	144.5	67.53	339.79					
N	67.63	145.2	72.53	344.69					
D	70.19	145.6	66.59	341.09					

Thereafter, they rose each year until 1937, at which time they were nearly 20 per cent above their 1933 volume. There was a decline of nearly 10 per cent in 1938, and an increase in 1939 and 1940. In 1940 sales were about 2 per cent less than their 1937 volume. Thus, in the best year, 1937, sales were less than 20 per cent greater than in the worst year, 1933. This difference represents a much smaller amplitude than has been observed in sales fluctuations in the previous empirical chapters. Peaks and troughs in production occurred in the same years as those in sales and the fluctuations were of similar amplitude. Inventory levels followed roughly the same cyclical pattern as did sales, except that their turning points tended to lag behind turning points in sales by several months.[5] Again, however, one is impressed by the relatively small amplitudes recorded. The largest inventory level in Table 1 is only 31 per cent larger than the smallest level.

The price index in the table indicates correspondingly small fluctuations. The average absolute monthly change over the entire sample period was 0.53 per cent. This is the smallest value of this measure recorded in the four industries studied. In contrast with the cement and tire price indexes, however, this index shows no tendency to change in large, discrete jumps. In this respect, the shoe price index is more like the southern pine lumber price index than it is like the others studied. In broad outline, the shoe price index followed much the same cyclical pattern as did the price indexes studied in previous chapters. From January 1932, the beginning of the sample period, until May 1933, the index fell steadily and showed an overall decline of 15 per cent. From May to September the index rose rapidly and then, until October 1937, more slowly, with small decreases in a few months. By October 1937 it was one-third higher than its minimum level in 1933 and 13 per cent above its January 1932 level. A small decline was registered during the 1937 to 1938 recession, then a steady rise until the end of the sample period in December 1940. By that time it was only a few points below its peak level in October 1937, and 10 per cent above its initial level in January 1932.

In part, the small amplitudes observed in these data undoubtedly result from the nature of the product and industry they represent. Nondurable consumer goods normally display smaller cyclical fluctuations than do durable consumer goods, and the latter in turn display less instability than producers' durables. The three products studied in the previous empirical chapters are all more durable than shoes, and at least the first two are extensively used to produce durable capital equipment. Furthermore, the three products are closely associated with industries (automobiles, and construction) which were relatively unstable during the 1930's. In part, however, the small amplitudes of the series in Table 1 are accounted for simply by the fact that the data are seasonally adjusted, and thus one cyclical movement has already been removed.

[5] See [46], Chapter 7.

2. Sources of Data

As was stated above in Section 1, all the data used in the calculations in this chapter are taken from Mrs. Mack's study. Since the sources, coverage, accuracy, and adjustment procedures for each series have been described by Mrs. Mack in thorough detail in Appendix B, pp. 263–283 of [46], only brief comments will be made here.

The price series in Table 1 is series 8, p. 264, in [46]. This series was originally compiled by the National Industrial Conference Board, on the basis of reports from stores in almost one hundred cities giving retail prices for a small number of popular men's and women's shoes. The base of the index is July 1914 = 100. This series is used by Mrs. Mack starting with the year 1924, but prior to 1932 it is available only as a five-month centered moving average. This is obviously unsuitable for structural estimation, and therefore the sample period for this study starts in January 1932. The other series described below are also available prior to 1932, but since the price series can be used only from 1932 on, no observations in any series are used prior to that date.

The sales series in Table 1 is series 29, p. 268 in [46]. This index was computed by the National Bureau of Economic Research from sample data originally collected by several Federal Reserve district banks. The banks reported estimates of the dollar volume of department store shoe sales, seasonally adjusted, in their respective districts. Hence the national index constructed by the National Bureau was also seasonally adjusted. The National Bureau deflated the dollar volume index by the price index described in the previous paragraph to obtain an estimate of the physical volume of sales. Thus, in this chapter, for the first time in this book, the sales and inventory series were obtained by dividing a dollar value index by the price series that is also used as a variable in the calculations. It is clear that, if the price index is inaccurate, this procedure introduces the possibility of "spurious" correlations among the variables in the model. It is not, however, clear that this procedure is in principle less defensible than the procedure employed in compiling the data used in other chapters. The physical volume indexes used in other chapters give weights of one to certain physical units, such as a tire. In compiling the index used in this chapter, physical units are weighted by deflated selling prices. The two procedures may lead to very different results. For example, selling prices of two tires covered by the tire sales data in

Chapter 11 may differ by a factor of five. The procedure followed in compiling the sales index used in Chapter 11 gives a weight of one to each tire, whereas the procedure followed in compiling the index used in this chapter gives a weight five times as large to one tire as to the other. Which of these, or many other, procedures is correct is an aggregation problem to which the writer has no solution.

The inventory series in Table 1 is derived from series 50 (end of month), p. 272 in [46]. Mrs. Mack's index expresses inventory as a percentage of its own base year level, and this index was multiplied by 4.8, which Mrs. Mack gives as the approximate ratio of inventory to monthly sales. Series 50 was also constructed by the National Bureau of Economic Research from sample data supplied by several Federal Reserve district banks. The number of district banks reporting inventory data was smaller than the number reporting the sales data described in the previous paragraph and Mrs. Mack remarks ([46], p. 101) on their possible inadequacy. The price series in Table 1 was used by the National Bureau to deflate their dollar inventory index as well as their dollar sales index. This is the correct deflator because, according to Mrs. Mack ([46], p. 272), "department stores typically value inventory at selling price rather than at cost."

There is also available a "production" index, series 62, p. 273 in [46], providing estimates of shoe receipts by department stores. However, it was constructed independently of the indexes described in the two previous paragraphs and gives different weights to men's and women's shoes from those used in the other indexes. Therefore this index does not satisfy the identity $z_n - x_n = \Delta I_n$. Since the theoretical models assume definitions of the relevant variables such that this identity holds, series 62 is not used in the calculations. Instead, production is defined by the above identity, inserting values of x_n and ΔI_n obtained from the series described above and presented in Table 1. The production series in Table 1 is constructed in this way.

3. Regression Analysis

The regressions estimated from the data in Table 1 are the same as those estimated in the previous empirical chapters.

$$z_n = \beta_{10} + \beta_{11}x_n + \beta_{12}z_{n-1} + \beta_{13}I_{n-1} + \epsilon_{1n} \tag{1}$$

$$p_n = \beta_{20} + \beta_{21}x_n + \beta_{22}z_n + \beta_{23}I_{n-1} + \beta_{24}p_{n-1} + \epsilon_{2n} \tag{2}$$

$$p_n = \beta_{30} + \beta_{31}x_n + \beta_{32}z_n + \beta_{33}I_{n-1} + \epsilon_{3n} \tag{3}$$

The estimated regressions are

$$\hat{z}_n = 4.855 + 0.850\ x_n + 0.420\ z_{n-1} - 0.073\ I_{n-1} \tag{4}$$

$$(7.459)\quad (0.133)\qquad (0.082)\qquad\quad (0.027)$$

$$R^2 = 0.563 \qquad d = 2.27$$

$$\hat{p}_n = -0.437 - 0.031\ x_n + 0.061\ z_n + 0.005\ I_{n-1} + 0.978\ p_{n-1}$$

$$(2.070)\quad (0.040)\qquad (0.022)\qquad (0.009)\qquad\quad (0.019)\qquad (5)$$

$$R^2 = 0.982 \qquad d = 0.48$$

$$\hat{p}_n = 43.036 - 0.096\ x_n + 0.172\ z_n + 0.282\ I_{n-1} \tag{6}$$

$$(9.716)\quad (0.204)\qquad (0.114)\qquad (0.034)$$

$$R^2 = 0.523$$

With one or two exceptions, these regressions follow the pattern established in the previous empirical studies. In the production regression, each coefficient is significant at the 5 per cent level, whereas in the price regressions several coefficients are not significant at this level. The R^2's for the two price regressions are the largest computed for corresponding regressions in any of the four industry studies. On the other hand, the R^2 for the production regression is much the smallest computed in any of the studies. The d-statistics for (4) and (5) show very different patterns of residuals for the two regressions. The d-statistic for (4) is nonsignificant at the 5 per cent level, whereas that for (5) is significant at the 1 per cent level. The surprising thing about these results is not the strong evidence of positive autocorrelation among the residuals in the price regression, which has been found in most of the other price regressions, but the lack of evidence of such autocorrelation in the production regression.

In the production regression (4) each coefficient has the sign predicted by the theoretical arguments in Chapters 7 and 8. Contrary to the expectation established in Section 1, the coefficient of lagged production is not smaller relative to the other coefficients in the production regression than in the other empirical studies. This, in conjunction with the small R^2 computed for this regression, creates a suspicion that lagged production plays the role of a proxy for some excluded variables in this regression. As has been found in most of the other production regressions, the coefficient of lagged inventory is relatively small in absolute value. It was suggested in Section 1 that this may reflect the influence of seasonal and style changes on the pattern of shoe buying.

In the price regressions (5) and (6) there is much less consistency with a priori expectations. The coefficient of lagged price in (5) is large and positive, a fact that is consistent both with theoretical considerations and with the findings in the other empirical chapters. However, the coefficients of production and lagged inventory in (5) and (6) have signs that are wrong on the basis of theoretical considerations and the opposite from those typically found in the other empirical chapters. The explanation of these findings appears to be as follows. In (5), the coefficient of lagged inventory is considerably smaller than its standard error and therefore nonsignificant at the usual significance levels. Thus, the evidence provided by this regression is that inventory has no discernible influence on price. If any such influence exists, it is probably of a seasonal nature, since large inventories probably induce retailers to lower prices only of shoes that are going out of season. But, since the data are seasonally adjusted, this relationship does not show up in the regression. The significantly positive coefficient of lagged inventory in (6) is undoubtedly accounted for by the positive correlation, shown in Table 2, between lagged inventory and lagged price. Hence, in (6) lagged inventory assumes part of the role played by lagged price in (5). Although the coefficient of production has the wrong sign in both (5) and (6), it is not significant at the 1 per cent level in either case, and it is significant at the 5 per cent level only in (5). Hence, the evidence also suggests that production has little effect on price. As in the case of lagged inventory, any effect of this type is probably seasonal in nature, owing to the inconvenience of changing the order-delivery schedule in the middle of the season, and therefore does not show up in seasonally adjusted data.

The final remark on the regressions has to do with the coefficients of sales in (5) and (6). This is the only industry in which the estimate of this coefficient has been negative. In Chapter 7, Section 4 it was argued that this should be the case when movements in sales are mainly in response to price changes rather than to exogenous factors. The process of seasonal adjustment implies the removal of one of the largest exogenous factors from the sales data, and it is therefore not surprising that movements in the adjusted variable are largely responses to movements in price. In any case, this effect is small, and

TABLE 2

ZERO-ORDER CORRELATIONS FOR DEPARTMENT STORE SHOE DATA

	2a Production Equation					2b Price Equation				
	z_n	x_n	z_{n-1}	I_{n-1}		p_n	x_n	z_n	I_{n-1}	p_{n-1}
z_n	..	0.664	0.625	0.317	p_n	..	0.461	0.327	0.715	0.990
x_n	..	..	0.566	0.599	x_n	..	..	0.664	0.599	0.449
z_{n-1}	..	..	..	0.493	z_n	..	..	..	0.317	0.293
I_{n-1}	..	..	..	..	I_{n-1}	..	..	..	..	0.715
					p_{n-1}	..	..	..	..	..

neither b_{21} nor b_{31} is significant at the 5 per cent level. Perhaps the most interesting fact concerning (6) is that, in spite of the difficulty of interpreting the coefficients, it explains more than half of the variance of p_n, considerably more than is explained by this regression in the other empirical studies.

The raw correlations among the variables in the regressions are shown in Table 2. It can be seen from Table 2a that neither x_n nor z_{n-1} dominates the production regression, but that each makes a contribution to the explanation of z_n. Furthermore, even though I_{n-1} is positively correlated with z_n, this correlation is explained by the fact that I_{n-1} is also positively correlated with the other explanatory variables in (4), and its partial correlation with z_n is therefore negative. Table 2b shows clearly the domination of (5) by p_{n-1}. The correlation between p_n and p_{n-1} is much the largest in the entire table, and its square is almost as large as R^2 in (5). However, the correlations between p_n and the other variables in (5) and (6) are also substantial, and they are respectively greater than those calculated for any other industry except southern pine lumber. In particular, the correlation between p_n and I_{n-1} is quite large, its square being nearly as large as R^2 in (6). I_{n-1} has the same correlation with p_{n-1} as with p_n and thus its function in (6) is to act as a proxy for p_{n-1}.

The graphs of the regressions (4) and (5) are shown in Figures 1a and 1b. Figure 1a confirms some of the impressions reported above. In particular, it shows that both x_n and z_{n-1} make substantial contributions to $\hat{z}_n$, but that I_{n-1} contributes almost nothing. The predictions follow the cyclical movements in z_n fairly well, but $\hat{z}_n$ shows some

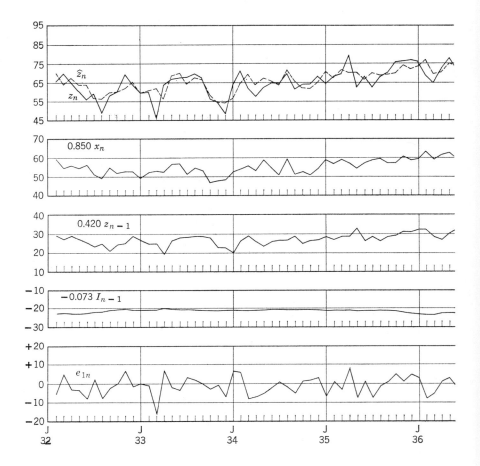

tendency to lag one period behind z_n at turning points in the latter, particularly in the earlier part of the sample period.

Figure 1b again shows clearly the domination of (5) by p_{n-1}. The other three explanatory variables in (5) make almost no discernible contribution to the prediction of p_n. This graph also shows that it is because p_n moves in the same direction for several consecutive periods that p_{n-1} provides such a good explanation of p_n. As in the previous industry studies, the graph shows that (5) lags behind all the turning

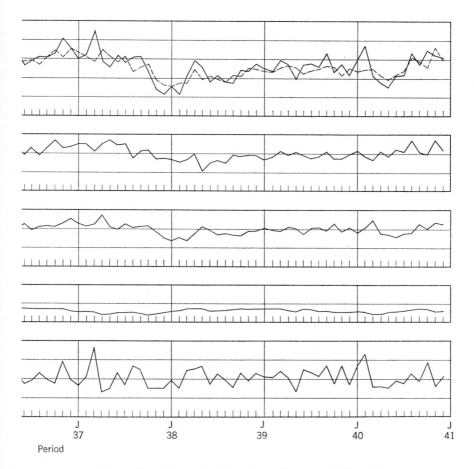

Figure 1a. Production Equation. Department Store Shoes.

points in p_n. The most dramatic movement in price is the rise that took place around the middle of 1933 and, as is true of the similar movements observed in the other price series, the regression largely fails to predict this movement. The more gradual price rise that culminated in 1937 is predicted with somewhat greater success, though again the tendency for $\hat{p}_n$ to lag behind p_n is present. The tendency for $\hat{p}_n$ to lag behind p_n also explains the very high autocorrelation among the residuals shown in the bottom panel of Figure 1b.

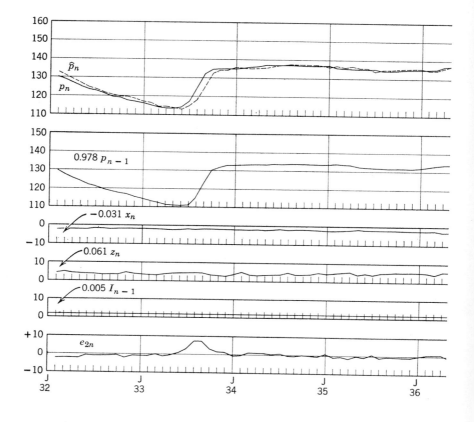

4. Comparison with Naive Forecasts

In this section the comparisons made in previous chapters between the forecasting ability of the regressions and that of several naive forecasts are presented for the department store shoe data. The first of the comparisons involves the use of squared correlations to measure the percentage of the variance of the dependent variable which can be explained by the naive or regression forecast. The comparison is presented in Table 3. From the top line in the table it can be seen that, as was true in previous chapters, the regression (4) represents a substantial improvement on the naive forecasts by this measure. Regression (4) explains 28 per cent of the variance of z_n that is not explained

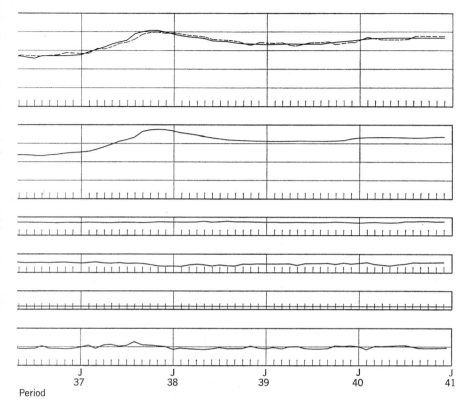

Figure 1b. Price Equation. Department Store Shoes.

TABLE 3

COMPARISON BETWEEN REGRESSION FORECASTS AND NAIVE FORECASTS

	Naive Forecasts	Naive Forecasts	Regression Forecasts
Production	$\mathrm{corr}^2(z_n, z_{n-1})$ $= 0.391$	$\mathrm{corr}^2(z_n, x_n)$ $= 0.441$	R^2[from (4)] $= 0.563$
Price	$\mathrm{corr}^2(p_n, p_{n-1})$ $= 0.980$		R^2[from (5)] $= 0.982$

TABLE 4

COMPARISON BETWEEN REGRESSION FORECASTS AND NAIVE FORECASTS

	Naive Forecast	Naive Forecast	Regression Forecast
Production	$\dfrac{100}{N} \sum \dfrac{\lvert z_n - z_{n-1}\rvert}{z_n}$	$\dfrac{100}{N} \sum \dfrac{\lvert z_n - x_n\rvert}{z_n}$	$\dfrac{100}{N} \sum \dfrac{\lvert z_n - \hat{z}_n\rvert}{z_n}$
	$= 8.02$	$= 6.69$	$= 6.02$
Price	$\dfrac{100}{N} \sum \dfrac{\lvert p_n - p_{n-1}\rvert}{p_n}$		$\dfrac{100}{N} \sum \dfrac{\lvert p_n - \hat{p}_n\rvert}{p_n}$
	$= 0.53$		$= 0.55$

by z_{n-1}, and 22 per cent of the variance of z_n which is not explained by x_n. Of course, (4) still leaves unexplained nearly half of the variance of z_n. From the bottom line in the table it can be seen that p_{n-1} explains virtually as much of the variance of p_n as does (5). Of the variance of p_n not explained by p_{n-1}, (5) explains 10 per cent, but the difference between the two variances is too small to be considered significant.

The second comparison involves the average absolute percentage forecasting error and is presented in Table 4. Again, we see that the production regression involves substantially smaller forecasting errors than do the naive forecasts. The average forecasting error of the regression is 25 per cent smaller than that of the naive forecast z_{n-1}, and 10 per cent smaller than that of the naive forecast x_n. It is interesting to note that, in spite of the relatively small R^2 of the production regression, its average forecasting error is the smallest of the four such regressions except for the one calculated for southern pine lumber. As is to be expected from the results presented above, the comparison involving price is much less favorable to the regression forecasts. Indeed, this is the third of the four industry studies in which the regression forecasts have yielded slightly larger average errors than the naive forecast p_{n-1}. In this case the average error of the regression forecast is 4 per cent greater than that of the naive forecast, although the difference is presumably too small to be significant.

Chapter 13

SUMMARY AND CONCLUSIONS

THE MAIN PURPOSE of this book has been to formulate, analyze, estimate, and test a model of the short-run price and output policies of a firm in an imperfectly competitive market. This chapter summarizes and evaluates the findings. The first step is to trace the thread of the theoretical argument through Chapters 1 to 8, indicating the principle results and insights they contain. The second and more important step is to bring together the empirical estimates and tests of Chapters 9 to 12, to show their relationship with the theoretical analysis of the earlier chapters.

Chapter 2 presented some preliminary analysis of the firm's decision making in the presence of uncertainty. Two important points were made in that chapter. First, many of the firm's decision problems are so complicated that it is either not possible or not worthwhile for the firm to compute exact solutions. Therefore, a rational firm should often approximate its true decision problems by simpler ones that it can solve without excessive computational and data-gathering costs. The implication is that the economist's problem in constructing models of firms' behavior is to discover and analyze the simpler decision problem that the firm has used as an approximation of its true problem. The models of price and output policies in the succeeding chapters were formulated in the spirit of this argument. Second, it is rarely worthwhile for the firm to make perfect forecasts of variables relevant to its decisions, since it is expensive to collect and process information for forecasting purposes. However, it was argued, when the firm balances the advantages of better forecasts against the costs of improving its forecasts, the resulting expectations should be statistically, if not numerically, correct, and expectational errors should have stable statistical properties.

The purpose of Chapter 3 was to show that in some circumstances the assumption of stable statistical properties of expectational errors enables the economist to estimate decision rules in which expectational variables appear, without first estimating the dependence of the expectations on observable variables. The basic step in this approach is the use of the value of the variable itself as a proxy for the decision maker's expectation or forecast of that variable. It was claimed that in many cases this procedure is preferable to the more usual assumption that expectations are generated by a simple mechanical autoregressive scheme. In more stringently defined circumstances it might also be possible to estimate the expectation itself from the estimated decision rule. Such an estimate, called the implicit expectation, is the value of the variable which, if it were the expectation, would lead the economist to predict from the estimated decision rule the decision that was actually taken.

Chapter 4 digressed from the path of the argument. There the assumption of correct expectations was applied to a model of production, sales, and inventory decisions of a firm in a perfectly competitive market. This analysis led to a dynamic model of market price adjustment, and it was shown that a competitive market price must be unstable upwards in the vicinity of equilibrium if expectations are correct in either a numerical or a statistical sense.

Chapters 5 and 6 presented the basic model employed in all the subsequent analysis and estimation. This model pertained to the price, output, and inventory policy of a firm in an imperfect market. The following assumptions were made: (1) The firm's demand curve is downward sloping and contains an additive random term whose probability distribution the firm knows; (2) Each period the firm incurs production and storage costs that depend on that period's production and terminal inventory respectively; (3) The firm approximates the effect of its current operations on its future profits by a function that attaches a cost to any shortage occurring in the period, and a value to any inventory remaining at the end of the period; (4) On the basis of these cost and demand conditions the firm maximizes the mathematical expectation of its short-run profits. It was shown that two rather simple decision rules for price and output policy result from this model. These decision rules were analyzed extensively, and it was shown that the resulting price and production levels might be above or below those indicated by the traditional static model. Important circumstances were presented in which the price predicted by the model with uncertainty would be lower than the price predicted by the static model.

In Chapters 7 and 8 the model was extended and analyzed in further detail in preparation for empirical estimation and testing. First, a dynamic cost depending on the rate of change of output was incorporated in the decision model. Then linear approximations of the price and output decision rules were derived for the purpose of regression analysis. Chapter 8 reported the results of ten sampling experiments conducted to test the adequacy of the linear approximations and the use of the observed value of the sales variable as a proxy for the firm's sales expectation (as suggested in Chapter 3). In the sampling experiments, artificial time series of the price, output, sales, sales expectations, and inventory variables were generated from special forms of the decision rules. Although these forms employed several linear cost relations for computational convenience, important nonlinearities were retained. The linear approximations of the decision rules were then estimated from these series, once using the true expectations and once using observed sales as a proxy. The results indicated that the approximations were very good when the true expectations were used. When the current sales variable was used as a proxy for expectations the approximation was still good, although considerable bias was introduced in the estimates of the coefficients of the expectations variable and a smaller bias was introduced in the estimates of coefficients of the other variables. The attempt to estimate the expectations from the regressions that had been fitted with the proxy proved unsatisfactory. This suggested strongly that even when the use of the proxy permits a good estimate of the decision rules, it is unwise to place much faith in the resulting implicit expectations. The sampling experiments also confirmed that the identifiability of the decision rules depends on the presence of an additive exogenous term in the demand equation.

Chapters 9 to 12 presented four empirical studies in which the linear approximations of the decision rules were estimated and tested, using monthly or quarterly time series for four United States industries during the interwar period. The remainder of this chapter brings together these estimates in order to present an overall evaluation of the results. Detailed comment on the estimates has been made in each of the last four chapters and is not repeated here. Instead, the pattern of success and failures that emerges in all the empirical studies is emphasized, some possible reasons for the failures are given, and some possible directions for further research are suggested. For ease of reference, the estimated coefficients of the price and output decision rules are presented in Table 1. The numbering of the regressions corresponds to the numbering in each of the empirical chapters except in the case of cement. The right-hand column under cement refers to the estimates of the coefficients calculated when the shippers' forecasts rather than current sales were used as the proxy for demand expectations. The relations between the estimated and theoretical decision rules can be summarized as follows.

The production regressions containing observed sales as an independent variable are mostly satisfactory, and they provide considerable support for the theoretical model. With one exception, each of the estimated coefficients satisfies the restrictions as to sign and magnitude implied by the theoretical model. The one exception is the coefficient of lagged inventory for the southern pine lumber data, and this coefficient is nonsignificant at the 5 per cent level. Furthermore, all the production regressions forecast production substantially better than do the naive forecasts that were employed for purposes of comparison. With the exception of that for department store shoes, all the production regressions have R^2's large enough to indicate that most of the important factors are included in the regressions. Finally, in the cement industry, the one case in which a comparison is possible, current sales appear to be a much better proxy for demand expectations than are the shippers' forecasts.

These results suggest that production regressions of the type estimated in this study will also be relatively successful in other applications. It appears that important factors are omitted only in the case of department store shoes. It is not possible to say whether the relative lack of success in this case results from the use of seasonally adjusted data, from the use of the price series to deflate the other variables in the study, or from fundamental differences between retailing and industrial operations. It seems quite likely, however, that a very different approach from the one used here is required to explain order-delivery decisions in retailing. In the case of industrial applications, the above results leave the impression that substantial improvement in the explanation and prediction of production decisions must rely heavily on the availability of better estimates of demand expectations. In many firms, monthly and quarterly adjustments in production are un-

TABLE 1

Estimates of Price and Output Decision Rules

Equation and Dependent Variable	Coefficient	Southern Pine Lumber	Cement Using Current Sales	Cement Using Shippers Forecasts	Pneumatic Tires	Shoes
(4)	b_{10}	14.683 (1.802)	68.8 (6.179)	−48.8 (20.273)	52.489 (20.650)	4.855 (7.459)
z_n	b_{11}	0.594 (0.086)	0.791 (0.068)	0.255 (0.102)	0.389 (0.047)	0.850 (0.133)
	b_{12}	0.343 (0.095)	0.156 (0.026)	0.478 (0.121)	0.559 (0.053)	0.420 (0.082)
	b_{13}	0.009 (0.034)	−0.234 (0.068)	0.553 (0.132)	−0.033 (0.023)	−0.073 (0.027)
	R^2	0.769	0.964	0.531	0.808	0.563
	d	1.33	1.98	1.82	1.39	2.27
(5)	b_{20}	6.971 (0.651)	47.7 (9.988)	43.9 (9.850)	0.157 (0.837)	−0.437 (0.070)
p_n	b_{21}	0.764 (0.062)	0.015 (0.012)	0.008 (0.007)	0.001 (0.001)	−0.031 (0.040)
	b_{22}	−0.572 (0.063)	−0.016 (0.013)	−0.010 (0.007)	0.001 (0.002)	0.061 (0.022)
	b_{23}	−0.286 (0.021)	−0.032 (0.014)	−0.031 (0.014)	−0.001 (0.001)	0.005 (0.009)
	b_{24}	0.910 (0.034)	0.560 (0.100)	0.601 (0.105)	1.005 (0.021)	0.978 (0.019)
	R^2	0.980	0.571	0.572	0.968	0.982
	d	1.57	2.27	2.22	1.65	0.48
(6)	b_{30}	21.354 (8.720)	100.6 (4.531)	97.1 (4.523)	31.983 (2.186)	43.036 (9.716)
p_n	b_{31}	0.525 (0.354)	0.015 (0.017)	−0.003 (0.009)	−0.010 (0.006)	−0.096 (0.204)
	b_{32}	0.900 (0.352)	−0.017 (0.018)	0.002 (0.010)	0.003 (0.006)	0.172 (0.114)
	b_{33}	−0.224 (0.120)	−0.040 (0.019)	−0.025 (0.020)	0.018 (0.002)	0.282 (0.034)
	R^2	0.403	0.124	0.105	0.353	0.523

doubtedly very responsive to changes in expectations, and the use of observed sales is probably a fairly crude proxy for this purpose. Thus, the results of this study strengthen the widespread belief among economists that the study of expectations is an important area for further research.

The price regressions also display a consistent pattern, but one that is much less favorable to the theoretical model than are the production regressions. With the exception of cement, each of the estimates of (5) has a higher R^2 than any of the production regressions. However, all the price regressions are dominated by the term in lagged price, and if they are estimated without this term, as in (6), the R^2's are much lower. Furthermore, the estimates of the nonprice terms in (5) and (6) are unsatisfactory in several ways. Considerable evidence has been presented in the last four chapters to the effect that these terms make only relatively small contributions to the explanation of price. In addition to this, in only two of the industries, southern pine lumber and cement, do the nonprice terms obey the sign restrictions imposed on them by the theoretical model. In the other two industries, pneumatic tires and department store shoes, these terms are nonsignificant and/or have the wrong signs.

These results give the strong impression that the inadequacies of the price regressions are much more fundamental and pervasive than were those of the production regression. For example, it does not seem likely that better estimates of demand expectations would greatly improve the success of the regressions in signaling major movements in price. The estimates of the price regressions suggest, instead, that there is very little information in short-run data on inventories, production, and demand expectations that is useful in explaining price movements in these industries. It is mainly for this reason that no alternative forms of the price regressions have been estimated in this study, even though a number of possibilities have been suggested. There are many possible explanations of the inadequacies of the price regressions, and several factors are almost certainly at work. Some of these factors are discussed in the following paragraphs, roughly in the order of the writer's intuitive estimate of their importance.

First and foremost are data deficiencies. In each industry, all the physical volume series were collected by the same agency and for much the same purposes. Therefore, within each industry, the physical volume data show a high degree of consistency as to coverage, definition of product, and general sampling procedures. However, in three of the four industries (southern pine lumber is the exception) the price series were collected by different agencies and for very different purposes. This fact introduces a serious risk of inconsistencies of coverage, relative weights, and so on between the price and physical volume series. In one industry, pneumatic tires, such a discrepancy is known to be present; similar discrepancies may be present in others as well. In addition to these factors, however, there are several reasons for thinking that the price series may be less accurate than the physical volume series. It is well known that many price indexes showed smaller price declines during the early 1930's than actually took place, because they failed to record hidden discounts and other "unofficial" price concessions. Furthermore, the notion of price is often a much more complex one than the notion of a unit of physical output. For example, whether it is the appropriate unit or not, the notion of a pneumatic tire is a relatively well-defined concept. The notion of its price, however, is made ambiguous by physical differences such as size, price discrimination, or the handling of transportation costs. A final factor having to do with the reliability of the price series is that many of those that are available on a monthly basis during the 1930's were collected by employers' associations for the purpose of administering industry-wide price agreements. Therefore, the sample of available series is biased toward those industries in which prices were the result of collusive agreements, and such agreements are notoriously insensitive to short-run market changes. Thus, part of the reason that the price regressions fail to indicate much effect of the nonprice variables on price is that the sample of available data is biased against industries in which this effect is important.

In addition to possible inadequacies in the data, it is probably also true that price decisions are inherently more difficult to represent than are production decisions. There are several reasons for believing this. The fact that there exists a vast operations research literature on production planning, but almost none on price planning, suggests that it is much more difficult to reduce price decisions than production decisions to rules and formulas. Furthermore, production planning and organization are more professional matters than is price planning. Many people pursue courses of training in colleges and technical institutes to qualify as production engineers, but there are no price engineers. Finally, the analysis in Chapters 7 and 8 showed that the price decision rule in the model developed in this book is intrinsically more complicated than the production decision rule. There is no obvious linear approximation to the price decision rule to correspond with (8) of Chapter 7 for the production decision rule. Also, the sampling experiments in Chapter 8 showed that the price regression is much more sensitive to specification errors than is the production regression.

In conclusion, it is interesting to ask what considerations it would be desirable to take into account to provide more adequate explanations and predictions of short-run price changes. First, and most obvious, would be to take into account the effects of changes in costs. In many ways, cost changes constitute the most obvious single factor to consider in explaining price changes. The only reason they have not been included in these studies is that the purpose of the entire book has been to study the dynamic adjustment of output and price on the basis of fixed cost functions. The fact that the available data also include the effects of changes in costs is simply an unfortunate result of economists' inability to conduct controlled experiments. For the purpose of explaining observed price and output changes, costs certainly ought to be included. Nevertheless, it is my conjecture that the inclusion of cost variables would still leave unexplained a considerable proportion of the price changes recorded in the samples studied in this book. For example, the upward surge which appears in each price series about the middle of 1933 can hardly have resulted from increases in costs. It seems likely that a considerable part of short-run price movements must be explained by pervasive, but noneconomic, factors. Another part must probably be explained on the basis of detailed information concerning the organization and administration of price-making arrangements, and some of this information undoubtedly appears in variables that are specific to individual industries.

REFERENCES

1. Abramovitz, Moses, *Inventories and Business Cycles,* New York: National Bureau of Economic Research, 1950.
   Ackoff, Russell L. *See* under Churchman, C. West.
2. Allen, R. G. D., *Mathematical Economics,* London: Macmillan and Co., 1956.
   Arnoff, E. Leonard. *See* under Churchman, C. West.
3. Arrow, Kenneth J., "Alternative Approaches to the Theory of Choice in Risk-Taking Situations," *Econometrica,* XIX, October, 1951, pp. 404–437.
4. ——, "Decision Theory and Operations Research," *Operations Research,* V, December, 1957, pp. 765–774.
5. ——, "Utilities, Attitudes, Choices: A Review Note," *Econometrica,* XXVI, January, 1958, pp. 1–23.
6. ——, "Toward a Theory of Price Adjustment," *The Allocation of Economic Resources,* Moses Abramovitz et. al., Stanford: Stanford University Press, 1959, pp. 41–51.
7. Arrow, Kenneth J., Theodore Harris, and Jacob Marschak, "Optimal Inventory Policy," *Econometrica,* XIX, July, 1951, pp. 250–272.
8. Arrow, Kenneth J., and Leonid Hurwicz, "On the Stability of Competitive Equilibrium," *Econometrica,* I: XXVI, October, 1958, pp. 522–552; II: and H. D. Block, XXVII, January, 1959, pp. 82–109.
9. Arrow, Kenneth J., Samuel Karlin, and Herbert Scarf, *Studies in the Mathematical Theory of Inventory and Production,* Stanford: Stanford University Press, 1958.
10. Arrow, Kenneth J., and Maurice McManus, "A Note on Dynamic Stability," *Econometrica,* XXVI, July, 1958, pp. 448–454.
11. Arrow, Kenneth J., and Marc Nerlove, "A Note on Expectations and Stability," *Econometrica,* XXVI, April, 1958, pp. 297–305.
    Arrow, Kenneth J. *See* under Enthoven, Alain C.
12. Baumol, William J., *Business Behavior, Value and Growth,* New York: The Macmillan Co., 1959.
13. Bellman, Richard, *Dynamic Programming,* Princeton: Princeton University Press, 1957.
    Block, H. D. *See* under Arrow, Kenneth J.

14. Bryant, Ralph Clement, *Lumber, Its Manufacture and Distribution,* 2nd ed., New York: John Wiley and Sons, 1958.

15. Cagan, Phillip, "The Monetary Dynamics of Hyperinflation," *Studies in the Quantity Theory of Money,* ed. Milton Friedman, Chicago: The Chicago University Press, 1956, pp. 25–117.

16. Churchman, C. West, Russell L. Ackoff, and E. Leonard Arnoff, *Introduction to Operations Research,* New York: John Wiley and Sons, 1957.

17. Cohen, Kalman J., *Computer Models of the Shoe, Leather, Hide Sequence,* Englewood Cliffs, N. J.: Prentice-Hall, 1960.
Cohen, Kalman J. *See* under Modigliani, Franco.

18. Darcovich, William, "Evaluation of Some Naive Expectation Models for Agricultural Yields and Prices," *Expectations, Uncertainty, and Business Behavior,* ed. Mary Jean Bowman, New York: Social Science Research Council, 1958, pp. 199–202.

19. Dorfman, Robert, Paul A. Samuelson, and Robert M. Solow, *Linear Programming and Economic Analysis,* New York: McGraw-Hill Book Company, 1958.

20. Duerr, William Allen, and Henry J. Vaux, eds., *Research in the Economics of Forestry,* Washington: Charles Lathrop Pack Forestry Foundation, 1953.

21. Durbin, J., and G. S. Watson, "Testing for Serial Correlation in Least Squares Regression," *Biometrika,* I: XXXVII, December, 1950, pp. 409–428; II: XXXVIII, June, 1951, pp. 159–178.

22. Dvoretsky, A., J. Kiefer, and J. Wolfowitz, "The Inventory Problem: I. Case of Known Distributions of Demand; II. Case of Unknown Distributions of Demand," *Econometrica,* XXIV, April, 1952; July, 1952, pp. 187–222; 450–466.

23. Eisner, Robert, "Expectations, Plans, and Capital Expenditures: A Synthesis of Ex Post and Ex Ante Data," *Expectations, Uncertainty, and Business Behavior,* ed. Mary Jean Bowman, New York: Social Science Research Council, 1958, pp. 165–188.

24. Enthoven, Alain C., and Kenneth J. Arrow, "A Theorem on Expectations and the Stability of Equilibrium," *Econometrica,* XXIV, July, 1956, pp. 288–293.

25. Fellner, William, *Competition Among the Few,* New York: Alfred A. Knopf, 1949.

26. Ferber, Robert, "The Railroad Shippers' Forecasts," *University of Illinois Bulletin,* L, June, 1953, pp. 1–140.

27. Friedman, Milton, *A Theory of the Consumption Function,* Princeton: Princeton University Press, 1957.

28. Friend, Irwin, "Critical Evaluation of Surveys of Expectations, Plans and Investment Behavior," *Expectations, Uncertainty, and Business Behavior,* ed. Mary Jean Bowman, New York: Social Science Research Council, 1958, pp. 189–198.

29. Haberler, Gottfried, *Prosperity and Depression,* new revised and enlarged [4th] ed., Cambridge: Harvard University Press, 1958.

30. Hahn, F. H., "Expectations and Equilibrium," *Economic Journal,* LXII, December, 1952, pp. 802–819.

31. Harling, John, "Simulation Techniques in Operations Research—A Review," *Operations Research,* VI, May–June, 1958, pp. 307–319.

    Harris, Theodore. *See* under Arrow, Kenneth J.
32. Hicks, J. R., *Value and Capital,* 2nd ed., Oxford: Clarendon Press, 1946.
33. Hicks, J. R., "The Process of Imperfect Competition," *Oxford Economic Papers,* VI, February, 1954, pp. 41–54.
34. Hirsch, Werner Z., "Manufacturing Progress Functions," *The Review of Economics and Statistics,* XXXIV, May, 1952, pp. 143–155.

    Hohn, Franz E. *See* under Modigliani, Franco.
35. Holt, Charles C., Franco Modigliani, and Herbert A. Simon, "A Linear Decision Rule for Production and Employment Scheduling," *Management Science,* II, October, 1955, pp. 1–30.

    Hood, William C. *See* under Koopmans, Tjalling C.
36. Houthakker, H. S. "The Scope and Limits of Futures Trading," *The Allocation of Economic Resources,* Moses Abramovitz et. al., Stanford: Stanford University Press, 1959, pp. 134–159.

    Hurwicz, Leonid. *See* under Arrow, Kenneth J.

    Juréen, Lars. *See* under Wold, Herman.

    Karlin, Samuel. *See* under Arrow, Kenneth J.
37. Katona, George, *Psychological Analysis of Economic Behavior,* New York: McGraw-Hill Book Co., 1951.
38. Kendall, Maurice George, *Contributions to the Study of Oscillatory Time Series,* National Institute of Economic and Social Research, Occasional Paper IX, Cambridge: The University Press, 1946.

    Kiefer, J. *See* under Dvoretsky, A.
39. Koopmans, Tjalling C., "Allocation of Resources and the Price System," *Three Essays on the State of Economic Science,* New York: McGraw-Hill Book Co., 1957, pp. 1–126.
40. Koopmans, Tjalling C., and William C. Hood, "The Estimation of Simultaneous Linear Economic Relationships," *Studies in Econometric Method,* ed. William C. Hood and Tjalling C. Koopmans, New York: John Wiley and Sons, 1953, pp. 112–199.
41. Lerner, A. P., "The Concept of Monopoly and the Measurement of Monopoly Power," *The Review of Economic Studies,* I, June, 1934, pp. 157–175.
42. Levy, Joel, "Optimal Inventory Policy When Demand is Increasing," *Operations Research,* VIII, November–December, 1960, pp. 861–863.
43. Lundberg, Erik, *Studies in the Theory of Economic Expansion,* New York: Kelley and Millman, 1955.
44. Lutz, Friedrich, and Vera Lutz, *The Theory of Investment of the Firm,* Princeton: Princeton University Press, 1951.

    Lutz, Vera. *See* under Lutz, Friedrich.
45. Machlup, Fritz, *The Basing-point System,* Philadelphia: The Blakiston Company, 1949.
46. Mack, Ruth P., *Consumption and Business Fluctuations,* New York: National Bureau of Economic Research, 1956.
47. Manne, Alan S., "Programming of Economic Lot Sizes," *Management Science,* IV, January, 1958, pp. 115–135.

48. Marschak, Jacob, "Towards an Economic Theory of Organization and Information," *Decision Processes,* ed. R. M. Thrall, C. H. Coombs, and R. L. Davis, New York: John Wiley and Sons, 1954, pp. 187–220.

Marschak, Jacob. *See* under Arrow, Kenneth J.

McClain, Hartsel G. *See* under Mills, Edwin S.

49. McCloskey, Joseph F., and Trefethen, Florence N., eds., *Operations Research for Management,* Baltimore: The Johns Hopkins Press, 1954.

McManus, Maurice, *See* under Arrow, Kenneth J.

50. Metzler, Lloyd A., "The Nature and Stability of Inventory Cycles," *Review of Economic Statistics,* XXIII, August, 1941, pp. 113–129.

51. ———, "Business Cycles and the Modern Theory of Employment," *American Economic Review,* XXXVI, June, 1946, pp. 278–291.

52. ———, "Factors Governing the Length of Inventory Cycles," *Review of Economic Statistics,* XXIX, February, 1947, pp. 1–15.

53. Mills, Edwin S., "Expectations, Uncertainty, and Inventory Fluctuations," *The Review of Economic Studies,* XXII, 1954–55, No. 57, pp. 15–22.

54. ———, "The Theory of Inventory Decisions," *Econometrica,* XXV, April, 1957, pp. 222–238.

55. ———, "Expectations and Undesired Inventory," *Management Science,* IV, October, 1957, pp. 105–109.

56. ———, "Uncertainty and Price Theory," *The Quarterly Journal of Economics,* LXXIII, February, 1959, pp. 116–130.

57. Mills, Edwin S., and Hartsel G. McClain, "A Study of Optimum Assembly Runs," *Operations Research,* IX, January–February, 1961, pp. 30–38.

58. Modigliani, Franco, and Kalman J. Cohen, "The Significance and Uses of Ex Ante Data," *Expectations, Uncertainty, and Business Behavior,* ed. Mary Jean Bowman, New York: Social Science Research Council, 1958, pp. 151–164.

59. Modigliani, Franco, and Franz E. Hohn, "Production Planning Over Time and the Nature of the Expectation and Planning Horizon," *Econometrica,* XXIII, January, 1955, pp. 46–66.

60. Modigliani, Franco, and Owen H. Sauerlender, "Economic Expectations and Plans of Firms in Relation to Short-Term Forecasting," *Short-Term Economic Forecasting,* A Report of the National Bureau of Economic Research, Princeton: Princeton University Press, 1955, pp. 261–359.

Modigliani, Franco. *See* under Holt, Charles C.

Morgenstern, Oskar. *See* under von Neumann, John.

61. Muth, John F., "Rational Expectations and the Theory of Price Movements," *Econometrica,* XXIX, July, 1961, pp. 315–335.

62. National Bureau of Economic Research, *The Quality and Economic Significance of Anticipations Data,* Princeton: Princeton University Press, 1960.

63. Nerlove, Marc, "Adaptive Expectations and Cobweb Phenomena," *Quarterly Journal of Economics,* LXXIII, May, 1958, pp. 227–240.

64. ———, *The Dynamics of Supply: Estimation of Farmers' Response to Price,* Baltimore: The Johns Hopkins Press, 1958.

Nerlove, Marc. *See* under Arrow, Kenneth J.

65. von Neumann, John, and Oskar Morgenstern, *Theory of Games and Economic Behavior,* 3rd ed., Princeton: Princeton University Press, 1953.

66. Ohlin, Bertil, "Some Notes on the Stockholm Theory of Savings and Investment," *Economic Journal,* I: XLVII, March, 1937, pp. 53–69; II: XLVII, June, 1937, pp. 221–240. Reprinted in *Readings in Business Cycle Theory,* The American Economic Association, Philadelphia: The Blakiston Company, 1944, pp. 87–130.

67. Saaty, Thomas L., *Mathematical Methods of Operations Research,* New York: McGraw-Hill Book Co., 1959.

68. Samuelson, Paul Anthony, *Foundations of Economic Analysis,* Cambridge: Harvard University Press, 1947.

Samuelson, Paul A. *See* under Dorfman, Robert.

Sauerlender, Owen H. *See* under Modigliani, Franco.

69. Savage, Leonard J., *The Foundations of Statistics,* New York: John Wiley and Sons, 1954.

Scarf, Herbert. *See* under Arrow, Kenneth J.

70. Shaw, E. S., "Elements of a Theory of Inventory," *Journal of Political Economy,* XLVIII, August, 1940, pp. 465–485.

71. Shubik, Martin, *Strategy and Market Structure,* New York: John Wiley and Sons, 1960.

Simon, Herbert A. *See* under Holt, Charles C.

72. Smithies, Arthur, "The Maximization of Profits Over Time With Changing Cost and Demand Functions," *Econometrica,* VII, October, 1939, pp. 312–318.

Solow, Robert M. *See* under Dorfman, Robert.

73. Southern Pine Association, *Economic Conditions in Southern Pine Industry,* presented to U. S. Timber Conservation Board, July 1, 1931.

74. Stone, Richard, *The Measurement of Consumers' Expenditure and Behavior in the United Kingdom* 1920–1938, Cambridge: Cambridge University Press, 1954.

75. Telser, Lester G., "Futures Trading and the Storage of Cotton and Wheat," *The Journal of Political Economy,* LXVI, June, 1958, pp. 233–255.

76. Theil, H., *Economic Forecasts and Policy,* Amsterdam: North-Holland Publishing Company, 1958.

Trefethen, Florence N. *See* under McCloskey, Joseph F.

77. United States Department of Commerce, Bureau of Foreign and Domestic Commerce, Division of Business Review, *Supplement to the Survey of Current Business,* 1940, 1942.

78. United States Department of Commerce, Bureau of Foreign and Domestic Commerce, Division of Business Review, *Survey of Current Business,* Vols. VIII–XX, 1928–1940.

79. United States Department of the Interior, Bureau of Mines, *Minerals Yearbook,* 1932–1941.

80. United States Department of Labor, Bureau of Labor Statistics, *Wholesale Prices and Price Indexes, 1958,* Bulletin No. 1257, July, 1959.

81. United States Department of Labor, Bureau of Labor Statistics, *Wholesale Prices (of Commodities),* 1929–1942.

Vaux, Henry J. *See* under Duerr, William Allen.

Watson, G. S. *See* under Durbin, J.

82. Wold, Herman, and Lars Juréen, *Demand Analysis,* New York: John Wiley and Sons, 1953.

Wolfowitz, J. *See* under Dvoretsky, A.

INDEX